GET OFF YOUR ASSETS!

How to Unleash the Power in You

by Desi Williamson

KENDALL/HUNT PUBLISHING COMPANY
4050 Westmark Drive   Dubuque, Iowa 52002

Overview

Get Off Your Assets!

How to Unleash the Power in You

Why you should read this book

The purpose of this book is to help you unleash the power within you to go after your dreams. It is my opinion that everyone should have a dream. As children, we all grow up with dreams of what we would like to be in life. Nothing is too outlandish for the imagination of a child. It is in this atmosphere that the foundational blocks are laid that often, determine our course in life.

However, by the time many of us reach adulthood, the harsh realities of life set in, and we become cynical about the present and apprehensive about the future. Some people are prompted to give up on life for various reasons, including their environment, race, cultural background, upbringing, past failures, and a host of others. They don't believe they have a future.

The high rate of unemployment, fueled by changes in the corporate business structure, have many people scared to death about the future, but this is only part of the story. At the same time, opportunity abounds! There are more opportunities available today than during any other time in history. There are more ways to succeed in today's world because there has never been more information and technology available to those with the ambition to seek it out, the discipline to learn, the courage to take action, and the persistence to continue until they reach their destination.

Unfortunately, much of our communication today only focuses on the negative, giving people a very jaded outlook on the future. Why are some people succeeding while others fail? I believe that there are some fundamental reasons. Many people are failing because they are frozen in fear.

Because of fear, they don't take action, and thus they find themselves sitting on the sidelines of life, watching the game rather than participating. This fear causes them to settle for less than they could be or less than they could have as a result. They don't believe in possibilities. They don't seek out the people or information that could help them reach their goals. Could this be you?

GET OFF YOUR ASSETS!. . .How to Unleash the Power in You is a book about your self empowerment and personal development. I want you to know that regardless of your situation, you have the power to succeed. It's all a matter of what you focus on, how determined you are to have it, and the strategies you employ to get it.

Every person on earth has a wealth of potential. We all have special gifts that are unique to our own individuality. Many people that I come across during my travels readily admit that they are using only a fraction of their potential. This is probably true, to some extent, for us all.

It is my hope that this book brings back to mind some of the dreams that you have had for your life and put on the back burner. I'm confident that through the information in this book, you will find hope, empowerment, and possibilities for your life. If something is possible, then it is possible for you, too!

"SEEK AND YE SHALL FIND!"

My Little Black Box

The FAA states that it is mandatory that all aircraft have a flight recorder on board known as the "Black Box". Whenever there's a plane crash authorities can always be found madly scrambling to find this box because it contains valuable flight information and history as to the origin of problems and possible root causes explaining why the plane may have experienced difficulty. Once the black box is retrieved, and the tape inside is played, it can usually be determined why certain things occurred. From there, precautions can be implemented in order to prevent future crashes and subsequent fatalities. If the black box is not retrieved, it is impossible to ascertain the problems from an inside perspective and the authorities must investigate further and speculate as to the causes associated with the crash.

What's in Your Black Box?

On this flight called life, I believe that we each have a little black box that contains our past. In it, there are tapes that play constantly inside of our heads. Some of them terrible experiences from our past that if not retrieved and dealt with can cause us great pain throughout our lives. Every time we seek to move ahead, recordings from certain incidents pop on and play clear and vivid pictures of these negative situations. We experience the full emotional range, as if it's happening right now. For me, there was a specific tape that I had buried long ago because the pain was always too great to face. The tape was that of sexual abuse. The pictures were clear and resonant. A man named Frank Hayes, was sexually abusing a four year old little boy, that little boy was me. His mother, Miss Hayes, was my baby sitter, a kind and gentle woman who trusted him to watch me one day while she went to the store. He took me into the basement of their home and sexually abused me. I had become another statistic, childhood innocence lost, gone forever! I can remember it just like it was yesterday. I've never told anyone to this day. I kept it buried on the recorder in my little black box. I was always too ashamed to mention it. It made me feel dirty and unworthy.

I vowed all of my young life that when I became a man, if I ever saw him, I would kill him! I didn't have the courage to include this story in the first edition of this book because I was not yet healed. It hurt so badly to think of it because, like so many other abused children, I thought something was wrong with me. I must have been a bad little boy to deserve something so capricious.

Many times throughout my life, as I would attempt to raise myself up emotionally from my troubled past, this thought would raise it's ugly head. The more often it did, the deeper I would bury it into my black box. I could never enjoy my successes as fully and always regarded my failures as some kind of just punishment. Who was I to think that I deserved something better from life?

Then one sultry summer day I would meet my past head on. It had been a long, humid summer, as summers go in St. Louis. I had been running errands with my father the entire morning as we prepared the bar and restaurant for yet another grinding day. I emerged from the kitchen in the late afternoon and entered the bar area. The music was blasting and the cigarette smoke was so thick you could cut it with a knife. At the end of the bar, close to the front door, a familiar silhouette was sitting slumped over the bar. Even though I could not see him clearly through the cluttered mass of humanity and confusion forever present in bars, I knew who it was. Boom! Flashback to that awful day in that basement thirty four years ago. Once again my past shook hands with my present. What should I do? I knew that if I told my father, he would kill him, no question about it! Was it worth that? I thought about killing him myself. The years since the incident had blessed me with size and mass that made me an imposing figure compared to this scrawny looking man who appeared much larger than life when he sexually abused me. I could kill him easily with my bare hands. I went to meet my assailant face to face. It was his time to be held accountable for what he'd done to me. My first steps towards him were filled with anger and vengeance. I asked God to help me! I prayed, "Father God, please walk with me, handle this for me, it's too big for me to tackle alone!" I didn't know what would happen once I reached the end of that bar. It could have been drastic, some serious drama with disastrous consequences. I could feel my hands tighten around his throat, him gasping for air. Pay back for all my years of suffering! But something strange happened. The closer I got to him, a calming presence took control. It was the voice of God almighty himself telling me to, through him, handle this situation in a different way. When I got face to face with Frank, it was obvious that life had dealt him the hand he deserved. He was a beaten man who looked far older than his years suggested. You could see what a life of looking for something for nothing had led to. He could barely look me in the eyes. He was also shaking hands with his past as he sat there. Physically beating him up wouldn't change him or what happened, and would only lessen me as a man in the process. He was already beaten up by life.

I surprised myself by my approach as I calmly sat down. My father, not knowing what had happened came over and asked me if I remembered Frank. My dad and mother rented from Miss Hayes when I was a baby. He had known Frank all that time. When my father left us to attend to other matters, I told Frank that I remembered him, but for all the wrong reasons. As painful as it was, I replayed that day. I told him of the terrible effect that this act had on my life growing up. My eyes burned a hole through his as he sat there in stunned disbelief. He was numb! He sat there in shock, speechless as he met, point blank, with personal responsibility and accountability. God spoke to me that day. He said, "Let me handle this my way!" "I've already taken care of it!" "Trust in me for

vengeance is mine!" Even though I was perfectly calm looking from my outside appearance, inside I was shaking like a
leaf, heart pounding, bad intentions held in check by my
creator. God saved both of our lives that day. I told Frank that
I wanted to kill him, and he knew full well that if my father
had knowledge of this, he was as good as dead! Instead, I told
him that I was holding him fully accountable for his actions,
would pray for him, and that I'd forgiven him. It became
crystal clear that this had a far greater impact on him than any
beating could have ever given him. This was a monkey off my
back. It was now between him and a power more capable
than I of dealing with it.

Thank goodness! Victory at last! I had faced the first of
many of those old recordings in my little black box of life. Not
totally erasing them, but finally putting them in check, thus
reducing their power and control over my life. It freed me! It
will do the same for you. What's on the tape that's playing in
your little black box? So often these old recordings imprison
us and keep us from discovering our best selves. The shame
and self condemnation render us unworthy of anything
worthwhile because we don't think we deserve it. We blame
ourselves even though we know, intellectually, that it's not
our fault.

I would challenge you to deal with these tapes once and
for all. Confront the situation and the people involved with
the loving hand of God guiding you. Ask for his intervention,
and trust that, through him, you will handle it properly. If
there's anyone who has abused you in any way and it's possible for you to confront them, do so. Even if you have to go
to prison to make contact, find them! Tell them what they did
and how you feel without hatred or evil in your heart. It will
be hard! I know because I've been there. Pray about it and ask
for God's help in seeing you through it. He will not let you
down! Unbeknownst to us, he's already dealt with it long
ago. His power is absolute. It's usually us who must come to
terms. After you've confronted the issue and held those in

question personally responsible and accountable for their actions, pray for them, forgive them, let go and something magical will happen. As you truly forgive, the memory of these situations will have less impact. You may never forget, but that's not the most important thing. You will find that you've given yourself a special gift. The gift will come in the form of love, reverence, humility, active faith, and ultimately the freedom to soar to new heights because the tapes on the flight recorder of your life will no longer be your slave master, but rather your servant. The master key to greater enlightenment will be yours as you sit on the tarmac of a brighter and better future ready to take off and soar to new heights of deeper self understanding and personal development.

TABLE OF CONTENTS

ACKNOWLEDGMENTS

I would like to start out by saying how happy I am to be finished with this project. I have been through many trying times in my life, but this is clearly, one of the toughest things that I've ever had to do. Writing a book stretches you in so many ways, because it forces you to dig deep within the recesses of your being to find ways to express yourself when you're exhausted and out of emotional fuel. Here's to all of the people who filled my tank when it was empty. I want to thank my mother, Ann, who gave me life; it's great to have you in my life again. I want to say thanks and, I love you to my family, the members of which put up with so many inconveniences in helping me to realize my dreams. To my wife, Sue, who provided much needed inspiration during critical times. To my daughter, Talia, and son, Reece, who are the heart and soul of me and give me the strength to reach to heights greater than I could have ever imagined because I want them to as well.

To my grandmother, Nonnie, whom I love with all of my heart because she believed in me when nobody else did, gave me a home, loved me unconditionally, and gave me a chance to make something of my life. To my father, Maurice, who instilled in me through his actions what a real work ethic is all about, and who taught me that anything in life worth having is worth working for. To all of my uncles who taught me what being a "real man" is all about. I want to thank Renée Strom for discovering me at that breakfast speech and seeing things in me that I didn't see in myself. She accelerated my career through her guidance and support. And lastly, I want to thank all of the mentors throughout my career who, through their own examples, have helped to set the standards by which we are all measured. To outstanding people such as Jim Rohn, Zig Ziglar, Tony Robbins, John Johnson, Tom Hopkins, Danielle Kennedy, Jack Canfield, Mark Victor Hansen, Og Mandino, Robert Schuller, the National Speakers Association, Les Brown, Rick Rainbolt, Michael Chatman, Randy Gage, Dr. Jeffrey Lant, Harvey Mackay, and so many others who have made a difference in my life. I want to also thank my good friend, Victory Smith, and Saunni Dais Productions for thought provoking poetry which helped me through many a tough day while completing this project. Let us continue to be messengers of hope in making the world a better place!

INTRODUCTION

It's Not Where You're From,
It's Where You're Going That Counts!

"When you are inspired by some great purpose, some extra-ordinary project, all your thoughts break their bounds: Your mind transcends limitations, your consciousness expands in every direction, and you find yourself in a new, great, and wonderful world. Dormant forces, faculties, and talents become alive, and you discover yourself to be a greater person by far than you ever dreamed yourself to be."

—Patanjali

It seems a long way from 3920 St. Ferdinand in St. Louis, Missouri. This street was the first place I remember as home as a child. Long before it became fashionable to call a broken home dysfunctional, it was apparent to me that the household I lived in was different. Most of the children in my neighborhood had the typical family situation with a mother, father, 2.3 children, and sometimes as many as ten. This was the 1950s and 60s, and it seemed that black people had a disproportionate share of poverty and anxiety to deal with, brought about, I suppose, by the fact that racism was a sign of the times. Back then, my environment was totally black and unless I ventured downtown I could go for weeks and never see a person of a different race. The businesses were owned by black people, including the local department stores, barber shops, grocery stores, restaurants, gas stations, taverns, and shoe shine parlors. This is no longer true today. I can still remember going to my cousin Vernon's barber shop and listening to the older men discuss everything from sports to politics. Man, those guys could on for hours and never seemed to get tired of debating. I learned a lot about life on those Saturday afternoons.

I can remember learning some of life's early lessons about survival when we used to play marbles. It was always the same, who ever had the most marbles made the rules. We would draw a huge circle in the dirt and and ante up by placing an equal number of marbles into the ring. Then with deadly aim, everyone would seek to take the other guys' marbles.

Some kids would leave with marbles bulging from their pockets while others left with nothing. This was a good metaphor for life. It was at this point that I figured it out, "Life ain't fair!" My mother was only sixteen years old when I was born and my father was nineteen. This situation would have a profound effect on me for the rest of my life. From that perspective, you might say that we grew up together, babies raising a baby! I can vaguely remember my mother and father living together for a short period of time. We lived in a three bedroom house with a living room, kitchen, and bedroom all lined up like dominoes. For heat, we had an old kerosene burning stove that was suppose to heat the whole house, but rarely did, and I burned myself on it continuously, even though I was instructed not to play near it. My crib was in the same room as my mother and father's bed. I still see the shadows that cast themselves on the walls and ceiling while that old stove hummed, growing hotter and hotter.

By the time my third birthday rolled around, my mother and father had divorced. By virtue of the fact that they had married so young, it stands to reason that I would be in for a rough life even if they stayed together, for neither of them had very much experience at raising children.

After that, my mother always had several husbands and

boyfriends. She was certainly caught between trying to be a mother and living a life of the young kid that she was. Many times, she would leave the house to go out on weekends and stay out all night, leaving me at home alone. I was four years old. She would tell me to lock the door and not answer it even if Jesus Christ himself knocked on it. I would be so lonely and scared that I would find myself running up and down the street screaming and crying until the neighbors brought me in. They would keep me until she came back and the cycle would start all over again. My mother was a very beautiful woman and was always attracted to men who were abusive, alcoholic, and drug users, with few exceptions. She was married a total of nine times in her life. In my opinion, a person who marries that many times is both desperately searching for something and running from themselves. I would later find myself running as well.

In the interim, between her marriage to my father and her ninth husband, my mother had two other children, my brother, André, and my sister, Kumonte. My heart stills bleeds for my baby brother because he has grown up his whole life not really knowing whether or not my father was his. It was always thought that we had the same father, but at the same time, some speculated that his father was someone else that my mother was going out with. Sometimes older people think they're hiding things from kids, not realizing that eventually the truth comes out. My brother wonders about it to this day. Who was my little brother's father? Can you imagine going through your life with that question always lurking in the back of your mind? People wonder why he's bitter! My mother straightened it all out for me 30 years later. André and I are definitely blood brothers, with the same mother and father. I would not love him any less, were this not true. I don't remember when André was born. I just remember that he all of a sudden showed up one day. He was always tough, and even as a kid, man, he loved to fight! My mother had one rule when she was at work and that was that under no condition were we to be at someone else's house when she wasn't home. I remember one particular day when we were over at a friend's house who lived down the street. My mother came home earlier than we expected. I can still hear her calling us as she always did, "Desiiiiii!......Andre!!!!.....Desirray!!!!....Andre!!!!" We started to run out of the house, but André did not notice that there was a glass storm door in front of him. He smashed right through it! He emerged with a huge piece of glass jutting out of his stomach which would have caused most adults to pass out. He pulled the glass out of his stomach and didn't wince or cry. He was only four years old. When I say he was tough, I mean tough!

After my mother and father separated she married a semi-pro baseball player. He was an alcoholic, and when he drank, he would beat my mother badly. I remember one day being locked out of the house in the cold, on a blistery winter's day. I stood outside, knocking on the door for what seemed like forever, freezing my little buns off. I knew he was in the house and wondered why he didn't answer. He finally swung open the door, snatched me inside, and slapped me until my nose started to bleed, all for waking him up because I wanted to come in out of the cold! After many of the beatings, he would threaten me further by informing me that if I said anything to my mother, he would beat me even worse. This was the pattern of the men she would marry time after time! And the worse was yet to come! This would force me to grow up much younger than I should have had to. I learned how to cook, clean a house, wash clothes and diapers, and do whatever else was necessary to take care of my little brother and sister. When most kids would come home from school to play with their friends, I would come home, cook dinner for my brother and sister, clean the house, and get them ready for the next day. That was my responsibility! I was eight years old! This form of life continued for the next three years with different men and marriages. Finally, she married a man that I just couldn't stand! He would beat and kick my mother in front of me. They would make up, but he would always do the same thing all over again. I would think about killing him while he was asleep, but could never muster the courage. They would have wild parties where drugs were consumed and the house would be left in a mess. I always found myself cleaning up the aftermath, and then going to the laundromat to wash all of the clothes for everyone, my mother, this guy, my little brother, sister, and myself. A few days later, this guy beat my mother and me again. I made up my mind that night that I couldn't deal with this anymore. I wanted out!

I had always gone over to my grandmother's house to visit since I was a small child. Whenever it was time to leave, I would always cry because I didn't want to go back home to the negative situation that existed with my mother and her men. I felt so sorry for my mother as well. She was searching for love and her children would always pay the price along with her for the choices she made. A few days later, on April 17, 1968, I would do something that would transform my life forever. I was told by my mother to clean up the house after another party while the abuser was in the bedroom asleep. I cleaned that house until it shined like new money. I knew that it would be the last time I would do so. I was getting out of there! If for no other reason, I was leaving for my own survival, physical as well as emotional. I was a sad little boy for most of my life. I wanted a chance at happiness. Lord knows, there had to be something better.

When I finished cleaning the house, I packed my clothes in brown paper grocery bags, called a cab, and left for my grandmother's house. One of the hardest decisions I've ever had to make was to leave my little brother and sister as I rode off in that cab, but at the age of eleven, I wasn't mature enough to take them. My father was given legal custody of me, but had no rights to my brother or sister. My grandmother told me that the authorities could take them back, even though she would have taken them, too, in a New York minute. I felt so much hurt and pain in my life as a child. I thought about suicide so many times growing up. I'm absolutely sure that had my grandmother not taken me in, I would be in one of three places: on drugs, in jail, or dead!

This decision marks a critical turning point that would change the course of my life forever. It is at this point that the Desi Williamson that you see today was born.

I feel compelled to share this part of my life because quite often successful people are perceived to be perfect people with not a hair out place. Nothing could be further from the truth! We are human beings with life stories that are often filled with sadness and misfortune. It is out of this pain that many of us are compelled to make a difference in the world by helping others to see that, regardless of their past circumstances, they can realize their dreams. I don't share parts of my past because I seek sympathy from you, but only to let you know that you can use your past either as a crutch or as fuel to create a burning desire to make your life better. I am grateful for everything that has happened to me in the past because, in those misfortunes, I was able to explore depths of my being that might have otherwise gone undiscovered. In moments of challenge, you will find the courage that lets you know that, with God's help, you can handle anything! When you come to accept your past as a learning and character building experience, you move from the realm of blame and condemnation to one of living life to the fullest, with the goal of becoming all that you can be. It is through the sharing of pain, which is common to the human experience, that you learn to appreciate the sweetness of victory. The more obstacles you encounter and overcome, the more character you will develop as a result. You must use your past as a launching pad to a brighter future. Let the pain in your life make you smarter, stronger, wiser, and more caring.

Many of life's lessons cannot be taught in a classroom. You've got to live them! The more character you develop, the bigger the contribution you can make towards leaving this world a better place than you found it!

If I ever have the opportunity to speak in your town, please come and visit with me and give me a hug. Let's get to know each other, if only for a moment. My goal is to be a catalyst for the maximization of human potential. I want you to realize that you are a special person with your own unique gift. The world needs it! Perhaps in you, someone else will see themselves. Perhaps through you, they will find the courage to discover and share their gifts. My wish is to play a part in that process. I see myself as a messenger, providing some of life's most powerful elixir. . . hope!

WITH EXTREME PURPOSE

*"Trial Boss, from whom
do you receive your
government?"*

*"The Will in overdrive,
focused with carnivorous
intent!"*

*"What is the purpose of
the path you have cleared
and blazed?"*

*"My Will hath one burden. . .
to mirror that upon which it
has glazed!"*

—©*Saunni Dais*

THE POWER OF PURPOSE

Far better is it to dare to do great things, to win glorious triumphs even though checkered by failure, rather than join the ranks of those poor miserable souls who neither suffer much nor enjoy much, for they live in grey dim twilight that knows neither victory nor defeat.

—Charles Bernard Shaw

This book was written to help you get your dreams back, the dreams that you've had, but dare not entertain for fear that success is something that happens to other people. Well, I'm here to say that success is not in short supply. It's available in abundance and it is your God given right! While there have been many books written on motivation, and they all serve a good purpose, it does take more than motivation to succeed. Recently, there's been criticism of the concept of motivation and, in particular, motivational speakers. This is not without, I believe, a certain justification. People get all excited and wonder, after leaving the seminar or reading the book, where do I go from here? What do I do next? If you're not careful, it won't be long before that high feeling is gone and you again find yourself struggling for emotional survival. It is my goal in this book to give you some "How Tos," coupled with your own individual action plan on this journey. This way you can empower yourself to achieve your dreams. I would only ask that you read this book with an open mind. Take out of it the ideas that you like, consider the rest, and then take massive action towards building your life to order.

YOUR PAST CAN LEAD TO A BRIGHT FUTURE

When I was younger, I was a terrible athlete. I wanted so much to be a football star, but was small, slow, and not very aggressive. I wanted a way out of the negative environment surrounding me. Poverty, drugs, and violence were the order of the day. So I set my sights on a goal, a vision, a journey into a better life. I knew that a football scholarship would give me that chance. It's strange sometimes how an unfortunate incident can lead to something very good in life. I was put back from the fifth to the fourth grade because in Missouri they had a law that when a child moves from the city to the suburbs, the child automatically gets put back one grade. I think this sprang from a belief that the surburban schools were so superior to the city schools that the transferred student would not be able to keep up.

When this happened, I was destroyed. I felt so stupid, as if I had really done something wrong. It's hard to believe now that my self-esteem could have been so low. I couldn't seem to do anything right. All the other kids seemed to be smarter, better looking, and have more athletic skills than I. I went out for Little League football and got pounded into the ground.

The other kids laughed at me because I was so awkward. I will never forget trying to tackle a kid named Jimmy Williams. He was like a little ten-year-old version of Jim Brown. He was big for a kid his age, fast and powerful. I was totally in awe and jealous of him. One day in practice, when I tried to tackle him, he ran over me as if I were a gnat and bloodied my nose. I cried during the bus ride home that night, because everyone at practice made fun of me, told me that I was a scrub and had no chance to make the team. I was a laughingstock. To this day, I've never been that humiliated. So the next day I quit to avoid the embarrassment of being cut. That ate at my soul for the entire next year. I was a quitter! I swore that the next year I would go out for football again and that I would never quit again, no matter what!"

YOU'VE GOT TO START SOMEWHERE

All that winter I dreamed of making that team. It became an obsession. It was all that I could think about. I saw myself succeeding, and through trial and error discovered something that would serve me for the rest of my life: the power of visualization! When that next year came, I made the team and was one of it's best players, but not one of the best athletes. I would come to practice early and stay late. I worked on my own outside of practice. I slept, ate, and drank football. I knew the starting lineups for every NFL football team and most of the colleges. I found that if you're dedicated enough to something, you will eventually find a way to succeed. Well, it was surprising to everyone in St. Louis, when as a senior in high school, I showed up about seven years later on the All Metro Team of the *St. Louis Post Dispatch* as well as many other all star teams. I can't remember how many people would say, "Is that Desi Williamson? I don't believe it! He was a horrible athlete as a kid!" I'll never forget running into Jimmy Williams, the super star Little League player, shortly after appearing in the Sunday edition of the newspaper. I hadn't seen him since Little League. I stood a full head taller and outweighed him by at least forty pounds. I was now the star and he was the one who stared in envy. He couldn't believe how I had changed! I left feeling so good and learned a valuable lesson. *Just because things are doesn't necessarily mean that they will always be.* We all develop at different times in our lives and should never judge ourselves based upon our current circumstances, because that does not represent the sum total of what we can become. It is in that thought that we should find all of the encouragement that we need to keep on truckin'!

YOU DON'T ALWAYS GET WHAT YOU WANT

I was fortunate enough to be awarded several scholarships to different schools around the country and chose the University of Minnesota. It is a very special place to me for many reasons. The Twin Cities is a great place to live, and when I visited the campus during my recruiting trip, they showed me a film. It profiled the fact that there were more than 47 *Fortune* 500 companies based there and that the campus was located in a major metropolitan area. Although the football program was not the greatest, they did compete in the Big Ten, and I saw the chance to play and earn a letter as a freshman, which I ultimately did. I felt like I could go to some other schools and possibly go to a bowl game every year, but where would I live when football was over? Most of the other big schools were located in small towns where the opportunities would be limited when the band stopped playing. Few schools in the country matched the University of Minnesota when I looked at the whole package. There was also another young man there who greatly affected me, named Tony Dungy. He was a freshman quarterback who spent time with me during my visit. More about him later. Every "Blue Chip" athlete in the country who has ever attended college has the dream to play in the National Football League, and I was certainly no different. In fact, most top athletes would be so bold as to expect that as a given. I felt that way! After all, I was a starting linebacker seven games into the season my freshman year in the Big Ten, playing against schools like Michigan, Ohio State, and Nebraska. A year before, I was watching these same guys on TV, and now here I was, one of them! I just knew that four years later, I would be right there achieving the dream of playing on Sundays and having all of my friends and family watch me run up and down the field of the NFL.

One of the most disappointing days of my life came during the 1978 NFL draft. I sat there by the phone, as so many others had before me, waiting for it to ring, but it never did. By the time the end of the last round of the draft rolled around, it became apparent to me that my lifelong dream was not going to happen the way I thought it would. I was devastated! Everything I thought about myself was wrapped into football: my self-esteem, and my self-image.

It was the worst day of my life! Have you ever had a day where you didn't feel like getting out of bed? Well, the next day was that kind of day for me. My body said get up and my mind asked, for what? I was so embarrassed because it was something that I thought others expected of me. I felt as though I had let them down. To make matters worse, two of my "so-called" best friends came over to my house to formally roast me. They said, "What are you going to do now? Yeah, right, let's cheer for the next star linebacker in the NFL, ha! ha! ha!" They turned the heat up so high on me that morning that it was unbearable. I wanted someplace to hide. They were actually doing me a big favor, because both of these guys had been through the same thing the year before. They were high school All Americans in their own right and stars at the U of M as well, who also did not make it to the ranks of the NFL. Believe it or not, they were roasting me because they were helping me come to terms at a critical point in my life. I had to learn to move on! One of my friends told me that if going to the NFL would be the highlight of my life, I was in for a sorry life. How right he was!

CRITICAL DECISIONS

At the University of Minnesota, I played the role of "utility man" more than anything else. I played linebacker my first two years, defensive end my junior year, and started at right offensive guard my senior year. Offensive linemen in major college football at that time weighed between 250–275 lbs. I played the position at a stout 205 lbs. I always believed in the concept of "team" and played wherever the coach felt was best for the program. The last move would cost me dearly in terms of being drafted. The NFL drafts players by position, and no team in the land was going to draft a lineman the size of a running back. I had an agent, however, who was interested in representing me. He tried to position me as a player who could do it all, a sort of jack of all trades! He was able to get two offers on the table, one from the St. Louis Cardinals (now the Arizona Cardinals) in my home town, and one from the Cincinnati Bengals. Both teams said that they would pay me the standard scale for training camp and offered me a contract of $28,000 if I made the team. I told my agent to forget it. I knew that I could get a sales job that would pay me that, and I wouldn't have to risk my life in the process. I didn't realize it at the time, but that was one of the best decisions I've ever made in my life. Why? This forced me to deal with other areas of life for the first time! I had to develop other interests. Getting my degree became more important than ever before. I had always been a good student, and I went back to class even more committed. I was not going to let myself off the hook by not graduating. That would have been much more embarrassing than not making the pros. That was the reason I went to college in the first place. Football was only the ticket! This situation allowed me to put football in its proper perspective. Many of my teammates went on to get drafted, and I was envious, but I knew one thing. Every athlete has a life expectancy. Some aren't forced to deal with the reality of life until they are in their mid or late 30s. For some, it's a stark reality that is hard to adjust to when the cheering stops and they are no longer the center of attention. Some jocks never get over it! Colleges throughout the country are filled with career students and frustrated athletes who can't deal with the fact that it's over and time to move on.

I felt that the sooner I was able to wrestle with those demons and settle the score, the better off I'd be. A few years later, some of the guys that had gone on and played in the pros were now retired, with blown out knees, permanent migrane headaches, and worn out spirits. I still had my health and a new lease on life! I now realize that not getting drafted was one of the best things that ever happened to me.

Many times in life, when things don't go as we think they should, we need to remember that life is a book that has many chapters. As one chapter closes, another opens. It gives us the opportunity to discover other parts of ourselves that otherwise would have been put on hold while we struggle to hold onto something when it's time to give it up. This holds true whether you're dealing with a job, a relationship, or any other major decision in life. When we are able to open our eyes, we find that one situation will often lead to another more exciting one, if we are willing to just let go!

WINNERS PRACTICE THE ART OF ADJUSTING

Have your ever really been looking forward to something that didn't happen? Perhaps a big sale that fell through, a date that got cancelled, or a promotion that didn't materialize? What did you do? Did you lay down and die, or get off your assets and crank the effort up even higher? I was on a flight one evening and the plane was flying from Miami to Minneapolis, when all of the sudden it hit a pocket of turbulence. It went up and down, back and forth. It was enough to make you grab that little bag and lose your cookies! After the plane had landed and we were safely on the ground, it occured to me that the pilot never turned the plane around and went back home. He made what they call a slight "adjustment" to get us out of that turbulent air and safely to our destination in one piece. What a metaphor! Sometimes in business or in our personal lives, things don't necessarily happen the way we think they should. Sometimes even the best laid plans don't work out, and when they don't, you need to be prepared to make some adjustments in order to correct your course. Sometimes the course requires that you take a detour or a path that was not in your original plan. I believe that the view from the top is the same, no matter how long it takes you to get there.

HOLLYWOOD, HERE I COME!

I've always been a believer in the credo, "Shoot for the moon and land on a star." So, after not making it in the NFL, I packed up my bags and moved to Hollywood. I had taken the time to visit Los Angeles extensively during a West Coast trip, and I was really excited by all of the hoopla surrounding the Hollywood scene. It's exhilarating for anyone who goes out there for the first time. By driving down Wilshire Boulevard from the furthest eastern point out to the ocean, you quickly get a lesson in economics. From those two points, you find a drastic difference in the economic condition of people as you travel through the Crenshaw district to Beverly Hills and finally to the ocean. When you get to a street called San Vincente, you notice an immediate change, for you are now on the outskirts of Beverly Hills. It's hard to believe that some people could have so much and some so little, and only be separated by a few city blocks. It feels different from the moment you cross Beverly Blvd. You notice a distinct difference in this place from anywhere else you may have visited in the world. Every car is a Mercedes, BMW, Ferrari, Maserati, Rolls Royce, Lexus, or a derivative thereof. In fact, a Mercedes is known as the Volkswagen of Beverly Hills.

One of my lifelong dreams was to move to Hollywood and become an actor. What better time to do it than after not getting drafted by the NFL? I had a cousin named Fred Williamson, better know as "The Hammer," who had fashioned for himself a good career in the movies after playing several years with the Kansas City Chiefs. I figured that I was better looking than he was and all I needed was a shot. I had a couple of things going for me. I had earned my SAG (Screen Actors Guild) and AFTRA (American Federation of Radio and Television Artists) cards in Minneapolis.

In Hollywood, there exists a sort of Catch 22. In order to get that speaking part in a movie, you've got to be in the union, and in order to get in the union, you've got to get a speaking part on TV or in a movie. Fortunately, I had both. I went on audition after audition, and was fortunate enough to sign on with an improvisational comedy group called the L.A. Connection. I did some commercial work, hawking different products for various companies, in print ads mostly, and on TV. There's also a very dark side to Hollywood that is not apparent until you go there in search of your dream. There are so many wannabes out there that some people will sell their souls to get into the business. I went on several auditions that turned out to be cattle calls for pornographic movies. I was shocked to learn how many young men and women move out there each year with the goal of stardom and end up making a deal with the devil. There were acting and voice coaches of all types that would help you make your dreams come true, for a small fee of course! After the tinsel from Tinsel Town wears off, you soon discover that it is very plastic. There's almost a sickness to wanting to be on television or in the movies so badly that you would literally do anything to get there. Many people do!

Hollywood knows that, and preys upon that central human element in people that craves love and attention. There is no in between—you either love Hollywood or hate it! You either like what you see and feel it's for you or you don't. What was really interesting is that I saw many different people that you would recognize from various movies at parties, in bars, or in restaurants, and I learned a reality about the movie business. Many people equate seeing someone on television or in a movie with making it! The fact of the matter is that one television or movie role does not a career make. This hit me squarely in the face at a restaurant one night in West Hollywood. I went to the bathroom and noticed a gentleman standing in the next stall who was a featured actor in the movie *The Lady Sings the Blues,* starring Diana Ross. He looked like a bum off of the streets and certainly didn't display the kind of success associated with major motion picture employment. He appeared to be distressed. I asked him if he was who I thought he was, and he responded in the affirmative. I asked him how he was doing and he immediately begin to give me a seminar on the Hollywood scene. He told me about the fact that many people associate being in the movies with major economic success, but the fact of the matter was that most of the so-called actors in Hollywood are starving to death while they wait for the big break. He went on to explain that, even among the ones that work frequently, unless they are able to score a successful television series, or work regularly in movies, just barely scratch out a living. With the extremely high cost of living in Los Angeles, he said, unless you were willing to make a sacrifice and possibly risk the better part of your youth to pursue a career in the business, you should really rethink your plans. He warned that you might end up waiting too long for something that either may not be forthcoming or worth it in the end, depending upon how much you wanted to give up for a chance to become a star. He mentioned that he had several friends who knocked around out there for twenty years, only to waste the best years of lives in an effort to break into the movies and have their hearts and spirits broken. At the age of 24, I decided that I was not willing to sacrifice my youth for something that I had little or no control over. I wanted to establish a life for myself that would give me a foundation for the future. Many people have gone out to Hollywood to seek the dream and have found it. Many more have found disappointment.

The Law of Distinctions

I don't wish to discourage anyone who wishes to make acting a profession. That's not why I shared this story. The key thing I found in life is to discover your true motivation for wanting something. You have to find the right reasons! Only then can you determine what price you are really willing to pay in order to get what you want. This distinction is the difference between success and failure in any calling. You must decide whether you want something because it's a labor of love or because you want the end result. If you only want the end result, you will not be able to deal with the obstacles that you will surely encounter during your journey. I only wanted to be in Hollywood because I thought acting and being on television was cool. I didn't realize until I got there that most of the people who have made it were willing to roll the dice with their futures to make it happen. We all hear about people who were discovered at the soda fountain at the corner drug store, but that is rare. In any craft, you must be willing to sacrifice for however long it takes to succeed. I didn't love acting enough to put myself through the paces. I was impatient and not willing to live the life of a pauper in pursuit of that world. I had a great time out there, but decided to move on to greener pastures. The most important lesson I learned from that experience was to go out there and find out whether or not Hollywood was for me. Had I not gone, I would have lived with regret for the rest of my life. With that in mind, whatever it is that you want to do with your life, I would encourage you to just GO FOR IT! That is how you are truly able to make value judgements about what is right or wrong for you. We never really fail at anything! We make distinctions as to what course is the right one for us. Life is like a smorgasbord, and the only way that you can find out what different foods taste like is to put them in your mouth and chew!

The ability to make distinctions allows you to
move on to a more desirable station without
wasting valuable time on something that is not
in alignment with what you're committed to
or willing to sacrifice for.

—*Desi Williamson*

If You've Got An Itch, Quit Complaining and Start Scratchin'!

Throughout our lives we all reach crossroads, the forks in the road where critical decisions can determine the course of our lives. I decided that the best course of action for me was to build a career in sales. Sales was something that was exciting to me because it involved dealing with people, and I love people! It also took advantage of some of the skills most agreeable to my personality. It involved some degree of acting, because in order to deliver presentatons, I had to put a certain of amount of showmanship to work. It was clearly one of the best decisions I've ever made. I'm proud to say that I've worked for three of the top *Fortune* 500 companies in the country, as well as having achieved success in my own businesses. Little did I know at the time that each of the experiences I encountered at each juncture in my life would play a key role in me finding my true calling in life. That was the speaking and training business.

I've had some great jobs with some great companies, such as Johnson & Johnson, Johnson Wax Company, Rain Bird Sprinkler Manufacturer, Pepsi Cola, and Cadbury Schweppes. I also had many other jobs at different points, but always felt compelled to leave once I felt that I had plateaued. I had a chronic itch that needed to be scratched, and the remedy was always a new opportunity to learn something different. So often, people are afraid to make changes in their lives because they are comfortable with what they have. Unfortunately, if you don't have a dream that's bigger than your current situation, you will never grow and realize anything close to what your true potential is. Some may say that for me to move around so much was suicide in terms of future employment. That might have been true if things had not changed in the last thirty years. It used to be that having more than three jobs in five years was the kiss of death. Nowadays, if you don't have a varied backround with different levels of experience, you've got a problem. Why?

Because everything changes. You've got to have a game plan and know in advance what your outcome is going to be. You've got to have the courage to make a move when you get that itch in life that is sure to come. If you can anticipate your itches in advance, you can be prepared to change the course of your life when you sense that things are changing and are no longer meeting your expectations.

Sand and the Hourglass

It was strange! With every job that I ever had, I did something. I envisioned an imaginary hourglass with tiny granules of sand pouring out of it. When that last grain of sand hit the bottom of the hour glass, I knew it was time for me to move on. I think that subconsciously I kept doing this because I wanted to maintain some kind of control over my life and what happened to me. I had that gnawing feeling that there was something more out there for me, and not moving at the appropriate time meant that I was losing ground. The sand and hourglass concept will allow you to reach into the future and take control of your life by anticipating what your next move is going to be rather than waiting around to see what is going to happen. Chances are that it won't be much!

Massive layoffs will continue to be a part of the American landscape, and companies everywhere are telling people to become empowered to take control of their future. I had no idea at the time that my hourglass mentality would serve me so well. It turned out to be in perfect alignment with the future. Lifetime employment is a thing of the past. You must be willing to corral your future and make the appropriate move at the right time. Make sure that you always give more than you take in everything that you do. Give your employer everything you have to offer. Learn as much as you can, and use what you've learned to craft a better future for you and your family. Corporations are not out to deliberately ruin your life. They must continue to reinvent themselves in order to remain competitive and stay in business in this global economy. You must operate with enlightened self-interest. It's just a reality of life. You will be that much further ahead in the game!

You Need a Personal Challenge

As I mentioned previously, there's been much criticism on the subject of motivation. Sometimes I feel inclined to agree. Have you ever read a motivational book, gone to a seminar, or listened to some tapes and felt energized? More than likely you felt like you could tackle the world, didn't you? What happened after a short period of time? If you're like most people, you found that the feeling didn't last. As soon as you hit your first adversity, your attitude was right back were you started. That's because being truly motivated comes from more than just a feeling. To have a feeling that lasts, those feelings must be grounded in something much stronger. In order for electricity to work properly, it must be properly grounded with the use of a grounding wire. Only then will it transfer the proper amount of current to its respective locations. Motivation is the same way! It must be grounded in a thing called PURPOSE! Webster defines purpose as 1) The object toward which one strives or for which something exists; goal aim. 2) A result or effect that's intended or desired. 3) Determination, resolution. To have a definite purpose is to have a grounding rod for your life. Without one, you will find yourself a frustrated person who drifts aimlessly through life taking whatever comes your way, usually after the people who have a definite purpose have dined at the table of opportunity.

How To Find Your Purpose

Many times, purpose can be manifested by life's circumstances. The first key is to ask six basic questions. The power of questions can change your life!

1. WHO?
2. WHAT?
3. WHEN?
4. WHERE?
5. WHY?
6. HOW?

When you answer these questions, you will find compelling reasons or causes to become involved in. It's the natural way the human mind works. In finding the answers to those questions, you determine:

1. Who can help you in your mission?
2. What do you want and what do you need to do to get it?
3. When will you take the necessary action?
4. Where will the action take place?
5. Why are you involved in this activity? Why do you want this?
6. How will you go about taking the actions that will address or solve the problem?

I believe that each of us must be compelled by some kind of personal challenge. Even if we aren't crystal clear on the challenge, these questions will cause you to think. If you keep asking these questions about whatever it is you're dealing with, you will find the personal challenge which will ultimately lead to your purpose in life. I believe that all noteworthy accomplishment comes from some kind of personal challenge. James Ramsey Alman was a famous explorer and member of the 1963 Mount Everest expedition. His contention was that challenge is the core and mainspring of high achievement. If there's a mountain, someone will try to climb it. If there's a river, no matter how wide, somebody will try to cross it. And if there's a record, somebody will eventually break it. Take the four-minute mile. Since the beginining of track and field, it was thought that it was humanly impossible to run the mile in under four minutes. Then finally on May 6, 1954, Roger Bannister broke the barrier by running the mile in 3:58. Interestingly enough, after that, 37 other runners ran the mile in under four minutes. Why? One of the reasons is that after Bannister achieved this milestone, other people had a stronger conviction than ever before. They created in themselves an even stronger purpose because someone else demonstrated what could be done when one has a strong enough reason.

Another example would be the football rushing record of the incomparable Jim Brown of the Cleveland Browns. He rushed for more than 12,000 yards in his short nine-year career. This was a record that stood for almost 20 years until a young man by the name of Walter Payton, of the Chicago Bears, came along and blew that record away with more than 16,000 yards. Why had so many others failed to break the barrier? One of the underlying factors was probably that he played with more conviction and purpose than anyone else before him. He played the game with a sense of purpose and commitment that has been rarely seen since. Jim Brown once said in an interview that many players in today's game don't have passion. They run out of bounds, lay out on the field, and accept the fact that they can be hurt. He went on to say that many players are so concerned about getting hurt that they don't go all out each and every time their cleats touch the field. If you ever had the pleasure of seeing Jim Brown run, you know what I'm talking about. It was a thing of beauty. He'd run over, under, very seldom around, and most of the time straight through the opposing players to get to that end zone. I don't ever recall him running out of bounds to avoid contact. Walter Payton played with same level of intensity and purpose.

Greatness in any form requires performing with a greater sense of purpose than anyone else. It takes that level of commitment to succeed. There were many players who were faster, stronger, and had better talent surrounding them than Jim Brown and Walter Payton. Purpose is an intangible that can't be measured, but one thing is certain, when a person has it, extraordinary things happen!

For the longer I live, the more convinced I become that the biggest difference between the feeble and the powerful, the great and insignificant, is will, a purpose once fixed, and then victory or death.

—Unknown

Another example of purpose is the Jackie Robinson story. It was August 25, 1946, and Branch Rickey, the general manager of the then Brooklyn Dodgers was staring out of the window with a vision. He was sickened by the amount of prejudice, hate, and malice in the world, particularly as it related to major league baseball. At that time, blacks were not allowed to play in the major leagues and were relegated to playing in their own Negro league. This infuriated Rickey, who believed that baseball was an American sport, and that every citizen, regardless of race or cultural backround, should have the opportunity to compete in that great game. Rickey also had a hidden agenda. He knew that this would help to break a pattern of bigotry in society as a whole, and that baseball would be the perfect metaphor.

As Rickey thought about who would be the first black man to break into the majors, one name kept coming into his mind with almost monotonous regularity. The name was Jackie Robinson. Late that afternoon, Jackie came storming into Rickey's office upon his request. The two men sat across the desk from each other eyeball to eyeball. Finally, Rickey asked, "Well, Jackie, can you do it?" Robinson responded, "Do what?" Rickey challenged, "Can you play in this league?" He said "Jackie, what we're trying to do will be met with lots of resistance. People will try to destroy the goodwill we wish to bring. Your own teammates will try to sabotage you, people will spit in your face, insult your family as they sit in the stands, and they will call you a nigger! And what's more, Jackie, you cannot fight back!" He went on to explain to Robinson that if he were to fight back, then it would solidify the sterotypes and propaganda that black people could not perform under pressure. Rickey explained that the focus would be taken off of Robinson's playing and placed on his behavior.

Rickey informed Robinson that his play on the field would have to do all of the talking. Robinson proved more than up to the challenge. As Rickey had promised, Robinson's detractors came in all forms. Opposing players would spit chewing tabacco all over his face when passing him on the field. They would throw balls at his head while he was in the batter's box. He was not allowed to eat in the same restaurants with the team, and frequently had to stay with friends or family because the hotels would not allow him to sleep with the team. Many times, other baseball teams would threaten to boycott the game if the Dodgers showed up with Robinson in the lineup. On one occassion, his own team members threaten to boycott play unless Robinson was released. They too had miscalculated the power of purpose and of an idea whose time has come. Rickey went on to conduct a team meeting in which he verbally ripped them apart. He asked many of the perpetrators where their parents came from. Many said their parents were immigrants who came to America in search of a better life. Rickey then asked those players what right their parents had to pursue the American dream if they believed that people should be refused the opportunity to play a great American sport such as baseball because of the color of their skin. Rickey went on to further inform them that Robinson would play on the team, with or without them.

As Rickey promised, the public did their part by ripping Robinson in the press and to his face by doing anything they

could to get him to retaliate, but he always heard a voice re-
verberating in his head. It was the voice of Branch Rickey, re-
minding him, "Remember, Jackie, no matter what, you can't
fight back! You've gotta let your play on the field do the talking!" Robinson went on that same year to become major
league baseball's rookie of the year and it's most valuable
player. Every time you see a Barry Bonds, Dave Justice, Ben-
ito Santiago, or a Kirby Puckett step to the plate and take a
swipe at that ball, remember that it all got started because two
men of different races who were filled with purpose met in a
room in 1946 and made a decision that changed the world.

If they can do all of that with the ignorance they faced at
that time, do you think it's possible for you to make a difference in this world? The answer is, "ABSOLUTELY!"

> *I do not wish to walk smooth paths or
> travel an easy road. I pray for strength and
> fortitude that I may bear the heavy load.
> I pray for strength that I may climb the highest
> peaks alone and transfer every stumbling
> block into a stepping stone.*
>
> —*Unknown*

YOU'VE GOT TO KEEP ON KEEPIN' ON

Sometimes we act like the things that we have to deal with
are so hard. Whenever I feel sorry for myself, I think about
some of the people in the world who really paid the price,
some with their lives, that you and I might have an easier go
of it. Look at people like Abraham Lincoln, John Kennedy,
Martin Luther King, Mahatma Ghandi and Mother Teresa. They
were and are willing to die because they felt so strongly about
their purpose in life. Once your definite purpose is identified,
you will find it hard not to be excited, to get up early, and stay
up late. You will find a fire burning deep within you.

I think about my grandmother, Nonnie, the lady who

raised me. She had eight children by the time she was 24 years old. She later said that had my grandfather not died, she might have had thirty, because he was a man of action! He kicked her out of the house in the back hills of Tennessee, took all eight children from her, and left her with no money and no place to go.

She borrowed enough money from family to catch a bus to St. Louis. Once there, she found a job as a cook and housekeeper for a wealthy family, earning $32 per week. When telling me this story, she explained that getting her children back was her reason for living. It became an all consuming purpose backed by a burning desire. She saved her money and created what amounted to an underground railroad as she sought to free her children from the wrath of my grandfather. She would save her money and then go pick up one or two of them. Nonnie would then retreat, save a little more money, and go back to get the others by plane, train or automobile. What's significant about this is that it took her a period of seven long years before she got them all back in her possession, including my father. No matter how long it took, she was prepared to see her mission through. In the interim, she had many rough times. Sometimes her integrity as a lady was tested as men from this wealthy family would proposition her, and she would have to straighten them out, risking her job in the process of maintaining her standards. But in the end, she got her children back and gave me a chance in life to make something of myself. You may have these stories in your own family, heroes and heroines who have succeeded despite what seemed to be insurmountable odds. Chances are that the greater the odds were, the stronger their purpose and burning desire were. Even when things seem hopeless, you've got to keep on keepin' on, knowing that whenever you have a purpose, your conviction will be tested.

It's interesting to see this manifested in my own life. People see me now, travelling across the country first class, speaking to *Fortune* 500 companies, and assume that I've had some kind of charmed life. What they see is what they perceive to be a finished product, but they don't see all of the pain and turmoil that I've endured in becoming the person that I am now. More importantly, they don't see what paces I'm willing to put myself through in order to continue to grow and develop into the person that I wish to be. If my grandmother could do all that she did with limited resources, as well as the people in your own families, and those throughout the course of history who have overcome great obstacles so that we could have a better life, do you think it's possible for you to make a difference in the world with your own unique contribution? The answer is, "ABSOLUTELY!"

In fact, you have an obligation to do so. We are all in debt to loans that we can't pay back. The fact that you were born in or live in this country is a debt that you can never pay back. You owe it to your God to be successful and you owe it to yourself to be successful, but most of all, you owe it to whoever may be watching you. Somebody always is. Some people won't do something unless you do it first, as Roger Bannister exemplified when he broke the record in the four-minute mile.

> *Before you get the answers to*
> *something in life, you must first have the reasons.*
> *"Reasons come first, answers come second."*
>
> *——Jim Rohn*

A MAN AND HIS DREAM

I often think about the incomparable inventor, Preston Tucker. Have you ever heard of the Tucker automobile? It goes to show that you never know what having a resounding purpose can lead to. This story makes the point that many of the things that we enjoy today without much thought, someone else paid the price for years ago. Preston Tucker invented the padded dashboard, disc brakes, seat belts, and fuel injection. The Tucker automobile was a 1940s phenonmenon! It featured the prior mentioned enhancements, as well as head lights that would turn in tandem with the front wheels so that you could see around dark corners at night. Aerodynamically, it was designed like many cars of today. It was way ahead of it's time! Tucker had invented a better mousetrap and the big three automakers knew it. They were scared to death! Through the use of money, politics, and influence, the big three got together with the government. They tried to send Mr. Tucker to prison by claiming that he never intended to build a car but sold franchises to hopefuls with the idea of bilking them out of money. This was not true. Jeff Bridges, the actor, plays Tucker in the movie, "Tucker, A Man and His Dream."

Towards the end of the movie, Tucker is aquitted of all charges of fraud, but the court mandates that he can never build the car. Outside of the courtroom sat fifty Tuckers in a rainbow of various colors, the same ones that hours earlier he almost went to prison for never intending to build. As the people attending the trial hopped into the cars for a ride from an invitation extended by Tucker, Tucker's confidant said, "Look at the people, they love the cars! Preston, we could have built fifty million, but now there will only be fifty built." Tucker responds, "Fifty or fifty million, it's having a purpose, it's the dream that counts!" Tucker went on to create automatic ice dispensers for refrigerators and many other inventions that helped increase the quality if life for many generations to come. His purpose was in clear view.

Impact Law: From this day forward, promise that you will ask of yourself continuously, "What is my purpose in life?" Sometimes negative things happen in your life. This will cause you to do one of two things. You can quit or you can continue to search for the answers necessary to discover your true purpose in life. Only from this process will you find those compelling reasons that will cause you to take action towards becoming that extraordinary person that resides within you.

All will come to he who waiteth as long as he
works like hell while he waiteth

—Unknown

YOU'VE GOT TO HAVE A MACHANISM!

Sometimes when negative things happen to us, we feel as though we want to throw in the towel, give up, and go into a shell for the rest of our lives, vowing to never attempt to succeed again. Have you ever felt that way? You can certainly do that! Or you can set your jaw even tighter and create a new resolve to succeed with more energy and commitment than ever before. I've learned in life that a clear purpose is often what separates winners from losers. I believe that we should welcome adversity because it often stretches us to the point of personal renewal. In that renewal, we often find a stronger purpose to succeed than we may have had before. My father used to always say to me, "Son, if you want to succeed in life, you've got to have a machanism!" Now, I understand that the correct word spelling is mechanism, the definition of which means an instrument or process, physical or mental, by which something is done or comes into being. Trust me, although he pronounced it "machanism," he meant mechanism, but the story wouldn't have the same meaning if it were pronounced as it's spelled in the dictionary. You see, my father did not have much formal education. He never went to high school and barely finished the eighth grade. While we didn't spend much time together as I was growing up, I'll never forget the example he set for me in terms of his drive to succeed and accomplish his purpose. He had an incredible work ethic. I remember him always working a minimum of three jobs. He would work all day, get three or four hours of sleep, get up and then go on to the next job.

He did this for 15 to 20 years, always with the dream of one day owning his own nightclub. He once got a job working for a company called The Oberman Shoe Company, in St.

Louis. This company made insoles for shoes and competed with Dr Scholl's. The owner of the company bought a machine that would better automate the production process, but nobody knew how to operate it. The owner was going on vacation, and before he left, my father asked to speak with him. My father made Mr. Oberman a proposition that he couldn't refuse. He told Mr. Oberman that he would be willing to figure out how to operate the machine and fill that warehouse with inventory by the time he returned from his vacation, if he would be willing to give him a small percentage of the profits for working overtime to make it happen. Laughingly, old man Oberman agreed to the terms, figuring that my father was just talking and would eventually give up in frustration.

When Oberman returned from his vacation, he got the shock of his life. That warehouse was filled with insoles. He eyes grew to the size of silver dollars. He knew that my father, Maurice Williamson, was no ordinary guy. When my father approached him about the deal they had made previously, he reneged. He told my father that while he admired his ambition, he who has the gold makes the rules. His final words to my father were that he could never reach his maximum earning potential while working for someone else. After that, he told my father that he was welcome to stay or he could quit any time he chose. It was in that atmosphere that my father found resolution enough to pursue his purpose. It became a burning desire, an obession! He got a job as a waiter back in the days when the hotel business was booming. He told me that a waiter in those days could earn $300–$400 a night if they hustled. He did! He worked almost around the clock, saving his money. Over a period of ten years, he saved $120,000 in cash. He then bought three cabs, leasing two of them and driving one himself. He did that for three years, took the money from that venture, and bought a liquor store. When the city came and took the property on which the store sat via eminent domain, he realized his dream. He found a small building on Olive St. which is on the main drag heading towards the Gateway Arch in downtown St. Louis. There were three buildings on either side of this small building, with two big parking lots adjacent to them. He opened his nightclub in 1968 at the age of 32. He eventually bought the other buildings, as well as the parking lots, until he had purchased the entire city block. Maurice's Night Club has now been in operation for more than 28 years. During that time, everyone from movie stars to government officals has crossed the threshold of his door. He found his "MACHA-NISM!" and interestingly enough, he learned much about life from his days as a waiter. During those years, he waited on multi-millionaires and listened to their conversations. He learned about the different kinds of foods and wines they liked. He became a gourmet cook in the process. He didn't just see himself as a waiter. The entire time, he saw himself owning his own business. As far as he was concerned, he was already there. The steps in the interim were part of the process necessary to get the knowledge he needed. Since that time, he's always worked for himself. This is where I got the desire to have my own business.

Through watching him, I saw what raw determination was all about. Since then, many nightclubs have come and gone. Many a new owner to be has warned my father that their club would be the next to seal his fate. He simply laughs with a shrug of the shoulders, as if to say I hope you have paid as many dues as I have to learn the game. The clubs of his so-called competitors usually close within a few months or years because they only want the social status of owning a night-club. Few understand the price that has to be paid to be a long-term player. When he told me years ago that you have to have a "machanism," what he meant was that you have to find something that you enjoy doing and find a way to make your living doing it. Most people settle for the first job that comes along without really analyzing how the job could possibly help them accomplish some larger purpose. They find themselves in a vicious cycle of doing just enough to keep from getting fired, and the boss usually pays them just enough to keep them from quitting if they're any good to begin with. After years of this cycle, people usually find themselves frustrated and empty because they had dreams that died on the vine. They live with the ghosts of opportunity lost. You must find the discipline necessary to discover your purpose. This requires the courage to think big and to see yourself with a burning desire to achieve an objective born as purpose from those thoughts. From there, you will find the whys and subsequently the hows necessary to create your own "MACHANISM!"

WHO ARE YOU?

Here's an exercise: I want you to find a nice quiet room where you won't be disturbed and get yourself a pen or pencil and a pad of notebook paper. I want you to stay in the room until you find the answers to these two questions. I want you to write the answers down as explicitly as you can.

- **Question Number One: Who am I?**
                                (What is my personal identity?)
                                (What do I stand for?)

Rule: You cannot describe yourself by using labels such as President of XYZ Corporation or Doctor, Lawyer, or Indian Chief. I want you to describe who you are without using labels because it's easy to hide behind labels. Just let the pen flow and write how you feel about yourself. If we were attending your funeral, what would you want said about you? Remember, no labels! Go for it!

Key Learning: I usually discover from this exercise that people get very frustrated because many are thinking about the answers to what should be a basic question for the first time. I then ask people in my seminars to describe the emotions that they were feeling while going through this process. I ask them to use only one word to communicate it, and to express that word as if they were introducing themselves to me using that emotion as their first name. In other words, they say, "Hello, I'm frustrated," or, "Hello, I'm scared, afraid, confused, courageous, energized, lonely, loved, forgotten, heartbroken, sad, mad, glad . . . ." You get the idea? It's amazing that heads of corporations find themselves at a loss for words when they go through this exercise and their labels are taken away. Only then can we discover who we really are. Our identity is our grounding wire to living a balanced life and understanding the difference between the false and the real.

An example of a person that I really respect is a young man by the name of Tony Dungy. He was one of the main reasons I attended the University of Minnesota. I was impressed with him because he truly has his head screwed on correctly. He was a quarterback on my team for three years in college and we shared an apartment. Today he is a good friend. If you follow professional football, you know that he was destined to become one of the NFL's super star head coaches, and is considered by many to be one of the brightest coaches in the game today. To those who know him, none of this comes as a surprise. I remember when he played for the Pittsburgh Steelers.

He played with the likes of Terry Bradshaw, Mean Joe Greene, Franco Harris, and Lynn Swan. This was enough to impress anyone, right? I found it hilarious that whenever we were out together and people asked Tony what he did, he'd respond in a deadpan manner, "I'm a laborer!" The funny thing about this is that he was deadly serious. He never bought into star status because he always kept the reality of the game in the forefront of his mind. He used to tell me that, "Professional football is a business, and you're only as good as your last hit record!" He wanted to remain in touch with the real Tony and not lose sight of reality.

He thought the entire concept of stardom was ridiculous. He often commented, "A young man comes into the NFL looking for fame and fortune, but you better get the fortune 'cause that fame ain't nothing!" I'll always love him for being real, and no matter how much notoriety he gets from being the best at what he does, to those of us who know him he'll always be simply, "T. D.!"

Exercise: In this same room or quiet place, I want you to answer the next major question.

• Question Number Two: What is your purpose in life?

Rule: I want you to answer this question as if you could accomplish anything that you desire. In doing this, I want you approach this exercise as if failure does not exist. What would you write down as your purpose if you knew that for certain you could have it? There's no such thing as failure! That's the mindset I want you to have as you approach this assignment. Don't spend any time worrying about the what ifs, just write the things that come to your mind. The first things you write are normally the truest representation of how you really feel.

After this, I would like you to write a clarifying statement as it relates to these two questions:

1.) WHO ARE YOU? (Your personal identity)
2.) WHAT IS YOUR PURPOSE? (What do you want to accomplish in your life?)
   These two clarifying statements will help you chart a course towards building a future more in line with how you feel about life rather than taking whatever comes along.

My clarifying statements are as follows:

Who Am I? (Desi's Personal Identity)

I am a kind, loving person who cares about others and wishes to communicate that love through the art of persuasion and human interaction. I am an honest and trustworthy human being who believes in dreams, hard work, and success as a birthright. I am a focused, persistent individual who is not afraid of success or failure because I understand that one cannot exist without the other. I am a spiritual human being that believes in a higher power than myself and believes that my life is a direct reflection of how I think, dream, and behave. I have and will become what I think about most often.

What is my purpose? (What do I want to do with my life?) Desi's purpose statement:

My purpose is to grow and develop all of my skill to its full potential, and to continually learn and stretch myself to the maximum in order to achieve success and happiness in all areas of my life, including mental, spiritual, health, family, and financial. I want to make a positive contribution to the world and leave each situation that I encounter better than I found it.

Your purpose statement should focus on what it is that you want to become. Once we are clear as to exactly what we want to do with ourselves, we then have a template on which to overlay our activity and accomplishments. More importantly, if the answers to these two questions really represent what you value most in terms of your identity and purpose, you will find the answers because you have first found the reasons.

> *To have a purpose is the true joy of life. To have a*
> *purpose that's recognized by yourself as a mighty one.*
> *To be a force of life, rather than a feverish little clod*
> *of ailments and grievances complaining that the*
> *world will not devote itself to making you happy.*
>
> —*Charles Bernard Shaw*

WHAT IS YOUR VISION?

Queens and Kings, let your
wildest imaginings seduce for
you brighter days. Relax your
anger, close your eyes and smile,
see all the happy children lost at
play. Nuture your most positive
ideals, your dreams and the wonderful things you envision. Those
fueled by your heart's desires
shall be done with focus and
passion. Always be patient with
yourself and others . . this insight may help when you're feeling down. You are one of the
gifted and spirited, focus
on your VISION and it
shall abound.

—©Saunni Dais

PROGRAM YOURSELF
FOR SUCCESS

"Your imagination is your preview of life's coming attractions."

—*Albert Einstein*

There are varied opinions about the subject of motivation. Many critics harshly criticize the speaking industry because they claim that motivation is like taking a warm bath. As soon as the bath is over, you're right back where you started in the same old pile of stinkin' thinkin'. I understand why there's never been a statue constructed in honor of a critic. Most critics spend their time on the sideline writing about the game instead of tightening their belt buckles and getting a little bloody. I find it staggering that someone could find something wrong with the concept of being motivated, even temporarily. What other formula for success in life would they propose? Of course, most critics usually don't have any answers. Most of them don't understand that human motivation is a science. Within the confines of this science, there are varied opinions about what it takes to be motivated. Many of the opinions have validity because what motivates people varies. Successful coaches in sports understand that what may be a motivating factor for one person may be completely demoralizing for another. Some people need a pat on the back, others need a kick in the butt! Once you know what you're motivated by, you can then program yourself to get the kind of results you want from life.

Motivation won't let you do anything, but it will help you do everything better than negative thinking will!

—*Zig Ziglar*

FIND WHAT YOU LOVE TO DO AND MAKE A CAREER OF IT!

The Bureau of Labor Statistics recently wrote that 80 percent of the people working in today's labor force don't like what they do for a living. This is not a startling statistic! Why? The fact that 66 percent of all heart attacks occur on Monday morning between the hours of 7 a.m. and 9 a.m. is evidence that people are working at jobs that make them sick. We've been conditioned to go to school and get a job so that some way, somehow, we will be fufilled at some point in the future. Unfortunately, for most people the future never happens the way they thought it would because they left it up to someone else. Formal education is great, and I recommend it strongly, but we cannot forget that we are ultimately responsible for our own happiness. That includes the amount of joy we get from what we do for a living. Most colleges and universities don't teach us how to really utilize our passion to create a career that will best serve our own needs and the world's. Currently, one of this biggest issues in corporate America is the fact that so few companies are really maximizing the potential of their people for competitive advantage. This is because so few people derive any real joy from the work that they do. Only in recent years have colleges and universities begun to address the issues of entreprenuership and work as an expression of who we are as people. Many people want to work for a cause above and beyond survival or monetary benefit.

You spend more than one third of your life working. Doesn't it make sense to find something to do that gives you pleasure? Then why don't you? The answer just might be FEAR! It's very common for people to take the first job that comes along when they graduate from high school or college rather than really analyze what their true interests are and how to best utilize their skills. This happens because of the pressure to survive and the emphasis that's placed on finding a job as soon as possible. Quite often, people become involved in professions in which they really have no heartfelt interest, but pursue anyway because of pressure from family members or peers. Some think, my dad is a doctor, his dad was a doctor, and his dad was a doctor so unless I want my dad to hate me, I'd better be a doctor. We've all heard the stories about the premed or pre-law student who has a secret desire to become an artist, or the banker who really wants to be a rock star. Because of the outside pressures from others, however, they allow themselves to do something that they really don't enjoy, even if they are monetarily well compensated. What they don't realize is that an erosion of their dreams started to take place the day they compromised. It will only be a matter of time before the true source of their motivation for life is launched to the forefront. It can take 5, 10, 15, 20, or even 30 years before a person asks themselves the question, "Is this all there is to life? Many people suffer from depression, in many cases, brought about by a lack of motivation and meaning in their lives. When we enjoy what we do for a living, it's much easier to be motivated because that motivation is driven from the inside out rather than the outside in.

From that perspective, we have a greater measure of control over our emotions when our work reflects self-actualization and fulfillment rather than money, or the continuous approval of others.

THE SYMPTOMS OF DEPRESSION

If you have experienced four or more of the following symptoms for more than two weeks, you should seek a physical or psychological evaluation by a physician or mental health specialist. The feelings listed may be part of a normal grief reaction for someone who has recently experienced a loss. But professional treatment is warranted if the feelings persist with no improvement in mood.

- A persistent sad, anxious or "empty" mood.
- Loss of interest or pleasure in ordinary activities.
- Decreased energy, fatigue or feeling "slowed down."
- Sleep problems like insomnia, oversleeping or early morning awakening.
- Eating problems like loss of appetite or weight loss or gain.
- Difficulty concentrating, remembering or making decisions.
- Irritability.

- Excessive crying.
- Recurring aches and pains that do not respond to treatment.
- Feelings of hopelessness or pessimism.
- Feelings of guilt, worthlessness or helplessness.
- Thoughts of death or suicide or making a suicide attempt.

Source: National Institute of Mental Health Depression Awareness Program

Do you enjoy any of these kinds of feelings or emotions? I hope not! I certainly don't! Now, please don't misunderstand, I am not implying that every case of depression is brought about by someone's job. I'm merely conveying the message that in many cases this is true. The fact is that 80 percent of the people who occupy jobs in the American work force today don't like what they do. In many documented cases, this has lead to depression. How can we avoid this?

Let Your Motivation Become Your Passion

I've been speaking professionally now for five years. There's nothing else that I'd rather do. I truly understand now what was meant by the old adage, "Find something you love to do and you'll never have to work a day in your life." Every human being on this planet has something that they are good at, something that they can do better than anyone else and receive joy from at the same time. I admire people who excel at things that I'm not very good at, such as tennis, golf, nuclear science, physics, chemistry, art, and record production. The list goes on and on. When you find something that you do well, figure out how to make a career of it.

Can you imagine jumping out of bed each morning with enthusiasm and vigor because you can't wait to get on with the day's activities? There are many people who do just that every day. I'm one of them. You can be, too! Before we can move on to find our true motivation, we must reprogram ourselves from old ways of thinking.

"As you think so shall you become."

—*James Allen*

Why is it that for every dreamer there's a doubter? For every visionary, a crowd of skeptics? For every new breakthrough, those who are quick to criticize? It's human nature for some people to spend their lives bringing other people down to their level. They suffer from a form of mental illness that should require medical attention. It's called negative thinking. This is one of the main reasons why many people fail in life: because they have a bad mindset. They look for all of the resaons why something won't work rather than why it will. With this mindset, they're beat before the game even starts.

THREE LEVELS OF THOUGHT

Level One—Negative Acceptance

When negative acceptance sets in, you don't even have a chance. If you think you can or can't do something, guess what? You're right on both counts! If it's true that we have the power to choose how we feel, why do most people choose the negative? It's because *WE'RE BORN TO WIN, BUT PROGRAMMED TO FAIL!* We are programmed into the negative from the moment we come into this world. It starts with our upbringing. By the time you reach the age of 18, you've heard the world no 200,000 times, seen 30,000 acts of violence, and have recieved more than 12 million messages in the form of advertising telling you how to look, what to eat, and how to feel. No wonder most of us grow up with a negative image! This negative self-image will surely manifest itself into a negative person unless we intervene to break the pattern. The level of negative acceptance thinking is accented by words and phrases such as " I can't!", "It won't work!",

"We've always done it this way!"and "Nobody in my family has ever become anything, so why even try?" Sometimes loving but misguided relatives squash our dreams by telling us to "Just be a little more realistic,", "Be reasonable!"and "Don't get your hopes up too high!" And on and on. What's realistic or reasonable? Why should what they say or how they feel be a death sentence of mediocrity for you? I have discovered throughout the years that misery does love company. If you happen to find a dream strong enough to motivate you to accomplish something, it reminds some people of what they don't have the courage to do.

When my grandmother first took me in, many people, some in my own family, told her that I would only disappoint her, that I would never amount to anything, and that she was foolish to put hopes and dreams into me. Can you imagine somebody saying something like that about an eleven-year-old kid? What's worse is that I knew that they were saying these things about me. How do you think that made me feel? Well, I decided that rather than let this negative feedback put me down, I would use it as fuel to prove them wrong. Most of all, I used it to prove to myself that I was going to be somebody. My grandmother used to always tell me to keep on believing in myself regardless of what other people thought. I would ask you to do the same, no matter what other people might do or say. Keep on dreaming!

GIVE YOURSELF A FIGHTING CHANCE

Sometimes we can psych or talk ourselves right out of something without even giving ourselves an opportunity to succeed! I remember playing football at the University of Minnesota and playing against some of the top teams in the nation, such as Nebraska, Ohio State, and Michigan. It seemed that we were always in a state of panic when we played these teams. This included the coaching staff as well as the players. We would approach these games in fear rather than in full confidence, and this often resulted in us getting blown out of the stadium. We approached other teams much differently in our preparation. When we competed against teams like Illinois, Iowa, and, of course, Northwestern, we believed we would win. We did more often than not.

ALWAYS PLAY TO WIN!

We were in Ann Arbor, Michigan, one Saturday to play the University of Michigan, which happened to be ranked number two in the nation. The game was to be played on national television in front of millions of people. In fact, the day before the game, as we went through our pre-game drills, our head coach summoned us all and asked us to look around the stadium. He told us to breathe in the atmosphere because the next day there would be 100,000 screaming jackasses in the stands. When Tony Dungy, who was our starting quarterback and happened to be from Michigan, informed the coach that his mother was coming to the game, the coach immediately changed the statement, saying that there would be 99,999 screaming jackasses in the stands. Well, it was business as usual. We expected to lose and we did.

We were intimidated more by the history and swagger of the big, bad Wolverines than anything else. We went into the game with the attitude that if we could just keep the score down and avoid too much embarrassment, we would have gained a moral victory. Michigan had us down 35-0 at half time. Guys on our team were pulling up lame and just plain quitting. Finally in the fourth quarter, with a 46-0 lead in front of the entire nation on ABC, Bo Schembechler, the Michigan head coach, took a time-out with six seconds left and kicked a short field goal to make the score 49-0. This added to an already pitiful situation. He really rubbed it in! I can still remember our team walking off the field with our heads down, demoralized by all of the obnoxious fans and the shame that came from losing so badly. After the game, our coach walked across the field to inform Bo what a classless act it was to humiliate us so when the game was clearly out of reach. Bo told our coach to shove up his __ __ __... you get the point! The thing that stands out in my mind is that the game was lost long before we took the field. It was lost in practice and in all of the meetings that preceded the game. We were beaten before the game even started. No one believed we could win that game and we didn't. Was there really that much of a difference between their team and ours? Were they 49 points better? They were only because we thought they were. How many times have you have stopped yourself cold from taking action on something that you wanted for yourself, due to fear? Winning is a state of mind. If you don't believe that you can succeed, you never will. Belief in yourself is powerful medicine and the starting point for all achievement.

So Close, But Yet So Far

The ensuing year brought many unpleasant disappointments. We lost many games that would have allowed us to have an outstanding season and finished toward the middle of the pack with a 6-5 record, despite the fact that Tony Dungy led the Big Ten in passing and total offense.

We again faced the top ranked Wolverines of Michigan in the seventh game of the season and played them tough only to lose in a very tight game 27-21. After fumbling inside of the Michigan 20 yard line in the game's closing moments, the Wolverines recovered the fumble and ran out the clock, dashing all hopes of a 28-27 Minnesota upset. We believed in ourselves, but not enough to win the big one!

What Goes Around Comes Around!

The next season rolled around, and because of our ineptitude the previous year, we were picked to finish next to last in the Big Ten conference, ahead of only the downtrodden Northwestern Wildcats. It's great to see them finally have some good fortune for a change. After struggling through our first seven games to a 4-3 record, we were once again facing the mighty Michigan Wolverines, who were a perfect 7-0 and ranked number one in the nation. We were 35-point under - dogs, and for our seniors, myself included, this would be our last opportunity for redemption.

A strange thing would happen the week before the game. The previous week we had barely beaten Northwestern 7-3 at our homecoming, and the coach wanted to make some changes. One of them involved moving me from defensive end and having me start as our right offensive guard. If you follow football, even a little, you know that offensive linemen weigh 260 to 300 lbs. I weighed a paltry 205 lbs. The coach felt like we needed leadership on offense, and the fact that I played the position in high school was a plus as far as he was concerned. I practiced the entire week at that position, mostly with the idea that I would be pulling and trapping the opposition. That week of practice was a disaster. We were running around like Keystone Cops, unorganized, unpredictable, and scared. The Friday before the game we looked like F Troop, with guys jumping off side and making all kinds of mental errors. The coach sent us in and I could see the look on his face! To add insult to injury, I was to be playing across from two players who were All Big Ten and All American respectively. One was a defensive tackle who played several years with the Cardinals, Curtis Greer, and the other was an All American linebacker, Ron Simpkins, who played for the Cincinnati Bengals. Who would have given me a chance against these guys, let alone our team against theirs? The answer is no one! No one except us!

The morning of the game was always a weird time. We were always awakened by a call from the front desk and usually took a walk outside in the frigid Minnesota air. This was a home game at Memorial Stadium, which we called "The Brick House." After our walk, we usually ate our pre-game meal, which consisted of roast beef slices, dry toast, scrambled eggs and honey. After that, we taped ankles and joints, and held meetings by position. In the bus on our way over to the stadium, the seniors on our team made a vow to let it all hang out. The night before the game, we received one heck of a speech from George "Butch" Nash, who was one of our assistant coaches and a Minnesota football legend. He had coached too many All Americans to name. He told us to play like our lives were on the line. He told us that for once in our lives, we should give it everything we had, and do our best, because that's all that anyone could ever expect of us. The next morning, on the way over to the stadium, I kept remembering the sour taste in my mouth from the years before. I remembered how everyone cried in the locker room for bringing such shame to a once proud University of Minnesota football program. We all kept saying, "Let it all hang out!"

Our theme song that year was "Brick House" by the Commodores, featuring Lionel Richie. We played it on the bus and that bus was rocking! There was a buzzing sound in the air, an eerie feeling inside that told you something was happening. You could feel that something was going to be different about this day. We just didn't know what it was. When we went out to start the game, there were only about 40,000 fans in a stadium that held 65,000. That made no difference to us. We felt like nothing mattered. It wouldn't have made a difference if the place had been empty. We were going the play for ourselves, regardless of the outcome.

Michigan kicked the ball off to us to start the game and we quickly drove 65 yards to score and take the lead, 7-0. During the play that scored the touchdown, I got whacked in the nose and blood poured everywhere, all over my jersey, pants, and face mask. I knew one thing for sure: nobody was going to take me out of that game. Mark Carlson, our quarterback, said that after looking at me in the huddle, he felt like passing out. This was our opportunity to have that one shining moment that everyone talks about. I wasn't about to be cheated out of it, blood or no blood! The intensity after this drive was electric. Would we be able to keep it up? The fans were going crazy, but everyone expected the mighty Wolverines to come back and put us in our proper place, back in our gopher hole! The next thing they knew, it was half time and we had added a field goal to lead 10-0. The stadium was a madhouse with the fans going wild! We came out to start the third quarter and found the stadium packed. People had been listening to the game on the radio and decided to come and see if this was really happening. More than 25,000 tickets were sold at halftime and we were looking at the first packed house of the year. Everyone pretty much figured that we would come to our senses, so would Michigan and the final score would be Michigan 35: Minnesota 10. Somebody should have told us! Michigan kicked off to us to start the second half. We drove the ball 80 yards without throwing a pass, and kicked a field goal. The score was 13-0.

When Michigan finally got the ball back, there were only 3:58 seconds left in the third quarter. We were dominating the best college football team in the nation! Bo Schembechler, the coach who had so badly embarrassed us two years before, stared on in stunned disbelief. We scored once more, with a field goal in the fourth quarter, to seal the one of the biggest upsets in college football history. Before the game ended, I remember staring across the field at the nation's number one team and saying, "How does it feel? Now you jerks know how we felt last year, so soak it up and deal with it, 'cause we are kicking your butts!" We cried in the huddle as the game wound down, because for the first time in many of our lives, we felt like winners. Final score: Minnesota 16: Michigan 0. It was the first time that they had been shut out in 25 years. In the locker room after the game was over, there were lots of tears, mostly from joy and happiness. My coach came up to me and gave me a big bear hug with tears in his eyes and said, "Son, you're what college football is all about!" That same year, we defeated the University of Washington, which featured a quarterback named Warren Moon, and UCLA, which featured a host of super stars who would later go on to find fame in the NFL. We went on to play in the Hall of Fame Bowl, which was the first bowl game that the university had gone to in more than 16 years. Redemption at last!

What was so different about this team? We were basically the same guys who had been so miserable the year before. The difference was that we finally decided to move past the level of negative acceptance that held us back in the past and start believing in what was possible. Our backs were against the wall and we had nowhere to go but up. Sometimes when people are the most desperate, they perform the best. It's like the story of the 90 lb woman who lifts a 2,000 lb car off of her child and then pulls the child to safety. It's been said many times that sports transcend life. I believe that to be true, because sports is an expression of the human condition. There are ups and downs, winning and losing, and situations that help people determine what kind of character the have within. I learned that day that I have every right to expect just as much success as anyone. So do you!

Don't ever let anyone turn you around on your dreams because you never know what can happen. The incident with the Michigan game taught me how to be a winner. I've thought about that day many times when faced with other challenges. Think about times when you've accomplished something and really felt great about yourself. Capture the mood. What did the atmosphere feel like? What kinds of emotions were evoked from those feelings? Take those feelings, embrace them, remember them, and hold them always in the forefront of your mind to be recalled any time you may doubt yourself. The most powerful form of belief is self belief. As Napoleon Hill once said, "Whatever the mind of man can conceive and believe, it can achieve! " I say it will achieve. If you don't achieve something it's because deep down inside, you don't believe!

Many times we think that success only happens to other people. This type of mindset guarantees failure. So, do everything you can to eliminate negative thinking and negative people from your life. They will destroy your hopes and dreams if you allow them to. Beginning today, rededicate yourself to becoming better than you were yesterday. Renew any dreams that you may have placed on the back burner and never, I mean never, think about giving up on YOU!

DON'T QUIT!

When things go wrong as they sometimes will
When the road you're travelling seems all uphill
When the funds are low and the debts are high
When you want to smile and you have to sigh
When the pressure is bearing down again
Rest if you must, but don't you quit
Life is queer with its twists and turns
And every one of us sometimes learns that
Many a failure would have turned about
When they might have won had they stuck it out
Don't give up though the pace seems slow,
You might succeed with one more blow
Because success is failure turned inside out
The silver tent or the cloud of doubt?
You'll never know how close you are
It may be near, when it seems so far
So stick to the fight when you're hardest hit
It's when things seem worse, that you must not quit!

—Anonymous

Level Two Thinking—Regret

Many people suffer from the dreaded disease of regret because they don't have the courage to take action. So they sit on the sidelines of life and take whatever is left over after decisive people are finished. Many large companies have suffered from the wrath of regret. It doesn't matter how successful you may have been in the past, because the minute you think you've arrived, you're ready for the return trip back home.

Think about a powerful company like IBM. Just a few years ago they were held up as the pinnacle of corporate success. Companies would send their people out to IBM to find out what they were doing. These companies would go back home and do the same things. More often than not, they would work. IBM had figured out the combination to open the safe. Inside was massive success. The problem was that they rested too long and did not pay attention to what was happening in the marketplace. It began to change!

Two guys out in Cupertino, California, by the names of Steve Jobs and Steve Wozniak, had a vision. They wanted to take these huge mainframes that could fill a room, condense them, and place one in the hands of every person around the globe. They started a small company, and now their sales are in excess of eight billion dollars anually. Do you know the name of this company yet? It's Apple Computer! Before this, there were certain assumptions made, such as hardware will always be the driving force behind the computer industry. Is this true today? The answer is no! Apple set IBM back on its heels. We shoulda, we coulda, if only we had, why didn't we think of that? These comments often characterize regret. I'm sure that IBM felt that way. They are making a tremendous comeback, which is the mark of a true champion, but much of the pain could have been eliminated had they paid more attention to detail and continually demanded more of themselves in the form of creativity and perspective. You and I must do the same if we are to reach our goals in life. That's the challenge of success. It's fleeting. That's why we must constantly seek to improve ourselves if we are going the stay ahead.

I spent several years in the beverage industry with PepsiCo, Inc. It was always interesting to watch the dynamics between Pepsi and Coke. I felt like I was watching two twin brothers duke it out in a heavyweight fight. One throws a right, so does the other. One ducks, so does the other. They know each other's moves exactly. The only problem with that is they always wind up in the same place, in a dead heat. Tied and continiung to argue about who's number one! I felt like I was watching the old TV show, "What's My Line?", with Gary Moore, where the question was, Will the real number one please stand up? At the beverage companies, it was, No we're number one! Wait a minute, we're number one! Pepsi....We've got Michael Jackson! Coke.....We've got Michael Jordan! Pepsi... We've got the right one baby, UH! UH! Now I happened to be sitting in the audience the night that the Right One Baby commercial was premiered at the annual Pepsi Cola Bottlers convention and I thought, "That's got to be the stupidest commerical I've ever seen!" Good thing I wasn't in marketing then. It's one of the most recognized commercials in the history of advertising. While Pepsi and Coke were arguing about who was number one, however, the marketplace was changing. Baby Boomers, those born between 1946 and 1964, began to become more health conscious and question everything that went into their bodies. They questioned whether or not drinking tons of water loaded with sugar and caffeine was good for them. As a result, they started making other choices. They started drinking more teas, juices and water. Think about it! If someone had come to you thirty years ago and said one day you will go to the store and buy water, you would have probably said, "You're crazy, man, water's free!" Now you go to the supermarket and you are literally inundated with rows and rows of water. There's sparkling water, natural water, distilled water, and flavored water. There was even an entire beverage category created, called new age, that included drinks such as Gatorade, Powerade, and All Sport. Meanwhile, three window washers in upstate New York by the names of Leonard Marsh, Hymen Golden, and Arnold Greenberg, were watching this trend. Instead of being filled with fear and not doing anything, they kept asking the operative question, "How can we capitalize on the changes in the marketplace?" They created a product called Snapple. Have you ever heard of that? The company was subsequently sold to Quaker Oats which made all three men fabulously rich. Snapple is selling more than one billion dollars worth of its fruity tea drinks annually. Pepsi and Coke found themselves lamenting, we shoulda,.... we coulda,..... if only we had,.... why didn't we think of that?

Conventional thinking would say that there's no use in trying. You can't compete with the big boys. Conventional thinking often leads to mediocrity. You've got to be able to see an opportunity and take action on it if you really want a chance to succeed.

After that, beverage industry experts felt that the tea market was cornered because not long after the Snapple miracle, Pepsi inked a muti-million dollar deal with Lipton Tea. Coke countered with its own multi-million dollar deal with Nestea. Many people thought it foolish to attempt to compete with these two industry giants without tons of cash for marketing.

Enter Mike Schott and his new hit, Arizona Tea. He didn't have a multi-million dollar advertising budget, so he used a wild and very colorful 24 oz. can. It leaped off of the shelves and captured the attention of the American consumer to the tune of more than 300 million dollars a year.

> *" Don't ever let anyone tell you what can't be done,*
> *because people are finding ways every day to do*
> *the seemingly impossible. The key is to find what you*
> *believe to be a good idea. As long as it's legal and*
> *does not violate the rights of your fellow man, go for it!"*
>
> —*Desi Williamson*

EXCUSES, EXCUSES, EXCUSES
WHATEVER YOU'RE GOING TO DO, GET ON WITH IT!

> *"There are costs and risks to a program of action,*
> *but they are far less than the long range risks*
> *and costs of comfortable inaction."*
>
> —*John F. Kennedy*

It's amazing how many excuses people have for not taking action on their dreams in life. Some say "I'm too young!" Then when they start to mature, they say, "I'm too old!" Well, guess what?

You'll never be any younger! Each day spent is one less day you have do whatever it is that you plan to do with your life. I was giving a seminar in San Jose, California, not long ago, and one of my participants was an 85-year-old woman. She was vibrant and full of energy. When she shook my hand, she almost broke it! She had more pep than people half her age. She didn't think she was too old at all. She bought a home and took out a 30-year mortgage. That's optimism! She was going back to college to get her degree because she never went to school due to the depression and the obligation of raising a large family. She was just getting started on another chapter of her life at a time when most people are waiting to die. She could have said, "Well, I'm going to wait until conditions change or get better!" But she didn't have much time left to play with any more. While you might think that you have got lots of time, you don't have much time to play with any more either. I don't care if you're young! People have become so conditioned to wait and let circumstances determine what they're going to do that they constantly postpone the action point, waiting for conditions to change. You don't wait for something to happen, you make something happen! When you make something happen, you change the condition.

Many people suffer from a disease called the Mañana Syndrome. I'll get around to that tomorrow. I'll do it some other time. I don't feel right about it right now. That happened to me not too long ago. My agent called me. We split up some duties and I was supposed to call a couple of people. One of them was a person that I really didn't feel like talking to. Have you ever had someone like that? You say to yourself, "I don't feel right about it right now!" I then thought to myself, "There is only right now!" So I picked up that phone and called that person immediately, but nobody was there! I called again and got the wrong person, but in an instant, I found myself postponing something I had to do then! What most of us don't realize is that by making a decision not to do the major things that could improve our lives, we're postponing our better future. This becomes a terrible pattern of behavior, and the older we get, the harder it is to take action and get the ball rolling.

I have a friend who has this disease. He always talks about what he is going to do, but he never follows up his dream with action. This friend of mine was recruited to the University of Minnesota at the same time as myself, and we were both in the class of 1974. He never took school seriously, and eventually flunked out. After that, he always seemed to have negative things to say about the university. I've learned over the years that a good friend is someone who will slap you around mentally when you need it. This means that they won't allow you to dodge responsibility. They tell you like it is because they love you and want you to face what's real. Only then can you deal with the situation as it is and make the necessary changes to improve the situation. This comes from taking full responsibility for what happens to you. I decided to be a real friend and tell him like it was. I told him that the only reason he felt so negatively about the university was because he had unfinished business there. I suggested that he go back to school and complete his education. He said,"By the time I graduate from college, I would be 44 years old!" I said, "How old are you going to be if you don't go?" The answer is, of course, the same, 44! He suffers from the same disease as many people do, procrastination. Now is the time to make things happen in your life. Pick a direction and go. Any one will do. Some people would ask, "What if it's the wrong direction?"

My answer to that is always, "You'll find out more quickly! There's no substitute for action. If you make a mistake, you'll learn from it. Sometimes in life it's just as important to learn what not to do as what to do! If you succeed in your undertaking, it builds momentum and gives you the confidence to try something esle. One of the key components for success is MASSIVE ACTION! The question is not, Can you do something? It is, Will you do it? Are you really willing to discipline yourself to take the actions necessary to expand your horizons by continuing your education, learning a new language, taking self-improvement classes, getting a license to sell real estate, putting together a new resume, or making whatever changes needed to improve the quality of your life? The main question is, Are you willing to take charge of life now and be responsible for your results?

That's how you eliminate the pain of regret. When you take action, win or lose, you set up in your mind that action is it's own reward. When you act, you get a result and are given the formula for the next action that could lead to larger possibilities. Some people keep shoulding, and shoulding, and shoulding, until they should all over themselves!

Perhaps Charles Bernard Shaw said it best:

> *"People are always blaming their circumstances for what they are. I don't believe in circumstances. The people who get on in this world are the people who get up and look for the circumstances they want, and, if they can't find them, they make them."*

You must be willing to be accountable for your life. Over the course of the last 28 years, my father has owned a bar and restaurant in St. Louis. I've seen many a broken man and woman in my time. Many were alcoholics or drug addicts. As a youth, I was always curious as to why and how their lives turned out to be such tragedies. Some I watched grow from beautiful young women and handsome young men with promising futures to outcasts. When I asked them about the reasons for their plight, it was always interesting to note that very few of them would actually take responsibility for their condition. It was always someone or something else that was to blame. There were very few who would step forward and say that they were the reason.

My little brother has been in and out of reform schools and correctional facilities all of his life. I know that for many years he blamed me for running away from home when I was eleven and leaving him behind. He blamed my mother and father for the lives they led as young people. I agree that he got a raw deal as a child. When you finally grow up, you realize that few people come from ideal families. One night an amazing thing brought tears to my eyes. Calling me from the state penitentiary at 1:30 in the morning, my brother said he finally knew the reason that he was in the joint. He said it was because of him. He admitted that even with the bad breaks he'd endured, he knew right from wrong. I got down on my knees and thanked God. For the first time, I felt that he really had a chance at life because he was taking the first step to maturity and accountability for self. If only I had! If only they wouldn't have! Had I not had so many bad breaks! If I had only gotten started when I was younger! I'm too old! I'm too young! These are all the laments of the loser, the failure, the person who is never really willing to pay a price. I read a poem a few years ago that I often recall when thinking of these kinds of people.

> *I bargained with life for a penny*
> *And life would pay no more*
> *However I begged at evening*
> *When I counted my scanty store*
> *You see, life is a just employer*
> *It will give you what you ask*
> *But once you have set the wages*
> *Why, then you must bear the task*
> *I worked for a menial's hire*
> *Only to find dismayed*
> *Any price I would have asked of life*
> *Life would have willingly paid*
> —*Jessie B. Rittenhause*

WINNERS VS LOSERS

There are lots of words you can think of for a loser. We can call them all kinds of things. Helpless, pitiful, unsuccessful, also ran, enslaved, lazy, degenerate, sorryful, mediocre, and on and on. When someone says the word winner, you automatically know what that means. You don't have to wonder, "What did they mean by that?" The word winner has a ring to it and you need not say more. The difference between winners and losers is not that winners are smarter or have any greater natural ability. Most winners have one simple ability, the ability to decide what they want and take the actions necessary to make it happen. It's all a matter of choice, not chance!

We human beings are the most intellectual creatures on earth because we have the power to choose the course of our lives. No other animal has that option. Other species must depend solely on the instinct to survive. That's not true with people. They can make something out of nothing. They can turn pennies into fortunes, or take the most dire circumstances and transform their lives into successes, creating opportunity for others in the process. We all have an obilgation to leave this world in a little bit better condition than we found it. The true test of a successful life is not how long we live, but how we live. When we seek to contribute to a greater cause than ourselves, it is virtually impossible for us not to benefit in the process.

Life means to have something definite to do
A mission to fulfill. And in the measure in which we avoid set-
ting our life to something, we make it empty.
Human life, by its very nature, has to be dedicated to something.

—Jose Ortega Y Gasset

"The future belongs to those of us who
know and perform!"

—*Desi Williamson*

Level Three Thinking—Integration

The highest level of thinking is called integration. It says, **I CAN!**, **I WILL!**, and **I MUST!** achieve success. It is my birth right to maximize my potential and become the best person that I possibly can. According to Webster, the word integrate means 1.) The organization of organic, psychological, or social traits and tendencies of a personality into a harmonious whole. In my estimation, level three thinking comes when you are truly attuned to 1.) Who you are as a person, 2.) What your chief aim is in life, and 3.) What price you are willing to pay to make your dreams come true. The majority of today's corporations operate with a mission statement. This is a declaration of the direction of the organization. It is posted throughout the company as a reminder of what the company stands for. I believe that our lives are the same way. If someone were to ask you for your personal mission statement in life, would you be able to give them one? Without one, it will be difficult for you to remain consistent in your values, actions, and results.

My mission statement reads as follows:

> "To aid individuals in personal development and growth by offering information, ideas, and solutions that help them achieve measurable results in reasonable time as they strive to achieve excellence in all areas of their personal and professional lives."

Your mission statement differs from your purpose statement in that it focuses on what you want to give, whereas the pupose statement should be focused on what you would like to become or do. I would suggest that you find a quiet place and author a mission statement that reflects what you would like to do with your life. The operative question is, What do you want to accomplish in your life at this point? Your mission may change depending upon your situation at a given point and time in your life. For example, a couple trying to raise three children may have different individual mission statements before the children are all grown and have moved out than they would have afterwards. As your situation and priorities change, it is possible for your mission statement to change. The key thing is to take the time to think about your life without waking up every day as a creature of reaction and habit. You will be surprised at the clarity and sense of purpose you will have after completing this exercise. You will feel much freer and in control of your destiny. After you have penned your mission, place it somewhere so that you can see it often. It will remind you of why you're doing what you're doing when your dobber is down and you have cause to question yourself.

As we strive to achieve this level of integration we may need to tune in to everything that happens to us and use it to realize our mission in life. Every year on New Years Eve, CNN has a special report in which they review the lives of famous people who have died that year. I often marvel at some of the accomplishments of these people. Most of them have achieved excellence in their fields while others have become infamous rather than famous. The one thing that sticks in my mind from this show is that regardless of their accomplishments, these people are no longer with us. They're dead! It's a stark reality that each of us is given a finite amount of time on this spinning planet. No one of us knows when the last grain of sand in the hourglass will hit the bottom and the game is over. This hits especially hard when people close to us die and we are forced to deal with the question of why are we still here. Is there some special reason for us to live when so many people have died before us? Perhaps their futures appeared brighter and more promising than our own. The power of observation is very powerful if we take the time to let it work. We will gain deeper insight and appreciation for life if we our allow the power of reflection and introspection to work for us.

In St. Louis, there was a kid that I played football and basketball against. He went to Vianney High School, a rival of Christian Brothers High School, better known as C.B.C, where I went. This guy's name was Randy Frisch. He was a big, scrappy guy with curly red hair who stood about six feet five inches and weighed in at around 275 lbs. He was known as a bully. He was a stud on the football field and a brute on the basketball court. I didn't like him from the first time I laid eyes on him. Have you ever met someone like that? You said to yourself, "Even though I don't know this person, if I met them, I probably wouldn't like them?" As it turned out, my perception of him was all wrong. Even though he carried this swagger, I later learned that it was more out of confidence than arrogance. He was a good guy! He was like a big teddy bear, but he could also project a mean streak if you got on the wrong side of him. I saw this manifest itself several times when people gave him a hard time in public. They would soon learn that he was no one to fool around with, but he would never provoke anything himself. Over the course of the next few years, we became really good friends. He went on to the University of Missouri on athletic scholarship. One year later, I graduated from high school and went to the University of Minnesota. We continued to work out through the summers and man, did we push each other. We lifted weights at the same club and ran together during those humid Missouri summers to the point were we would almost pass out. We became so close, I really loved this guy! Well the years passed and we both were doing very well. During Randy's senior year, his team was awesome. Mizzou upset Alabama in their home opener and went on to beat Nebraska and three other teams ranked in the top ten that year. Randy was a defensive tackle and had a great year. Later that year, he was drafted by the Pittsburgh Steelers and was doing well in training camp. He was slated to play behind a guy named "Mean Joe Greene" on the most dominant defense that's ever been assembled in the history of professional football. We were all very proud of Randy and were looking forward to seeing him play in the fall. He and I had just completed our final summer workout only three weeks before I got the good news from Tony Dungy, who was also at that training camp, about how well my home boy was doing. Tony said that Randy was going to make the team. The following week, the Pittsburgh Steelers played the Philadelphia Eagles in a preseason game. Randy played very well. That night, after the game, Randy was driving back from their practice facility in La Trobe, P.A., when an oncoming truck swerved recklessly out of it's lane and hit Randy head on. He was killed instantly! My buddy was dead!

I got the news the next day as I was preparing to leave St. Louis to report to Minneapolis for my senior year. I got a phone call about 7:30 AM in the morning. It was Randy's mother. She was crying so hard, I could feel the pain as if I were there in person. When I hung up the phone, I walked out on the front porch and collapsed in a chair and cried for hours. I couldn't believe it! I kept playing these visual tapes in my head of our working and hanging out together, thinking of the brotherhood that was established between us.

My grandmother came out on the porch and asked me to come inside. She sat in a large living room chair and I sat down in the same chair with my head resting on her lap and cried some more. I asked why God let me live and took Randy away when he had so much to live for. He was about to live out a childhood dream. The same one I had, along with so many other kids, to play in the National Football League. Nonnie explained to me that God has plans for all of us, but sometimes chooses to use us in different ways, ways that we sometimes don't understand. She told me to learn from all of the things that Randy and I did together and remember that each day is not promised to any of us. She said that I should observe and learn how to take the things that happen in life and use them to become a better person. What I learned from this experience is that as long as we are here on earth, God has a purpose for us. That purpose is to contribute to the betterment of the world. We sometimes act as if we have forever to do something, until we lose someone very close to us. Then we are jolted into the reality of the temporal aspects of life. Why not take advantage of life now? Why wait until something drastic happens in order to get yourself to move off of the mark? One of the key factors in integration is learning to love yourself. I'll never forget that summer day when I got the news about Randy, because on that day, I promised myself that I would make something of my life. I looked up and down my block and one thing hit me squarely between the eyes. Most of the kids my age were dead! Most of them died due to violence. They were murdered! I wanted to make something of myself for those who had never had a chance. —Robbie, Greg, Jewell, Terrance, Kieth, Sandra, Preston, John, Roni, Lamont, Norvell, Reggie, Larry, Alvin, and all the others who never saw their 21st birthday. This book is a tribute to the many more who are in bondage to alchohol, drugs, and violence. Integration means bringing to the forefront all of the lessons of life and using them to live with a greater sense of passion, purpose, commitment, and meaning.

EXAMPLES AND WARNINGS

I had three uncles that were awesome. All three were extremely handsome men who were multi-talented. Like my father, they lacked formal education, but all of them had an inner drive to succeed. They worked very hard as young men, always holding two or three jobs. They all saved their money, eventually operating their own businesses, which included liquor stores, dry cleaners, convenience stores, night clubs, and restaurants. Unfortunately, they all died young. Two of them never saw their fiftieth birthdays. They lived too hard, never ate right, didn't get enough sleep, and drank a little too much. This lifestyle caused each of them to die young. I saw this growing up and made the decision as a very young kid to live life at a slower pace. It doesn't matter how successful you are or how much money you make, if it kills you in the process, YOU LOSE! I really miss my uncles and think of them all of the time. They were special men! If I saw how they lived and took nothing away from their lives and subsequent deaths to help make myself a better person, what did they die for? I learned things from them about life that I'm still applying to this day. To my Uncle Rudy, Uncle Wilbur, and Uncle Brother, know that wherever you are, I love you. The lessons you taught me not only in death, but more importantly in your lives, will live on for many generations to come as I teach them to my children and they pass the learnings on to future generations of the Williamson family. I look forward to seeing you all at some future time. From this moment on, I challenge you to become a student of observation. Let's not allow the valuable lessons in life pass you by without asking yourself how you can use them to become a better person.

EVERYTHING IN ITS PROPER PLACE

I attended the funeral of a young man by the name of Charles Mason when I was twelve years old. I didn't know him personally, but he was a member of my church. He was only 34 years old when he died from a nervous breakdown. My grandmother and I were riding back home from the funeral when I asked her what a nervous breakdown was and why Charles had to die at such a young age. She told me that a nervous breakdown came from a lack of balance in life. She went on to tell me that the way to have balance in your life is to make sure that everything is in its proper place in your mind. Now, my grandmother is not an educated woman in the formal sense, but she has more wisdom than anyone I've ever met. I've never forgotten that day, and whenever something gets out of whack, I think about Charles, who doesn't have the opportunity to balance issues in his life. The fact that you and I are still alive leaves us with options. We should seek each day to take the full range of experiences that life will surely provide and integrate them into our lives.

If you are waking up each day and feeling as though you are leading a life of quiet desparation, you have plenty of company, but it need not be that way. Your apprehension may come from looking at your problems as permanent instead of realizing that, like life itself, they're temporary. We should arise each morning with anticipation and ulitilize the things we've learned. A journey of a thousand miles begins with a single step.

Back in the early 1980's when I was just getting my career started in sales, I often ate in the restaurant of a posh grocery store called Byerly's. Every morning that I was there, so was this very successful looking gentleman with striking features. He had a full head of thick, silver hair with a perfectly trimmed mustache to match. He was in his late sixties, and it seemed that our body clocks were the same because we always seemed to be sitting at the counter having the breakfast special at the same time. I got to know him and he was a fascinating man. He owned a multi-milllion dollar hair care products company and had a real passion for life. He always smiled and had a kind word for those he encountered along the way.

Even though it has been many years since I've seen him, he told me something I'll never forget. He mentioned that throughout his life he had often heard the comment, "If I only had the chance to live my life over!" He went on to explain that with the technology available in terms of health care, it was no big deal for people to live to be 100 years old or older. He said that when he was growing up a person was lucky to live to be much past the age of 55. He added that now people in their fifties or sixties do have a chance to live their lives over again. Younger people have even better odds. He further explained that the reason he was so excited about life was that he made a commitment years ago to take everything that he had learned in the first half of his life and use it to make the second half a masterpiece. He felt as though he didn't really begin to hit his stride until he was in his mid-fifties, and this was when his success really began to manifest itself financially as well as spiritually. I got a chill the after hearing this. It made perfect sense to me. Many people spend their lives worrying about getting older and try to live in the past, reminiscing about days gone by. Doesn't it make sense to awaken each morning with anticipation rather than apprehension? This gentleman's name is Maurice Spiegel, and his company is Lamar Hair Care Products. He may not remember me, but that's not important. He taught me a valuable lesson about life, and that's to look forward to each day. It sure beats the concept of just trying to survive. Some people have given up on life, not realizing that if you give up on life it will give up on you! Each day on this earth is but another opportunity to learn something more than the day before. A friend of mine once said that we are but a blink in the great eyeball of life. Get the most out of it! Don't be like some of the people that have joined the "Thank God's It Friday Club." Are these the same people that die and say, "Thank God it's over?" Don't let that be you! Like a squirrel that gathers nuts, gather as many experiences as you can so that you can integrate them into a wonderful life. Tony Robbins said, "The only value of the past is in how wisely we invest it in the future!" I couldn't agree more! The question is always, IF?

IF

If you can keep your head when all about you
Are losing theirs and blaming it on you;
If you can trust yourself when all men doubt you,
But make allowance for their doubting too;
If you can wait and not be tired by waiting,
Or, being lied about, don't deal in lies,
Or being hated, don't give way to hating,
And yet don't look to good, nor talk too wise;

If you can dream—and not make dreams your master;
If you can think—and not make thoughts your aim;
If you can meet with triumph and disaster
And treat these two impostors just the same;
If you can bear to hear the truth you've spoken
Twisted by knaves to make a trap for fools,
Or watch the things you gave your life to broken,
And stoop and build'em up with worn out tools;

If you can make one heap of all your winnings
And risk it on the turn of pitch-and-toss,
And lose, and start again at your beginnings
And never breathe a word about your loss;
If you can force your heart and nerve and sinew
To serve your turn long after they are gone
And so hold on when there is nothing in you
Except the Will which says to them "Hold on";

If you can talk with crowds and keep your virtue,
Or walk with kings—nor lose the common touch;
If neither foes nor loving friends can hurt you;
If all men count with you, but none too much;

If you can fill the unforgiving minute
With sixty seconds' worth of distance run-
Yours is the Earth and everything that's in it,
And—which is more—you'll be a Man, my son!

—Rudyard Kipling

SELF PYGMALION

Know that you think and act according to your esteem and beliefs. Be careful of what you and others tell them. Be faithful to your Self and your most grands plans so they will not fade and waste. Be a positive "SELF" Pygmalion! Capture the essence of what makes you happy. Replay its song over and over again. Focus and REFOCUS on those things that make you grow. Success breeds the best environ to WIN!

—© Saunni Davis

THE POWER OF
SELF-ESTEEM
(YOU AND YOUR INNER DIALOGUE)

"To be nobody, but yourself, in a world which is doing its best, night and day, to make you everybody else, means to fight the hardest battle which any human being can fight; and never stop fighting."

—E.E. Cummings

We live in a youth oriented society that often stresses the importance of looking youthful and taking care of our physical health. People spend millions of dollars on health club memberships, spas, and vitamins. It's amazing to me that at the same time, so little attention is given to our mental health. I believe that it's just as important to make sure that we are mentally fit. A huge part of being mentally healthy is self-esteem. How you feel about yourself will determine the quality of your life and the results you get from it. Many of us have low self-esteem because of our past. Sometimes it can take years to come to terms with those demons and move to the better future we deserve.

I was recently reading an article about Oprah Winfrey, who is one of the most successful and powerful women on the planet. In this article she explained that with all of her fame and fortune, an estimated net worth of $300 million dollars, an Emmy award-winning talk show, and her status as the only African American to own her own TV and film production facility, she was just coming to terms with her own self-esteem. Her willingness to share her past pain gave millions of Americans the courage and permission to clean their own slate, put the past in the proper perspective, and move on with their lives.

You are conditioned to feel the way that you do about yourself. From the day you are born, you are given feedback by your parents, if you had them, your relatives, and the outside world. From this feedback we form an opinion of ourselves. Feedback can come in many forms, all the way from the things that are said to us to the things that we see and are influenced by, as well as the impact from how we are treated by others. You should always be aware of the impact and influence that you may have on another person. Whether you realize it or not, somebody is watching. That's why it's so important for people in the public eye to be mindful of what they say and do because they are such a dominant force in shaping the self-esteem of our youth. I find it very upsetting when athletes claim that they are not role models, thus relinquishing their responsibility to project healthy images for our youth. It's a cop out to say "Pay me millions of dollars, plaster my face all over creation, but leave me alone when it comes to holding me accountable for my behavior." Do these people have a right to privacy? Absolutely! Do they have a right to a life without constant harrassment? Yes! But anyone that's a public figure has to understand that scrutiny goes with the territory. The future of our youth is at stake!

I Didn't Make You Up!

My little sister, Kumonte, was born from a marriage of my mother's after my father and she were divorced. When I ran away from home, my sister was just a baby. Over the course of the next 25 years I saw her only a handful of times. We talked on the phone once or twice during this time. When I finally saw her at a wedding in Los Angeles, it was the first times in our lives that we had a chance to really get to know each other. When we first saw each other, she ran into my arms with tears streaming down her face, saying to anyone that was in ear shot, "Hey, this is my brother! This is my big brother, you all!" She whispered into my ear that, throughout the years, when she told people that she had a big brother, they thought she was lying. "They thought that I made you up because they never saw you!" she said. She then looked around, shouting with joy, "I told you that I had a brother and here he is." She told me that she had been waiting for this moment for years. I was floored to think of the influence that I had on her without ever being around her. This taught me a valuable lesson about the power of influence and the affect that one single person can have on our lives. It starts from the moment we come into this world. Everything you come in contact with leaves its stamp on you. Self-esteem, like motivation, is a matter of conditioning. Just as physical conditioning is critical to health, good self-esteem is critical to mental health.

MENTAL MASTERY

We've all heard about the concept of mental conditioning, but few people purposely seek it. They leave it to happenstance, and that's very dangerous! Unless you make a concerted effort each day to question the information that comes into your world, you could very well open your mind up to things that aren't necessarily in your best interest. It seems that in this highly computerized society, we are on automatic pilot, reacting to the things that happen to us rather than operating from a position of control. There are four basic levels of competency:

FOUR LEVELS OF MENTAL COMPETENCY

Level One — Unconscious Incompetence

This mental condition is one of ignorance of skills and potential. People who have it are content to just get by. They know their personal development is deficient and they don't care. This kind of thinking is a recipe for disaster, no matter how successful you have been in the past. Everything is changing fast today and the bar for success continues to rise. Many people are frustrated by the fact that many of the skills necessary for success in the past, are obsolete today, but that's part of progress. They need to sharpen their attitude towards learning and take advantage of change.

Level Two — Conscious Incompetent

There's an old adage that says the admission of ignorance is the beginning of learning. At this stage, you know that you are incompetent and that your skill level does not match the things that you want for yourself in life. At this point you become willing to take those first steps towards education or reeducation in order to afford yourself the opportunities new skills could attract. Many times you will find that you must sacrifice old methods of behavior that had you trapped at the Unconscious Incompetent level, such as taking a class in the evening to learn computer skills as opposed to sitting at home or drinking beer and watching the sports channel. This approach works no matter what the endeavor. An example is the person who is frustrated by poor golf scores or the inability to swim but finally decides to take lessons and then improves, increasing self-esteem in the bargain.

Level Three — Conscious Competent

At this level you began to gain some skills, but you don't feel fully confident about what you're doing. It takes all of your energy and focus to pull something off. Remember when you first learned to ride a bicycle, while the training wheels were still on? Each time you pedaled, the bike got wobbly, your body shook, and you tried to maintain control. You were at a level where you knew what to do, but had not yet developed the skill to master bicycling. This level is the beginning of growth and personal development, providing that you don't stop the exploring. Masters in any walk of life constantly seek to learn as much as they can. At this point, you must constantly dedicate and rededicate yourself to learning everything you can about what interests you.

Level Four — Unconscious Competent

This is the highest level of mental conditioning. It is when you feel so confident you don't even have to think about it. It becomes a relfex action! If some one were to blindfold you, take you to your house, and tell you that if you could successfully operate with a blindfold on, you would win $10,000, do you think you could do it? If nothing was moved from it's normal place, chances are you could. That's because you know exactly where things are. You know where the toothbrush is, where your sock drawer is, and how far your bedroom is from the bathroom. You can see the hallway in your mind's eye, and you know exactly how many steps are necessary to get there, and whether you should turn right or left. You are unconsciously competent! Have you ever driven a car and noticed that you no longer have to look at the ignition in order to insert the key? You are on automatic pilot. Your hand simply guides the key into the ignition while you are yelling instructions out of the window for your kids to clean up their rooms. Vroom! The car starts while your attention is focused on a million other things. You are unconsciously competent! Have you ever gone to work and when you arrived at the office, someone asks you if you saw the terrible accident on the freeway or the building that was in flames near your exit? You look at the person and ask, what fire are you talking about? As a matter of fact, how did I get here this morning? You don't remember anything about the ride to work. You just know that somehow you got there! It seems sort of spooky, doesn't it? That's because as far as getting to your office, you have reached the Unconscious Competent zone. You can achieve this level of mastery in anything that you choose if you're willing to work at it. This comes from a commitment to continue to practice, drill, and rehearse at something until it becomes second nature. When this happens, you can operate with a great degree of control.

YOU'RE BORN TO SUCCEED, BUT PROGRAMMED TO FAIL

During the course of the last twenty years, I've had the opportunity to attend many seminars and listen to many speakers. Two of the speakers that have affected me the most are Jim Rohn and Zig Ziglar. Both speakers will tell you that what you think about will become what happens to you. Zig says that some people suffer from "Stinkin' Thinkin'!" Rohn says that you should stand guard at the doorway of your mind and question everything that comes your way. If the thoughts don't stand up to your scrutiny, then throw them out!

What if you invited me over to your house, and along with me, I brought a huge barrel of trash and dumped it all over your living room floor? Would you be slightly upset with me? Chances are that not only would you be enraged, you would probably also toss me out on my rump! Why is it that we let people dump trash into our minds and never question it? Some of the things that we read, listen to, and watch are bleeding us of our possibilities one pinprick at a time. We don't even question it, yet we wonder why we don't get the kinds of results we want.

The Programming Starts Early

When I was a kid, I had an unlimited imagination. I would dream about being everything that I thought I wanted to be, an astronaut one day, a rock 'n roll singer the next. The only limits at that time were my ability to dream. What happens to us along the way? We come in contact with a system that's supposed to educate us, right? It seems that so often we learn about the limitations of human potential rather than the possibilities. We are taught from early ages not to run in the streets or we'll get run over, to have our feet firmly planted on the ground, to be realistic about our potential, and to be practical in our approach. When I was in college, professors would come in on the first day of class and tell us how many people would receive A's, B's, C's and F's. It was amazing how close they were in their forecast. This alone should have told them something! It is human nature for people to rise to the level of expectation that is held for them.

Thank You, Miss Hayes

When I was a baby, there was a lady who used to babysit me, Miss Hayes. She was a wonderful woman. I remember her changing my diapers and telling me how pretty, smart, and capable I was. She would comment, "One day you're going to set the world on fire!" I've remembered this woman my entire life even though she has been dead for thirty years and I haven't seen her since I was seven years old. It's amazing what happens when you instill postitive messages into the minds of others. It can have a lifelong effect. I think of Miss Hayes often when dealing with my own children and try to give them that special gift that Miss Hayes gave me; a feeling of self-worth. Miss Hayes was a very wise woman. She could have taught our educators a thing or two about mental conditioning. I can still see her beautiful brown face smiling down at me with those big, round eyes the size of silver dollars. I will be forever grateful to her for her kindness and warmth. I will never forget her.

A Mountain of a Woman

My eighth grade teacher was a wonderful woman. Her name was Vernice Bates, but all her students called her Miss Bates. She stood six feet tall and always dressed impeccably. She was an excellent teacher who didn't take any stuff from anyone. I went to a very tough elementary school, known for its share of thugs and hoodlums. Many of these kids had no regard for authority on any level. It was different when they came into Miss Bates' class. She told us up front that we were bright, capable students and that she was going to push us to reach our full potential. She let us know, up front, what was expected and would see to it that you "walked the line!" She had a large yardstick that was covered from top to bottom with duct tape. When you got out of line she told you to bend over and look to the east. When this happened, you knew that it was more than geography that you were going to learn.

One afternoon, one of the kids in class was becoming disruptive. Miss Bates took out the yardstick and immediately took control of the class. She told the girl to bend over, look to the east and gave the girl 3 hard swats on the back side. The next day, the girl's mother stormed into class reading Miss Bates the riot act. Miss Bates told the child to get her coat and had the principal escort the mother and her child out. Miss Bates informed the child's mother the she was the boss in this class and that if she didn't like it, she should keep her daughter at home and could teach her herself. Two days later the mother came back with the child pleading with Miss Bates to allow the child to return. She vowed she would support her any way she could to see that her child behaved herself and did her class work. As strict as Miss Bates was, she was very kind and loved her students. She didn't believe in the concept of helplessness! She held you accountable for your behavior and let you know when you where falling short. Her classes were known for learning and discipline. To this day, when I come across people with whom I've attended elementary school, it is impossible to have a conversation without the mention of Miss Bates. She was a lady with high expectations for her students, strict standards of behavior, and the courage to stand up for what was right. She programmed us to win! Each day she told us that she had big hopes and dreams for us, and that we should always see ourselves doing great things. Many of the students, including myself, took her words of encouragement to heart. It's too bad that in today's world, we have litigated ourselves to the point where good teachers are afraid to teach because of a system that has taken their power away and does not support them in their attempts at training and discipline. It's time we rethink the values in our educational system so that our children can grow up disciplined and knowledgeable.

Our Mental Programming and the Media

Behavioral scientists tell us that more than 75 percent of all of the thoughts that come into our minds are negative. Much of this comes from the programming we receive from our cultural environment. Imagine how most Americans start their day. They awaken to the morning news, which is filled with reports of tragedies from the previous day. Afterwards, they augment that with a dose of the daily newspaper, which is filled with news of muggings, murders, rapes, high interest rates, inflation, higher taxes, increased debt, deaths, and bankruptcies. Then they go to work at a job that they probably hate or feel indifferent about, which is just as bad. This sounds pretty bleak doesn't it? Well it doesn't have to be that way.

Can you imagine loading up on all of that negative programming and then attempting to have a rich, dynamic life? It can't be done! You must learn to actively control the information that comes into your mind so that you don't get overburdened with programming that could destroy your positive outlook.

You Have the Power To Choose

I came down with the flu one time and was so sick that I couldn't get out of bed. Have you ever been there? You wake up and your mind says, "Let's go out there and make things happen!" But your body says to you, "Hey fool, I'm sick, what are you trying to do, kill me?" I think we've all been there. I made the worst mistake I could have made. I turned on day-time television to keep me company. You know how the television is on in the backround to keep you company and you fall off to sleep, but you subconsciously hear the programs anyway? Well, I did this. What a mistake! I'm not much of a television watcher and especially during the daytime . . . I'm too busy! In the backround there were shows coming on the television machine gun style. There was Ricki Lake, Sally Jesse Raphael, Jerry Springer, Montel Williams, Jenny Jones, and on and on! I couldn't believe the garbage that was coming across the airwaves. There were stories about rape and incest, mothers who were sleeping with their daughters' boyfriends, fathers who were dating their daughters' best friends, murder, and bizarre stories that depicted the lowest human behavior. I became infuriated! If I was ill at 8:30 in the morning, by the time 5:30 p.m. arrived, I was ready for intensive care, emotionally speaking. I thought to myself, why wouldn't some one make a show about the positive attributes of people? Why wouldn't the networks create shows about people who have succeeded in spite of great opposition, a show about single mothers who go back to school, get off welfare, and become productive citizens. Why not a show about fathers who are responsible, who pay child support and raise their children, about people who have started with nothing and built businesses that provide vital services to the communities, about kids that aren't involved in drugs, but are excited about going to school? Why wouldn't a show like that work? Why wouldn't people watch that? You would think that shows like that would get super high ratings and win awards. But they don't! Why is the American public so enamored with the sensational, the negative, and the hideousness of failure? It's because we are programmed to be excited about the negative. It makes people who don't have the desire or the courage to take a stand and think for themselves feel better. The old saying is true, "Misery loves company!" Is the easy way out to live in this dumpster of death? It requires little thought, very little energy, and no creativity. The key thing to understand is that you and I control exactly what we choose to focus on at any moment and time in our lives. Do you believe this to be true? If you do, that means that you have the ability to choose the ingredients that create the fabric of your thoughts, which control your actions and create your destiny. I'm not advocating that you throw your television out of the window and never read the newspaper, although for some people, that wouldn't be a bad idea. I'm merely suggesting that you guard against overloading your mind with this kind programming. Each day, many people are struggling for emotional survival because of the stimulus they receive from the outside world. Who else is going to see to it that you are mentally healthy? No one cares as much as you should. When we allow ourselves to be influenced by this kind of programming, it teaches us dependency, and programs our minds to look for excuses rather solutions.

CHECK YOURSELF

With two small children, it becomes more apparent to me each day that their mental outlook on life depends a great deal upon the example I set. This example is predicated more by what I do than what I say. I notice that when I'm working on a difficult task and they are watching, it is critical that I handle frustration in a way that teaches them patience and resiliency. It is very shocking to notice that they will respond just as I do when faced with their own little challenges. If they see me react impatiently when doing something, I will see that behavior in them. Many people wonder why their children grow up demonstrating dysfunctional behavior, but chances are those same patterns of behavior have been role modeled for their children over the years. That's why many people grow up asking isn't life awful, or why doesn't the little guy ever get the breaks? I am horrified to see how some uninformed people ridicule their children in public by calling them dumb, stupid, and clumsy. What kind of self-image are these children supposed to end up with? What if each day you were told how bright, beautiful, smart, capable, loving, kind, and needed you were? How do you think that would make you feel? Do you think you would have a different mental picture of yourself than if you were constantly told what a horrible person you were? Absolutely! That's why what we pay attention to is so critical to how we feel about ourselves and the world around us. Your self-concept determines whether or not you have impotent goals or ones that empower you. You can only have large goals to the extent that you see yourself capable and worthy of the goal. For that reason, how you think about yourself determines what actions you are willing to take. Your life will manifest these thoughts.

As You Think, So Shall You Be

Many years ago I read a passage from the book *As A Man Thinketh* by James Allen. In order to be more in tune with the times, it should probably read, *As A Man and Woman Thinketh*. This passage had a profound affect on my life. I had the good fortune to read it at the right time. I had just graduated from the University of Minnesota and was looking for some answers when I happened upon this book at a bookstore. One passage from the book stuck in my mind. I'd like to share this with you:

PASSAGE FROM *AS A MAN THINKETH*

—James Allen

The dreamers are the saviors of the world. He who cherishes a beautiful vision, a lofty ideal in his heart, shall one day realize it. Columbus had the vision of another world and he discovered it. Copernicus fostered the vision of a multiplicity of worlds and a wider universe, and he revealed it. To desire is to obtain, but to aspire is to achieve. Dream lofty dreams, and as you dream, so shall you become. For your vision is the promise of what you shall one day be. Your ideal is the prophecy of what you will at last unveil. For example, a young man may be hard pressed by proverty and labor, confined long hours in an unhealthy workshop, unschooled and lacking all the arts of refinement. But he dreams of better things. He thinks of intelligence, of grace, and of beauty. Unrest urges him to action. He utilizes all of his spare time and means, small though they are, to the development of his latent powers and resources. Very soon so altered has his mind become that the workshop can no longer hold him. It has become so out of harmony with his mentality that the workshop can no longer hold him, pretty soon it falls out of his life as a garment is cast aside and with the growth of opportunities which fit the scope of his expanding powers, he passes out of this phase of his life forever. Years later we see this same youth as a full grown man. We find him a master of the forces of the mind which he wields with unequaled power. Men and women hang upon his words and remold their character and sun like destinies revolve. He has realized the vision of his youth. He has become one with his ideal. And you, too, who listening to this story will realize the vision, not the ideal wishes of your heart, be they base or beautiful or a mixture of both. For you will always gravitate to that which you secretly most love. Into your own hands will be placed the exact results of your own thoughts. You'll receive that which you earn, no more, no less. Whatever your present environment may be, you will fall, remain or rise with your thoughts, your vision, and your ideal. You'll become as small as your controlling desire or as great as your dominant aspiration. In all human affairs, there are efforts and there are results. The strength of the effort is the measure of the result, chance is not. Gifts, powers, spiritual and intellectual possessions are the fruits of effort. They are thoughts completed, objects accomplished, visions realized. The vision that you glorify in your mind, the ideal you enthrone in your heart, This you will build your life by, this you will BECOME!

This passage is a gem that helped to give my life direction at a time when I needed it most. To many people, the concept of consciously thinking and projecting a larger self image of themselves is silly. They leave it up to someone or something else. What you focus on is what you get. That's why you must make sure that there are more positive stimuli going into your head than negative. There are so many wonderful things happening in the world. I believe that for every negative thing happening, there are a thousand things that are positive. That's how things get done! That's how bridges get built, curriculums get created, and things that improve the quality of our lives get invented. This is one of the most exciting times to be alive in this history of the human race. We have more technology, more opportunities, more information, and more assistance than ever before. The key is to understand that success is not in short supply. Remember that there's plenty of prosperity to go around. You just have to be willing to stake your claim.

YOU ATTRACT THAT WHICH YOU THINK ABOUT

I'll never forget an experience I had with a group of guys that I used to play basketball with a few years ago. We would shoot hoops for two or three hours at a time. Atferwards, we would assemble at someone's house to play cards, drink beer, and solve all of the world's problems. We would spend hours wasting time! It seemed that for most of the guys there, this was the closest thing to real work that they encountered. This went on every day, and I usually participated when I was not on the road doing my job. Then one day it hit me right between the eyes. I started to think about each guy in the room, fifteen all together. I noticed as I took inventory of this group, I was the only guy in the room with a job! I started to panic, my heart started to pound as if it were going to jump out of my chest. I thought to myself, "I've got to get out of here!" These were not bad guys, they just weren't highly motivated. I wanted more from my life than just talking about the conditions of life. I wanted to create them. As I thought about it, I realized that I had attracted these guys through my own passive outlook. I also realized that in order to attract people that I could learn from, I would first have to raise my standards. Most of us were from the inner city and came from backgrounds of dysfunctional families, poverty, drugs, and violence. We would always talk about how bad the conditions were and how awful the system was. No solutions, just problems! I got frustrated enough before I left to just explode all over the group. I said, "I'm sick and tired of always hearing about the negative in terms of what can't be done! Why don't we do something about it! Things aren't going to change by just sitting hear talking about the same things we talk about every time!"

It was like some alien force had taken control and was doing the talking for me. As I stormed out of the door, I felt mixed emotions. I felt vindication because maybe I had cut through some of the mental clutter, and at the same time, I felt remorse because maybe I had alienated guys that I had known for years. It made me feel good when I got a call later that evening. It was from the friend at whose house we gathered. He called to say that a spirited debate took place after I left and it was agreed that we were on a slow boat to nowhere. The group broke up shortly thereafter. Maybe that's the best thing that could have happened.

You and Your Self Talk

The movie *Fear Strikes Out* profiles the life and times of one of major league baseball's most gifted legends, Jimmy Piersall. The movie stars Anthony Perkins as Jimmy Piersall and Karl Malden as his father. In his seventeen years in the major leagues Jimmy Piersall had an impressive lifetime batting average of .272. He was a child prodigy that the scouts had been watching since his high school days. Unfortunately, before he racked up those numbers, he faced a much more powerful foe than 90 mph fast balls, and that was mental illness.

The story dials back to Jimmy's childhood. No matter what he did, it was never quite good enough for his father. He would get a game winning hit and his father would tell him, "Jim, you could have done better! Had you bore down and concentrated like I taught you, you would have hit a home run." Jimmy would then make a game saving catch in the outfield and his father would say, "Jimmy, make sure next time you see the ball all the way into your glove while you're making the catch. You could have dropped the ball and cost your team the game!" Nothing he ever did was good enough. No matter how hard he tried, he could never please his father. His father pushed until he pushed Jimmy over the edge. Jimmy loved his father to the point of worship and went out of his way to work extra hard to make him proud. After years and years of this negative self talk, Jimmy Piersall still made it to the ranks of professional baseball. He was that good! But the emotional price he paid from the negative self talk he inflicted upon himself caused him to have a nervous breakdown and almost killed him. This came from years and years of negative self talk that he had been conditioned with from his father.

Self talk is what you say to yourself, and about yourself. It affects your self-image. Your self-image is the accumulation of all of your attitudes about your chances of success or failure. This has a great deal to do with your performance as well as your willingness to try something again if you do not at first succeed. If you succeed at something, your self talk tells you that you are good at that particular thing and perhaps that it comes easily for you. You may find yourself saying, "It's just like me to do that!" or "You know, I've always been that way!" When you make comments such as this, you reinforce a positive image. This also gives you the confidence to speak positively to yourself in the future when faced with the same task. This creates a positive core belief system and a sense of certainty about possible outcomes. We can create positive self talk by the use of affirmations. An affirmation is a statement of fact; it is an internal, cognitive act that establishes a specific course, direction, outcome, or state of being for the future. It means to ratify or confirm something to be true. Some examples of positive affirmations are as follows:

> I am worthy of success!
> Each day in everyway, I'm getting better and better!
> I am a smart, capable person!
> I have tons of personal energy!
> I enjoy helping other people!
> I will succeed in my goals no matter how long it takes!

I will become the best person that I can be!
I deserve success!
I want success!
I am successful!
I am emotionally strong!
I love my life!
I am healthy and vibrant!
I am not getting older, I'm getting better!
I'm outgoing when I want to be!
I'm disciplined!
I make my own luck!
I always come through in the clutch!
Every day is my day, if I make it that way!
I carry my weather with me every day, it's my attitude!
My attitude determines my altitude!
I'm creative and spontaneous!
The only way that I can fail is if I quit!
I am very organized!
I get along with all kinds of people!
I respect and value people who are different from me!

This list is obviously not all-inclusive, but just imagine what each day would be like if you told yourself these things and reinforced them. What do you think your chances would be for a more positive self-image? I suggest that you take the time to write out positive affirmations regarding anything you want to do in life. For example, I had many challenges in finding the courage to sit down and write this book. Even though I had been successful as a businessman and professional speaker, I had never written a book. One of the things I did was to write affirmations about my goal of being an author. Here's what I came up with:

GOAL: To write a self-help book that will empower others to take control of their lives and realize their dreams by unleashing the greatness within them.

Affirmations:

> I am a good writer!
> I will not quit until this book is written!
> I love to write!
> I am committed to this undertaking!
> I am completing a labor of love!
> There are people who need my help!
> I have an obligation to serve my fellow man!
> I have pride in my work!
> I will deliver the best possible product!
> This book will teach me about myself!
> I am worthy of this book's success!
> I am an effective and efficient writer!
> I am a man of action!
> Do it now!
> People will feel my love come through this book!
> People will see and feel my honesty and sincerity!

Notice that I've placed exclamation points behind each statement because how you say something is important. This is also true in self talk.

The Three Components of Human Influence

1. Words—seven percent
2. Voice Quality (Tone and Pace)—thirty-eight percent
3. Physiology—fifty-five percent

You can see that 93 percent of communication is predicated not only by what we say, but how we say it. If I walked into a room and saw that you were upset about something, I could ask, "What's wrong with you?" or I could ask, "What's troubling you?" How I communicated the question will have a great deal to do with your response and how you feel from that point forward. Make sure that you speak with excitement about your affirmations. Make sure that from now on, when someone asks you how things are going, you tell them, GREAT! If you can't bring yourself to say that, then simply say, UNBELIEVABLE! That way you're covered no matter how things are going. How we use our bodies also plays an important role in helping us form positive self-images. From this moment on, walk with your back straight and your head up. Carry yourself as if you have already achieved your dream.

I AM THE GREATEST!

After Muhammed Ali captured the gold medal in 1960, he began a quest to become the heavyweight champion of the world. Many people thought that he was an arrogant blowhard. Muhammed Ali was a great athlete, not only because he could float like a butterfly and sting like a bee, but also because he was a master psychologist. When he proclaimed that he was the greatest of all time, Sonny Liston was actually the heavyweight champion of the world. Ali did such a masterful job of public relations that people started to tag him with the label "The Greatest" long before he defeated Liston and captured the crown. Before the fight, in the locker room, there was Ali with his right hand man, Bundini Brown. As Ali warmed up, Bundini would say over and over, "You're the greatest!", You're the man!", "Women love you!" "Children love you!", You're the champ!", and "You're so pretty!" By the time Ali got into the ring, he was worked up into such a frenzy that he was so much more mentally prepared for the fight than his oppostion. That combined with his God given ability made him an unbeatable combination. Ali was a master of self talk! The proclaimed "Lousville Lip" self talked and performed himself into one of the most recognized public figure on the face of the earth. He also, more often than not, psyched his opponents right out of their minds. Many of his opponents were much stronger men with greater punching power. This was often nullified by the mental games Ali played with them. The majority of these men were beaten long before the first round. They, too, believed he was the greatest. The key thing is that without the formal interpretation behavioral psychologists had given to the methods of affirmations and self talk, Ali was demonstrating these skills. For him they came naturally. Champ, I love you! Thanks for demonstrating to us all what self belief, self-esteem and self-respect are all about. You are the greatest of all time!

Affirmation Principles

There are some important principles to keep in mind when using affirmations in order to derive the greatest benefits. First you must READ the words aloud. This will trigger your subconscious to take command. The subconscious mind cannot distinguish between the false and the real. So the commands you give it is what it has to work with. The second thing you should do is VISUALIZE and see yourself performing the task down to the most finite details. The more detailed and clearer the picture, the greater the effect on your subconscious mind. As you read the affirmations to yourself, imagine seeing yourself cross the finish line with arms raised, fully achieving the goal of your choice. See this vision in living color, as though you are watching a movie. See it in slow motion, in fast speed, and at every possible angle. Allow yourself next to EMOTIONALIZE as you accomplish your goal.

What does the atmosphere look like? How does it feel? Who else is involved? In writing your affirmations, it's also important to:
1. Write them in the first person
2. Write them in the present tense as though they are already true and a part of your life at this moment
3. Write them using emotional words that clearly describe the mental picture you see of yourself reaching your goal.

After writing your affirmations, spend at least 30 minutes or more a day, preferably early in the morning or before you retire for the evening saying, picturing, and feeling your affirmations. I often use music, usually new age or soft jazz without lyrics. This helps me create a theme for my affirmations. I have several songs that I can simply listen to, and they automatically bring to my mind my affirmation, goals or visions. Another thing that I would strongly suggest is that you record your affirmations and listen to them often. This will again imbed these positives messages into your mind. Remember, there is an entire series of actions that must be taken:

READING—Just reading your affirmations will have only a ten percent impact on your subconscious mind, limiting the results that you get from the process.

READING AND VISUALIZING—This will anchor your subconscious mind further and allow you to achieve a fifty-five percent impact on your subconscious mind.

READ, VISUALIZE, AND EMOTIONALIZE—This will allow you to impact your subconscious mind 100 percent and reach your goals more quickly, enjoying the process as you succeed.

THE FLIP SIDE OF LIFE

I am not going to spend much time on the subject of negativity because I feel that too much time is already given to this subject. There are a couple of distinctions that I would like to make, however. The first one is that negative things are normal. I didn't say that they are good. Negative things are not a major component of success, but they are something that we must acknowledge. Just as you can tell yourself what a wonderful person you are, you can also beat yourself up and analyze all of your worse qualities. That is not what this book is about. In the level of negative acceptance thinking, you learned all about how to program your mind negatively, so from this point forward, we are going to focus on solutions. The solutions come from your own ability to give yourself permission to believe in yourself.

Do Something Different

It's amazing what a fresh, new approach can sometimes do for us. I would admonish you to change your approach. Even if you simply take a different way to work in the morning, that's a start. Break your old patterns of doing things and try something new. Try coming home and not turning on the television. Just enjoy the silence of your own company. I heard a profound statement: "Most of people's problems stem from their inability to sit in a quiet room alone." If you have family, try to enjoy an evening with them without interference from outside influences. Turn off the TV! When that happens, people begin to communicate with each other. Now that's a novel idea! If you're use to lumbering out of bed in just enough time to do everything, but always seem be running ten minutes behind, get up one hour earlier. Believe me, the trade-off in extra sleep is not worth the stress that constantly feeling overwhelmed will cause you. When you do something different from the norm, you will discover breakthroughs that will afford you the opportunity to learn more about yourself. You'll notice things that you didn't notice before. These distinctions will give you a new lease on life. One of the things that I enjoy as a diversion is to sneak into the movies during the middle of the afternoon. If I happen to drive by a theatre and a movie is conveniently starting, I will dart in there for a couple of hours and escape the pressures of the day for a little while. Another favorite diversion of mine is to go into a bookstore and get lost in different books. This is a great way to change your mental program. I read, which is a form of entertainment for me, and I learn a great deal at the same time. I get dual benefits from the same activity. I usually leave with a half dozen books to add to my library so the bookstore benefits as well.

You will find that no matter what the conditions are, successful people are doing something differently from unsuccessful ones. If the tax laws change, successful people don't complain about it, they take classes to learn how to take advantage of the new system's benefits. If interest rates go up, they find other ways to finance their ventures creatively. They don't sit around waiting for things to get back to the way they used to be. Back in 1982 when I started my real estate business, people told me that it was the wrong time to buy property because interest rates were 11 percent. They said that I would never be able to charge enough in rent to cover the debt service.

Since that time, I've bought and owned more than $1.5 million dollars worth of real estate and have become financially independent. What's even more exciting is that I'm just getting started. I simply did something different from the people who were stifled by conditions. I used creative financing, and found higher and better uses for properties. You can put a mouse in a maze and eventually you will find it at the end, munching on the cheese snack you placed at the end of it. . . Thank you very much! For some reason, many people look at the walls of life as permanent. You must take detours, sometimes right in the middle of your designated course, in order to reach your destination. What I'm suggesting is that you search for alternate routes ahead of time so that when you get sidetracked, you've thought about detours in advance. This will provide you with more options.

Unto the Conqueror I say:

Your "experiences" are the evidence that your Esteem and Dreams are Pygmalion to your day to day. Desires sires fire required to lift yourself higher. The "I-fullfilling Prophecy" will build your most passionate, emotional, and reccurring desires.

*If your mind can conceive,
then your heart believes,
that's what your spirit retrieves.*

Your Will shall read and deliver every message. It shall clear the way for your desire's passage. When the Will and Belief pair and bear fruit as one, sweet or sour, you'll embrace what your will has done.

—© Saunni Dais

YOUR POWER TO CHOOSE

"The person who is tenacious of purpose in a rightful cause is not shaken from their firm resolve by the frenzy of their fellow citizens clamoring for what is wrong or by the tyrants threatening countenance."

—*Horace 65–8 B.C.*

Sometimes, we've got to be willing to make difficult, unpopular decisions. This often involves people whose affect on us is negative. When I was younger, I had a friend named Greg. We did everything together! We loved sports and often would play baseball, basketball, and football all in the same day. He was an excellent athlete. We had dreams of one day going to college and making it big. Greg had one weakness. He was always attracted to people who had a negative influence on him. As long as he was away from these guys, he was fine. Unfortunately, he often found himself having to choose between doing what he knew was right and doing the wrong things in order to be accepted by a group of thugs. I decided at this point that I could no longer associate with him due to the people he hung around. I knew many of these guys, and they were bad news. Most of them had criminal records and were accidents waiting to happen. Many of them never saw their twentieth birthday! Greg eventually got involved in selling heroin. It broke my heart when I came home from college for a break to find that Greg was dead. He had been shot in the head at point-blank range in a house down the street from where we both lived. My friend was dead! I thought about how easy it would have been for me to be lying in that funeral home instead of him. Letting go of people who negatively influence our lives is a difficult choice to make. A lady once asked me at a seminar, "What do you do if you have negative relatives in your family?" I told her to love them from a distance! Yes, sometimes people in your own family can be the worst perpetrators of lowering your self-esteem. Sometimes they mean well in telling you not to expect too much or not to get your hopes up too high. What they don't understand is that, through their own ignorance, they are ruining your chances for success. They failed because they gave up. Now they are asking you not to try.

LEARN TO PROGRAM YOUR OWN MIND

You are a human computer. The human brain is the most powerful computer on earth. You must learn to think for yourself without letting the programming from outside influences determine your outcome. It's a personal choice. You must learn to run your own mental PC.

THE BRAIN IS THE MOST POWERFUL COMPUTER EVER

While sitting in my office one day, I was looking at my computer. I thought about what a great metaphor it is for how our brain works. It has three basic components that must operate in tandem in order for it to function effectively, just as the human brain has many parts that must function together for you to operate at peak efficiency.

THE SCREEN

The screen is a great metaphor for your behavior. I want you to imagine that you're watching a movie on your computer screen. You are the star of the show. The next time you think about your life, ask yourself a question. Is my behavior congruent with the things I want out of life? Do you like what you see? If you don't, know that you have the power to change it. How do you treat others? Is a situation better or worse because your are involved? Are you a positive force or a negative one? Are you part of the solution or part of the problem? If your life is not what you want it to be, why isn't it? Are you willing to do what it takes to change for the better? Many people want things out of life, but they don't have the discipline to make themselves do what it takes to get them. They want to make more money, but they do not develop themselves so that they are worthy enough to earn it. They want better health, but instead of joining a health club, or jogging after work, they resort to doing the same old things that got them to the unhappy place they now occupy. You must understand that you can make a difference in this world. It is your obligation to do so. Will you be the next person to step forward and make a difference? If we make an honest appraisal of ourselves, most of us would readily admit that we can do much more and become much more than we currently are. It's a fact that most of us only use about ten percent of our brain capacity. Some people even brag about it as if to say, "Hey look at me! I'm only using ten percent of my ability!" They proclaim this as though the statement has redeeming quality. I believe that one of the real keys to happiness is the feeling that comes from constantly growing and helping someone else do the same. You have the power in your hands to make a difference!

YOU CAN MAKE A DIFFERENCE

Never underestimate the power you have within you to influence someone and make a difference in their life. Someone is watching you! You may not even be aware of it. Maybe it's your kids or other relatives. Maybe it's a close or distant friend. It could even be a total stranger who is looking for some answers to life's challenges. Maybe it's someone on the verge of suicide who finds a ray of hope through watching something that you do or say. Whether you know it or not, somebody's watching!

Teddy Stollard is a young man whom you would have marked most least likely to succeed. He often reported to school with uncombed hair wearing musty old clothes. He appeared to be anything but a model student. He could often be seen in class staring out into space. When his teacher, Miss Thompson, asked him a question, he would often respond by mumbling back to in her monosyllables. Unattractive, unmotivated, and distant describes Teddy Stollard. Even though Miss Thompson said that she loved and treated all of her students the same, deep down inside, she knew that this was not true. She treated him differently, and she knew it! She often got some kind of perverse pleasure out of placing large red Xs next to his wrong answers on tests. Whenever she gave him an F, she did it with a bit of a flair by placing the F at the top of the page with a big red magic marker. She should have known better. She had his records! All the information on him was right there in them. The records read that in first grade, Teddy showed promise with his work and attitude, but had a poor home situation. In second grade, Teddy was showing signs of slowness. His mother was very ill. He received very little from home. In third grade, Teddy was a good boy, but very reserved. He was much too serious for a child so young. His mother died last year. In fourth grade, Teddy was slow, very slow. He was a good kid, but not up too par with the other kids his age. His father showed very little interest in him.

Well, the months came and went, and finally it was Christmas time. All of the children had bought gifts for Miss Thompson and had gathered around her desk to watch her open them. At the top of the pile, she noticed a big gift that was wrapped in an old brown paper bag and held together with thin strips of scotch tape. There was a note written on it that said, "To Miss Thompson, From Teddy Stollard." As she began to open the present, a large, gaudy, fake rhinestone bracelet fell to the floor with most of the stones missing. There was also a bottle of cheap perfume, the kind you buy at a five and dime store. All of the children began to laugh at the presents, but at least Miss Thompson had enough sense to silence them by placing the bracelet on one wrist, and taking some of the perfume and placing it on the other. She then smelled it and held up her hand to the class, as if to say, "Gee, doesn't it smell great!" And almost as if on cue, the class ooohed and ahhhhed as if to be surprised, but, the underlying tone was that of ridicule and humiliation of poor Teddy. At the end of class that day, Teddy hung around until the last student was gone. He then walked slowly up to Miss Thompson, who was preparing to go home. He looked at her and said softly, "Gee Miss Thompson, I'm sure glad you liked the presents! You smell just like my mother, and her bracelet sure does look pretty on you. I want to thank you and wish you a Merry Christmas." When Teddy walked out of the door, Miss Thompson dropped to her knees right there in that classroom and asked God for forgiveness. When the kids came to school the next day, they had a new teacher, for Miss Thompson was a changed woman. She made a promise to herself to be not just a teacher, but instead an agent of change. She vowed to give her students something that they could have long after she was gone, a piece of herself. She swore to herself that she would be there to help all of her students, especially the slow ones, and especially Teddy Stollard.

Over the ensuing months, Teddy caught up with a lot of the students in the class and passed more of them by. He became one of the best students in the class and surprised everyone, including himself. The years came and went, and Miss Thompson and Teddy lost track of one another. One day as Miss Thompson was preparing to go home, she notice that there was a note in her mailbox. It read:

"Dear Miss Thompson, I have just been told that I'm graduating second in my high school class and thought you should be the first to know." Love, Teddy Stollard

Four years later, Miss Thompson received yet another letter. It read:

"Dear Miss Thompson, I've just been informed that I'm graduating number one in my college class. I thought you should be the first to know. It was difficult because I had to work full-time while attending the University, but I liked it." Love, Teddy Stollard

Another four years later, Miss Thompson received yet another letter. It read.

"Dear Miss Thompson, as of today, I am Theodore Stollard, M.D. How about that? I thought you should be the first to know. I'm getting married next week, the 27th to be exact, and would love for you to attend. You're the only family I have now. Dad died last year."

Love, Teddy Stollard

She went to that wedding and sat right where his mother would have. She had earned the right to do so. She had given a part of herself to him that he could have long after she was gone. More importantly, she had given something to him that he could give to someone else. The chain of giving, loving, and learning keeps on going. This is what life is all about! Are you just going through the motions in your life? Or are you seeking to make a difference in this world? Believe me, there's no greater feeling in the world than knowing that you helped another person get to a place that they never could have gotten without your influence. Money can't buy it, for it is the essence of life. Someone is watching you! As you look at the screen, seek to demonstrate behavior that others will want to emulate. Become a role model. The world needs more of them! The world needs you!

THE KEYBOARD

All physical activity involves the senses. There are five basic senses: visual, auditory, kinesthetic, olfactory, and gustatory. The one I want to focus on is vision. There are two ways to see. Sight you see with your eyes, but insight you see with your mind. Anything created in this world was created because a man or woman had vision. They could see what others could not. The key is to understand that in order to be successful in anything, you must be able to see yourself with a much larger vision than you currently do. As long as you judge yourself by the standard of what you are now and what's available to you now, you will never move from your current circumstances. There are two ways to see, sight we see with our eyes, insight we see with our mind. Everything starts with the power of vision in your mind's eye, insight! Imagine a tiny acorn. What do you see? Many people would answer food for squirrels. Others might say that they see a mighty oak tree. Someone with insight would see commerce, industry, jobs, information, technology, and trade. It's called depth of vision. Most people only focus on what's immediately available to them. They're afraid to see themselves succeeding in a major way.

Think about your business or personal life. How do you want it to be? If you want to build a multi-million dollar business, or become an artist or a chemical engineer, don't look at where you are as much as where you can be. My grandmother always told me that it's not where you're from that counts, but where you're going.

BE CAREFUL WHAT YOU ASK FOR, YOU MIGHT GET IT!

The Peak Performers Network is a very successful seminar company that was founded by a sharp young businessman by the name of Dan Brattland. Its office happens to be based in Minneapolis, even though they operate throughout the country. The network conducts public seminars in which individuals become members for a set fee and are allowed to hear a cadre of professional speakers monthly throughout the year. I was a proud member of the network and went each month to hear the different speakers. It was interesting as well as educational. I would go not only to hear the message, but to get the feel for what doing it would be like from the speaker's perspective. I would go to the seminars and pretend that I was watching myself rather than the speakers who were actually on the platform that night. As I imagined that their standing ovations were for me, I tried to capture the feeling of what it would be like to be up on the stage. One day I made a silent promise to myself that I would some day be on that stage at the Minneapolis Convention Center giving a seminar. I didn't know how it would happen, I just knew that it would. I heard Les Brown, "The Motivator," say one night at a seminar not to worry about how something is going to happen. How is none of your business. I would have to concur! When you start to see a larger vision of yourself, it does something to your entire thinking process. Your thoughts cause you to act with a new boldness. You meet people that, otherwise would never have crossed your path. You find yourself in situations where opportunities present themselves and you ask yourself, "Where were they before?" The truth is that they were always there. You just did not see them. When I made that declaration to myself, I didn't realize that my prayer would be answered much sooner than I expected.

THEY'VE GOT THE RIGHT ONE BABY, UH, UH!

I was sitting in my office at PepsiCo, Inc. minding my own business, not doing anyone any harm, and not doing them much good either. I was simply wrapping up another day in the life of a sales manager. I was admittedly very tired from the days activities. I felt as though I was emotionally bleeding to death, one pinprick at a time, from the different problems that people had unloaded on me during the day. However, I did have my salvation. I had a ticket to attend a seminar that night, by Danielle Kennedy, sponsored by the Peak Performers Network. She is one of the most powerful speakers in the world. It was just what I needed to get my batteries recharged. I went to these seminars to dream, for I was trying to work my way free to one day be able to speak on a full time basis, which was part of my larger vision. The seminar was to start at 7 p.m., just enough time for me to get home and grab a quick bite to eat before heading downtown.

At 5:35 p.m., I got a call from Reneé Strom, who owns the Speakers Bureau in Minneapolis. She was excited and frantic at the same time. She was talking a mile a minute, telling me that I've got to get down to the convention center. I explained to her that I was going down there as soon as I went home and ate, because I was excited about hearing Danielle Kennedy. She told me that I didn't understand what she was saying. She went on to explain that Danielle Kennedy would not be coming because she was stranded on an airplane in Austin, Texas. She would not be able to make it in spite of a stellar effort. She said that Peak Performers needed a speaker for that night, and asked me if I would be willing to fill in for her. I asked her how many people would be there, and she told me 1,700. I asked her how long they wanted me to speak, and she told me 3 hours. I freaked out! I was so nervous that I couldn't think straight. I was fumbling and mumbling! I couldn't believe this was happening! I thought to myself, "Lord, I asked you for this blessing, but not now, OK? I told Reneé that I would call her back in five minutes because I needed some time to clear my head. She told me five minutes was all I had because if I decided that I couldn't do it, they needed to know as soon as possible so that they could find another speaker. When I hung up that phone, the negatives started speaking to me. They said who do you think you are? You're going to go down there and make a complete fool of yourself. You're not prepared. You've seen speakers who were good who couldn't carry three hours. You can't do it! Why don't you call her back and tell her that you can't do it because they didn't give you enough lead time. Then you'll be off the hook!

Fortunately, there was also another voice talking to me. It was the voice of opportunity, telling me that this was my chance to shine and I'd better take it! The voice kept talking. "Those folks haven't seen a real speaker yet! They don't have any idea what's about to happen tonight. I'm no stand-in! I'm the real thing." I called Reneé back three minutes and fifty nine seconds later and told her that I would do it. I left the office, pant cuffs smoking, and jumped on the freeway doing about 120 mph. I went home and changed, told my wife that Reneé would be by to pick up some tapes to sell at the seminar, grabbed some overheads, and headed for the convention center. My knees were knocking, and I felt like I was ready to start hyperventilating. When I walked into the room and saw 1,700 people, it looked like the entire population of the world. I thought wow! There are going to be 3,400 eyeballs looking at me. Talk about being under the microscope! When they began to introduce me, I thought about my football days. Before we took the field, the team would assemble in the tunnel. You could hear the thunder of the band jamming in the stands. You would look into the eyes of your teammates as if to say, "It's showtime!" Those are the thoughts that went through my head as I heard the announcer from WCCO radio introduce me. When he said, "Ladies and gentlemen, after tonight you'll see why he's known throughout the country as Mr. Impact! Please help me welome Mr. Desi Williamson." I exploded onto the stage and for the next three hours I was in a zone. When athletes talk about being in a zone, they're performing at their best. It seems as though there is someone else at the control switch guiding them through. It's as if some kind of divine intervention occurs. If you could capture and sell it, you would become rich overnight. That's what happened to me. The three hours went so fast, and the audience repsonded so well to me, that I was in shock to find them standing on their feet, bestowing upon me the most precious gift a speaker can receive, a standing ovation! A standing ovation cannot be manufactured. Either people liked you to that extent or they didn't. It's that simple! I cried as the audience stood to their feet and clapped. "They approved of me! I thought. I'm worthy!" That moment marked the beginning of my professional speaking career. I learned something very valuable about myself that night. Believe in yourself, no matter what! When your chance comes, be ready! Be careful what you wish for, because you might just get it! Sometimes we look at other people, celebrities in fact, and might find cause to ask, "Lord, why didn't you give me the ability to jump like Michael Jordan, dance like

Michael Jackson, or think like Albert Einstein?" Finally we come to grips with the fact that we've got to play this game called life with the uniform that God gives us. For the first time in my life, I felt as though I finally had the answer. I've got to become the very best Desi Williamson that I possibly can. And that's good enough!

DÉJÀ VU IS NOT AN ACCIDENT

I really believe in the power of visualization. Sit back in your favorite chair sometime and relax to some of your favorite music. Close you eyes and really think about something that you want to do in your life. Try to paint the picture as vividly as you can. How does it feel? What does the atmosphere look like? Who are the people involved? What do the surroundings smell like? The ability to be as specific as possible is very important during this little escape. The more specific you can be, the better results you will get. I did this one day as I imagined speaking to a special group of people in a very special place. It involved first-class accomodations, a limousine, the whole bit!

THE POWER OF YOUR MENTAL SOFTWARE

I was scheduled to speak at Disney World for the International Racquet Swim and Health Association. This organization represents health club owners and managers from all over the world. It's a huge event! As I boarded the plane to take my seat in first-class, a strange feeling came over me as if I had done this before. I knew that the flight attendant would ask me if I wanted something to drink long before she did. I looked at the magazines sitting in the rack with the feeling that *People* magazine would present itself in the pile and it did. Déjà vu was upon me. When I stepped off of the plane in Orlando, I suspected that there would be a man there with a sign that read "Mr. Desi Williamson." He was right there, at the appointed place, standing by the gate. I asked him what kind of vehicle we were driving to the hotel, all the while thinking to myself, "I know it's a stretch limousine." Guess what? It was! I couldn't help feeling spooky as I sat in the back of the limo, flipping all of the switches and enjoying the ride. When I got to the Swan Hotel, I was waited on hand and foot. The service was impeccable, just as I had imagined. The audience loved the speech and made me feel like part of their health club family. I had experienced this entire trip before in my mind's eye! I thought about what a powerful tool the mind is when we take the time to use it. That's the power of vision. If you can see it, you can do it!

THE DISKETTE
YOUR MENTAL SOFTWARE

We must learn to program our own disk. As I sat at my computer, I thought, "What a metaphor for the mind." The diskette represents your thoughts. Everything that's programmed into your head is just as permanent as the data programmed into the most powerful computer on earth. Think about the Super Bowl and what a spectacle it has become. Advertisers spend as much as one million dollars for a 30 second commercial. Why? They do it in an effort to control our behavior when it comes to buying decisions. These commercials all promise that your life will be better, all for the low, low, price of XYZ! Do they play the commerials just once and leave it at that? Of course not! They understand the power of learning through spaced repetition, so they play them over and over. And guess what? They work! It's called "frequency" in advertising lingo. Advertisers know that when you immediately associate their tagline with their product, they've got you. We all respond like Ivan Pavlov's dogs when we hear the commerials. Let's play a little game! Next to the tagline, write the name of the company or product that it represents.

THE HEARTBEAT OF AMERICA IS TODAY'S _____

THE KING OF BEERS _____

FINGER LICKIN' GOOD _____

WHAT THE BIG BOYS EAT _____

DON'T LEAVE HOME WITHOUT IT _____

QUALITY IS JOB ONE _____

THE REAL THING! _____

THE CHOICE OF A NEW GENERATION _____

BE ALL YOU CAN BE! _____

HOW DO YOU SPELL RELIEF? _____

NOT JUST FOR BREAKFAST ANYMORE _____

WINSTON TASTES GOOD LIKE A _____

The last commerical has been off the air for more than thirty years. Why do you still know it? Because you've been programmed to know it. The key thing is to be aware of the fact that each day we all receive more than 2,000 messages vying for a share of our mind. The key thing is to recognize that you can control your own software by programming your own mind and running it according to your own rules. You must learn to actively program your mind by the things you pay attention to and allow to become a part of your life.

I Am Very Accommodating

I ask no question.
I accept whatever you give me.
I do whatever I am told to do.
I do not presume to change anything you think, say, or do; I file it all away in perfect order, quickly and efficiently, and then I return it exactly as you gave it to me.
Sometimes you call me your memory.
I am the reservoir into which you toss anything your heart or mind chooses to deposit there.

I work night and day; I never rest, and nothing can
impede my activity.

The thoughts you send to me are categorized and
filed, and my filing system never fails.

I am truly your servant who does your bidding without hesitation or criticism.

I cooperate when you tell me that you are "this" or
"that" and I play it back as you give it. I am
most agreeable.

Since I do not think, argue, judge, analyze, question,
or make decisions, I accept impressions easily. I
am going to ask you to sort out what you send
me, however; my files are getting a little cluttered and confused. I mean, please discard those
things that you do not want returned to you.
What is my name? Oh, I thought you knew!

I am your subconscious.

—Unknown

YOU PRODUCE WHAT YOU PROJECT

The first thing that the average person does when they
come home from work is turn on the television. It's a statis-
tical fact that the average television is on in each and every
household eight hours a day. Now, if you sleep seven to
eight hours a day, work seven to eight hours a day, and watch
television the rest of the time, that's it! There isn't any more
time. Time is the most valuable resource on earth. The only
thing that you can do with it is use it! Television is a great in-
vention and can definitely be used to increase the quality of
your life if you watch it selectively. There are programs with
richness and vital information. If we carefully choose what
we watch, the television can be used as a learning tool. It can
also be used for entertainment, but, unfortunately, many people use it for a baby sitter, regardless of their age. When you
simply "veg out" in front of it each day, you're postponing the

opportunity to become more involved with your own life. What are you paying attention to? Who has you programmed on auto pilot? Once you are able to control what you focus your attention on, you can control what goes into your software and ultimately what you see in the results of your life. If you have programmed your disk with the idea of limited prospects for a bright future, then this will come true. There is so much in the way of toxic communication going around that you must guard your disk with your life. Your life depends on it! Some people bring their negative input everywhere they go. Have you ever met someone like this? They bring it to their jobs as if everyone there wants to hear about it. Here's my best advice about sharing negative experiences with the world. Leave them at home. Here's why. Eighty percent of the people you're telling don't care and the other twenty percent are actually glad it's happening to you! Some people walk through life with a permanent chip on their shoulder, waiting for somebody to bump into them. Certainly we all have days that we'd just as soon like to forget. There's a way to handle those days. I call them all unbelievable! From now on when someone asks you how you're doing, you tell them, "Unbelievable!" With that statement, you cover all scenarios whether they are good or bad. You carry your weather with you each day, packed in a forecast called your attitude.

I am often asked by businesspeople, What distinguishes top producers in any field from the middle of the pack? I would have to say, without reservation, that successful people are that way because they believe they are. They think, "Top producer, top producer, top producer!" For them, there is no other alternative. You'll find that they are very conscious of how they spend their time. They read, study, and talk to people who can help them continue to be a top producer! It's a way of life!

For many years, I was programmed to believe that I needed eight hours of sleep a night in order to be effective. On nights when I didn't get my eight hours, I was a basket case the entire next day! I spent more time worrying about the sleep that

I missed than I did accomplishing anything else. My disk was programmed to think "tired" so my body didn't disappoint it one bit. Now, I operate with a life that's filled with vitality because my disk is programmed to think energy and vitality rather than tired and exhausted. Let me ask you a question. In your business or whatever walk of life you currently find yourself, at the end of the year will there be top producers, those at the middle of the pack, and those at the bottom? I hope you said yes! You can pop your disk out of your head anytime you choose and program it with things that will add to the quality of your life. You can empower yourself to succeed by deciding, in advance, what kind of year you're going to have. It is a matter of personal preference. So try something different. Ask yourself some key questions about what you find yourself focusing on.

1. In what way will this experience help me to become a better person?
2. Is this effect positive or negative?
3. What will be the outcome if I continue to focus my time in this way?
4. How has my lack of focus in the past hurt me?
5. How has my focus benefited me in the past?
6. How can I use the power of focus to create an even brighter future?

If you believe that based upon this data, you have a lack of ambition and are not smart enough to make your dreams come true, you will eventually play this scenario out in your behavior. You will see the results of this kind of programming when you look at the screen and replay your life. You can program the types of commercials playing in your head so that they reflect a life of learning, growth, and achievement.

Another thing I believe to be central is to have fun. Many people don't succeed because they put too much pressure on themselves to succeed. Achievement should be fun. One of the things that we should each take time to do every day is laugh. No, not just a normal laugh, but a big belly laugh! On the count of three, I want you to think of something funny in your past, and laugh out loud as loudly as you can. One, two, three, Ha! Ha! Ha! Wasn't that fun? It's important to do work that you love to do. This will allow you to reach your full potential and give more to the people around you.

THE VALUE OF A SMILE

It costs nothing, but creates much.
It enriches those who receive, without impoverish-
      ing those who give.
It happens in a flash and the memory of it some-
      times lasts forever.
None are so rich that they can get along without it,
And none so poor but are richer for its benefits.
It creates happiness in the home, fosters goodwill
      in a business, and is the countersign of
      friends.
It is rest to the weary, daylight to the discouraged,
      sunshine to the sad, and nature's best antidote
      for trouble.
Yet it cannot be bought, begged, borrowed, or
      stolen, for it is something that is of no earthly
      good to anyone, until it is given away. And if
      in the hurly-burly bustle of today's world,
      some people you meet should be too tired to
      give you a smile, May we ask you to leave
      one of yours? For nobody needs a smile so
      much, As those who have none left to give.

—Unknown

I would encourage you to look around and count your blessings. Continually focus your attention on what's good about your life. For everything negative that happens in life, there are many more positive occurences. For every death, a birth. For every failure, yet another opportunity. For every dark night, yet the opportunity that comes with following day. That's how things get done! Massive changes continue to take place that make today one of the most exciting times in history to be alive. Then again, any time is the most exciting time in history to be alive. It's all in how you set up the software between your ears called your mind. If your life isn't what you want it to be, you must break the pattern of the kind of mental programming that's held you back. You must break free into becoming the best you that you can possibly be, and not worry about meeting other peoples' expectations about how you should live your life!

FACE IT

The apparent and tangible
are the gains evident and
within your embrace.
Dreams and plans in your
heart don't come easy.
You must go meet them
face to face.

— © *Saunni Dais*

INVEST IN YOURSELF
WITHOUT HESITATION

*"The growth of the human mind is still
high adventure, in many ways the highest
adventure on earth."*

—Norman Cousins

I am a strong proponent of the belief that you get what you expect. It's hard to believe that in a country as rich as America, people are finding it hard to make it. Do we have social challenges that allow some people the opportunity to excel with greater ease than others? Absolutely! That's a given! But in spite of all the obstacles that one could use as excuses for not excelling, there are people who throughout history have found ways to make their dreams come true. They not only found ways to survive, they learned how to succeed! There's a fundamental problem in this country with the way people think. Many people believe that there are only a finite amount of resources available. They do not recognize life's abundance. Poverty consciousness leads to poor education, high crime rates, and a lower standard of living on a permanent basis. For every person that you can point out who has challenges to deal with, I can point out someone who has overcome greater challenges by getting off the ground and going for their dreams.

I once saw a program on *60 Minutes* that profiled a lady by the name of Bonnie Consolo. She was born without arms. She is one of the most remarkable people that I've ever seen. She raised a family, went back to college and completed her education, and is now making a significant contribution to society. She learned to cook, drive a car, cut and comb her children's hair, and perform countless other activities that you and I take for granted. All with her feet! When they interviewed her, she was asked whether or not she missed having her arms. She said, "No, I don't miss having arms because I've never known what it was like to have them in the first place. The only reality I know is the one I'm currently living and that has always been without arms." She went on to say that you can't miss what you've never had. I thought to myself, "Wow, what a wonderful outlook on life this lady has!" And yet we all know people who are perfectly healthy, who experience far fewer challenges than this courageous woman, yet can't seem to get their motor running. The welfare rolls are now filled with second and third generation re-cipients who pass the same poverty mentality on to future generations. They don't believe in the concept of abundance because of the environment in which they live. Everywhere they look they see lack. They didn't see their parents get up and go to work, and as a result, they never learned the value of work. Work adds meaning to life, creating a sense of self-worth and accomplishment. When children are taught that society owes them something, it eliminates any chance they have to gain independence through their own efforts. The concept of something for nothing becomes a lifelong strug-gle to see how much they can get for the least amount of time and effort. This something for nothing mentality is not limited to just the people in lower socioeconomic standing. It per-meates our culture to the point where productivity is lower now than at any other time during the last thirty years. There's no question that we live in the richest, most powerful nation in the world. Unfortunately, success oftentimes breeds com-placency. Over the years, people have taken prosperity for granted to the point where they think that it should come nat-urally as it did in the past. Well, the past has caught up with us! The vast and far reaching changes in our world today have many people perplexed, furstrated, and afraid. There is hope, however, for people who are willing to use what they've got to get what they want.

More and more, we hear about how many thousands of workers will lose their jobs due to rightsizing, downsizing, re-structuring, and revitalization. If you happen to be on the re-ceiving end of a pink slip, all of these things have only one meaning, you're fired! As companies attempt to become more competitive, enabling them to compete in this global environment, they need people who can add value to their organizations. Many misguided people think that they should be rewarded for the time they've put in up until now. What they don't realize is that the company cannot continue to rest on past accomplishments. You must be able to demonstrate each day the value that you bring to the organization and its effect on the bottom line. In Jeffrey Madrick's wonderful book, *The End of Affluence*, he profiles the fact that by the year 2013, America will have lost more than $3.5 trillion dollars worth of lost productivity in the last thirty years. He goes on to point out that as of the fall of 1994, the average real wage had been falling for more than two decades. He added that the rate of growth in productivity was still historically low, the proverty rate had risen significantly, and America could no longer invest adequately in its future without a significant sacrifice in current standards of living.

In my opinion, the operative word in the above statement is SACRIFICE! Many people want to change their circumstances in life, but are unwilling to change themselves. They therefore remain victims, not of circumstances, but of their own way of thinking. People often complain about the fact that there's no job security. You know what? They're right! There's no security in terms of employment as it was known in the past. In those days, you were paid for survival, loyalty, and time. When America was number one in almost every economic category, life was good! Everyone was fat, dumb, and happy. They collected their paycheck every other week and attempted to survive until they reached retirement. This mentality seemed to fit the times. The company took care of you as long as you kept your nose clean and didn't miss too many days of work without a serious reason. Oh, how times have changed!

The people who have the hardest time with these changes are people who want to drag this old paradigm of thinking into this new world in which we now live. They're upset beause they weren't grandfathered in under the old program. They believe it unreasonable for the organization to expect a justification as to why they exist and what value they bring to the organization. So they're unattempting to approach the new millenium kicking and screaming instead of looking in the mirror and dealing with their own deficiencies. They find blame with everyone and everything for their lack of progress. They are not willing to pay the price to upgrade their skills. The cost is not high, it just seems high to those who don't have the courage or ambition enough to get off their assets!

TO SURVIVE OR SUCCEED? THAT IS THE QUESTION!

I was standing on the corner of 4th and Pike St. in downtown Seattle Washington many years ago. As I looked next to me, I noticed a young man who was begging. They called it panhandling in those days. I noticed that people were giving him dollars instead of the traditional coins that were usually reserved for those less fortunate souls. It dawned on me that he was getting exactly what he was asking for. He had extremely low expectations! He was healthy, handsome, and well-spoken. This young man did not look like a beggar. Rather intrigued with the situation, I stepped to the side and watched him in action for about fifteen minutes. Then I eased up next to him to strike up a conversation. He told me that he was 26 years old, had a college education, and earned more than $25 thousand dollars a year by begging. He said, "Some of my best customers are down here!" This implied that many of the same people rewarded him over and over, simply for the asking. When he walked away, I watched him for about six blocks. When he was out of sight, I asked myself a couple of questions. What would he do to survive? Answer: He would do anything! You can't get much lower than begging, especially if you are healthly and have the capacity to produce, which he surely did. What would he do to succeed? Answer: Nothing! He would do everything to survive and nothing to succeed. My question to you is, what are you willing to do to survive? What are you willing to do to succeed? The answers to these two questions will have a profound effect on you for the rest of your life.

You Get Paid For Value, Not Time!

"I don't like work, no man does, but I like
what is in work, the chance to find yourself.
Your own reality, for yourself, not for others,
what no other man can ever know."

—*Joseph Conrad*

The concept of entitlement is a dangerous one indeed. Many people working in corporations cringe when I tell them that they get paid for value, not time. They feel as though because they've been employed somewhere for x number of years, the company owes them a living. You must demonstrate the benefits of your employment. This goes for anyone, on any level, in any business! I tell managers that in order to really be effective, you must now spend no more than two days a week in your office. The other three must be spent out on the factory floor if you're in manufacturing, out in the warehouse if you're in distribution, or on the retail floor or in the field if you're in sales. You must spend time finding out what's going on so that you can become a resource as opposed to a roadblock. The ones who have a problem with this are those who feel that their tenure should afford them the benefit of sitting behind a desk pushing out memos and ordering people around. Those days are gone!

There is no job security. Experts tell us that the college graduates of today may be facing as many as 12 to 15 different careers during the course of their working lives. However, there is employment security. This is achieved by the constant upgrading of your skills through continuing education. This means that you cannot expect to compete in today's competitive environment unless you are willing to constantly improve yourself through personal development.

THANK YOU, MR. ROHN

I had the opportunity to attend a seminar back in 1980 that would change my life forever. It was taught by a man named Jim Rohn. After the seminar, I left with more than 15 pages of notes that I took home and fashioned into a plan that revolutionized my life. He taught me several fundamental principles about life that I'll never forget. Among the many things that he said were, "You can have more than you have if you become more than you are." Another one was, "Learn to work harder on yourself than you do on your job." Others included, "Don't wish things were easier, wish you were better!", "Don't wish for less challenges, work to gain more skills," and, "In order for your life to change, you've got to change." Once I was able to really peel back the onion and look at the essence of those statements, I finally realized that I had the formula for success in my life. Mr. Rohn became my mentor, even though I didn't meet him until thirteen years later. His philosophy of life helped put me on a path to achievement.

Empowering yourself to succeed involves taking full responsibility for how your life turns out. It's taking a proactive approach to increasing your skills to a new level each and every day. I'm sometimes amazed at how few people will attend a seminar that could change their lives unless their company or someone else pays the fare. Even then, they sit in the program the entire time with an attitude of indifference as if to say, "I'm only here because I have to be!" These are the same people who complain because of their lack of progress in life, not realizing that their own foolish ways are keeping them behind.

LEARNING IS A LIFELONG JOURNEY

When I graduated from college, I did one of the most boneheaded things a person could do. I drove by a dumpster, took all of my books, and threw them away. I thought to myself, "Man, I'm glad all of that learning junk is over with! Now

I can get on with my life!" I didn't realize that learning is a journey that is never ending. The minute you stop learning, you might as well be dead! This is so important because so many people have a negative attitude about learning. This affects every aspect of their life, especially their economic life. A perfect example is technology. Unless you know how to master computer technology, in the next few years, you won't be on the map as far as the world is concerned. Yet many people refuse to deal with the inevitability of this fact and bury their heads in the sand. Well, it's not going away! You will only limit your own market viability if you refuse to work on your skills. You will earn less income and be limited to opportunities commensurate with your skill. You can only blame yourself for your situation because you didn't have the courage and discipline to take action.

When you look around, you'll find that they've made it so convenient to learn that it's unbelievable. The technology centered around learning has made it possible for us to learn more things in a shorter period of time than during any other time in history. That's not without justification. Ten years ago it was thought that the capacity for information in this world doubled every five years. Five years ago it was thought to have doubled every three years. Today it is thought that the capacity for information in this world doubles every year. Now imagine what kind of condition you will have to be in to compete and earn a viable living if you don't make a personal development program an ongoing part of everything that you do in life. If you choose not to, no question about it, you will find yourself in serious trouble!

In the United States of America, there is a staircase of economic porportions. At the bottom of this ladder is the minimum wage, which is around five dollars in most areas of the country. At the top of the ladder is the highest paid CEO salary in corporate America. Over the last couple of years, that prize has gone to Roberto Gozuieta, the CEO of Coca Cola. He was paid $58 million dollars. That's what I call big bucks! Now, in comparison to what Coca Cola made it is not.

Coca Cola is a $25 billion dollar a year company. The reason that he can earn that much is because of the EVA (equity value added) and MVA (market value added) that he brings to the party. Whether society thinks he is worth that much is a moot point. The fact of the matter is that he is perceived to be worth that much by the only people who really count, and that's the shareholders of Coca Cola. In order to achieve that level of economic security, Mr. Gozuieta had to pay a price. He did not start out at the top of the company. He started as a chemist, and before that, he spent many years in school. He could not speak English when he first came to America, but that did not discourage him. He kept working on himself until he was worthy of the promotions that he garnered along the way.

You are charged with the responsibility of developing your own skills on a continual basis. It's no one else's job. It's all up to you! You must be commited enough to take the steps necessary to go back to school, to get the computer training necessary, to improve your reading skills, to increase the quality of your communication skills. You must be willing to become a better manager, to learn new leadership skills, to become a better parent or child, for that matter, to learn how to become a team player, to become better in your writing skills, and to learn better health practices. Don't wait for circumstances to kick your butt! Do it yourself, ahead of time, and you will be that much further ahead in the game.

DON'T CONFUSE COMMITMENT AND INTEREST

There's a huge difference between commitment and interest. When you're only interested in something, you will quit at the first sign of opposition or adversity. When you're committed, you will find away to reach your goals no matter how long it takes or what you have to go through. There's an old song that says, "You've got to be willing to go through something in order to get something!"

I'll never forget how my grandmother demonstrated her commitment to my education when I was in eighth grade.

One evening my grandmother, my father, and I were talking at the dinner table after supper. The conversation came up about where I was going to attend high school. My grand-mother had told me previously that I was going to have one of two choices. I could attend Christian Brothers Military or St. Louis University High School. She had mentioned it to my father earlier, but nothing serious had been discussed. When she brought this up as a topic of conversation that night, my father told her that I was going to attend the public school in our area like the rest of the kids in our neighborhood. My grandmother gritted her teeth and shouted, "Over my dead body!" I mean, everything in the world stopped for what seemed like hours. The clock on the wall stopped! The birds flying outside stopped in the air, frozen! The water I was pouring out of the pitcher stopped in midstream. My father's face was also frozen. There was nothing in my grandmother's face that even looked like compromise. He was stonewalled, shut out, and the game was over. It's was Nonnie-55, Daddy-0 at the end of the first quarter. The following week my grand-mother, with her wobbly, aching knees, and I took three different buses out to Christian Brothers Military Academy. She waited in the hallway three hours while I took the en-trance exam to this school and afterwards we took the long trek back home. I'm almost brought to tears as I write because the memory is as vivid as yesterday. That's what commitment is all about. The ability to do whatever it takes, no matter how long it takes. The view from the top is the same no matter how long it takes you to get there. How commited are you to building a better life for yourself? What are you willing to do to make it happen? The rewards you receive in life will be in direct porportion to your level of personal development and skill.

READING IS FUNDAMENTAL

I was surprised to read that today in our workforce, one out of five American workers is illiterate. How could that be? In the richest country in the world? There's absolutely no reason for this! There are too many ways to learn for people not to know how to read. I hope you are aware of this awful and pathetic statistic so that you can help others. A few years ago, the media profiled a sad story about Dexter Manley, an all pro defensive end with the Washington Redskins, who, with tear filled eyes at a press conference, admitted that he left Oklahoma State University without knowing how to read. I must commend Mr. Manley for his courage to step forward and expose an educational system that lets people through without learning to read. He did it with the objective of helping others step forward with the same affliction and address their problem.

Certainly illiteracy is a problem in our country, but another concern that's looming even larger is that of alliteracy. These are people that can read, but don't. The result is the same, ignorance. There are many books that can help people improve the quality of their lives, but people don't read them. This is astounding. Jim Rohn eloquently points out in his seminars that less than three percent of the American population owns a library card. Reading books can help you condense the amount of time it takes to do something from years to possibly months, but you must be committed enough to explore. Instead of going to happy hour, sometimes try going to a bookstore and you'll find it an exhilarating experience. Whatever your area of interest, there's a book on the subject. Many are written by authors who faced the same dilemma you're dealing with now. Whether it's building a fortune in real estate with no money down, creating a stronger bond with your family, or remodeling your bathroom, somebody has written a book on that subject. Now what do you suppose separates you from the answers that you seek about how to improve your life? It's called space! The only thing holding you back is your own ability to put your feet in motion. For this reason, I believe that it is essential to spend a portion of each day engaged in your own personal development program. Reading one hour a day will change your life. It will take your mind on journeys that you otherwise would never experience. Reading will allow you to explore dimensions of your own consciousness and help you become a more powerful person. Zig Ziglar has long been one of my favorite people. His contributions in the field of self-development speak for themselves. I had an opportunity to meet him at one of his seminars many years ago. It was impressed by the fact that even well into his sixties, he spends three hours each day working to increase his skills through personal development. Now that's commitment! Are you willing to invest the time it takes to get better? Are you willing to take control of your life now? I would encourage you to start now, right where you are.

BECOME A 21ST CENTURY PERSON

I am very blessed to have the opportunity to work with senior managers for some of the most powerful corporations in the world. I often ask human resource managers what they feel are some of the key skills needed to succeed in today's competitive environment. Some of the answers follow.

Communication Skills: The ability to express yourself one-on-one or in large or small groups is a skill that will help separate you from the pack. I've met people, too numereous to name here, who have a good educational backround, but lack the interpersonal skills necessary to succeed. Many are unaware that this vital skill is a shortcoming for them until someone is candid enough to point it out. They can bounce around for years in frustration, going from interview to interview, and often taking jobs that are far less challenging than their level of skill would suggest. You must continue to improve your oral and written communication skills. The higher you go in business, the stronger these skills need to be, for at each progressively higher level, there are people who are more adept at these skills. This is one of the primary skills that separates people who enjoy greater responsibility, faster advancement, and higher incomes from people with the same backround, but weaker communication skills. Starting tomorrow, craft for yourself a game plan that includes books, tapes, and classes on how to improve your communication skills. There are many associations, such as Toastmasters and The National Speakers Association, which happen to have local chapters in each state.

Computer Skills: As I mentioned before, many people are approaching the computer age kicking and screaming. It's just a fact of life that the world is going more and more high tech. You must become skilled in computer technology in order to succeed in the future. I was initially horrified at the prospect of having to learn about computers. I bought a computer and left in the box for weeks before summoning the courage to set up the system. After that I decided that if I was going to really become the kind of businessman that I wanted to be, getting on board the technology train was critical. I enrolled in a series of computer classes and immediately began to feel more comfortable with the technology. There's a super company called Executrain, with offices throughout the country, which does an excellent job in computer training. They also allow their graduates to come back for follow-up training at no cost. I recommend them highly. With each class, my skill level increased and now I find myself helpless without my computer. It's interesting what happens when we move past our fears and take the plunge! Whether you are working for a large corporation or engaged in your own small business, you need to be computer literate. Why not get started now? Go for it!

Become a Team Player: Teamwork is the cornerstone of success in today's business world. People who can successfully interact with others remain among the most attractive candidates for any organizaton. Interaction calls on many skills, such as communication, and listening, as well as the ability to subordinate personal interests for the good of the team. I've seen many instances in business where lack of teamwork destroyed the business. I once worked in an environment where the inability of management and the union to work together almost ruined the company. It wasn't until the very existence of the organization was put at risk that they realized if the company went out of business, there wouldn't be anything to argue about. They moved from the mindset of looking for who was right to trying to find out what's best. This example shows how people succeed at teamwork. When you learn to succesfully colloborate with other people, you have developed a universal skill. With this skill, you will be more marketable, because one of the most difficult things to accomplish in business is the ability to work together with other people towards a common objective.

Become Adaptable To Change: In my travels throughout the country, I often hear people say, "Man, I sure will be glad when this change stuff is over and things get back to normal!" I immediately tell them, knocking on my forehead with my fist, "Hello, this is normal!" You must understand that because the world is in a constant state of change, you must be open-minded enough to continue trying new things. I will be discussing change in detail in the next chapter.

THERE'S NO WAY AROUND EDUCATION

I believe that there are two kinds of education, formal education and street knowledge. One without the other is automatically weaker. For balance, you need both. We've all heard about or met an educated fool, a person who is well versed technically speaking, but lacks the common sense to walk around the block without getting lost. There's also the street urchin, the person who is streetwise to the ways of life, but doesn't know how to communicate. The only way to become proficient in both is to seek out knowledge in each area.

If you're lacking in formal education, you must find out what you're interested in. (See Chapter 1 on purpose) and then you must find out who has the knowledge in that area. After that, you must devote time, effort, and energy to pursuing this information. You must become unconsciously competent. Armed with this information, you can now figure out how to learn by doing. This often involves starting at the bottom level of an organization and learning the business from the ground up. I meet many young people who are far too impatient. They want to be CEO of the corporation right now! If you fit this description, regardless of your age, you must recognize that until you learn something, you don't know it. Unfortunately, no business, large or small, can afford to roll the dice of its future based upon what you think you know.

McDonald's Corporation has a program called "Hamburger University" that each potential franchisee must attend before they can began operating. These franchisees are people who have proven themselves successful enough to put together at least $500,000 in financing, yet they are willing to be taught by someone more knowledgable than themselves so that they increase their odds for success.

They start out by learning everything about restaurant management from mopping the floors to balancing the books. They don't learn by reading alone, they learn by doing as well. Only after they've successfully completed their graduation from "Hamburger U"are they unleashed on the public. Even after their graduation, ongoing education keeps them up to date with the changing trends in the marketplace.

I spend quite a bit of time talking with college athletes. It's very hard to get them to understand that most of them will not play pro sports. In all of the major sports, there are fewer than three thousand athletes who are fortunate enough to play professionally. At the University of Minnesota, each year they have a counseling day where several former pro football players and myself come in to talk with the players about the value of education. I'm always the last to speak among all of the presenters that day. It's amazing to see the look in the players' eyes when former players tell them that they have a better chance of hitting the lottery than they do of playing professional sports. They don't believe it. Each one thinks that he is going to be the one that makes it big. They don't take their education seriously and they end up in serious trouble. I end the day by telling them that I was once sitting right where they are, thinking the same thing: "I'm going to the pros!" I go on to say that, "Among all of the speakers you see here today, I'm the only one who didn't play pro ball." I continue by telling them that this is exactly where most of them are not going, too. This immediately gets their attention! They are no longer seated, slumped over in their chairs, and looking cool. I say, "Oh, I see that I have your attention now!" I play out a scenario for them by assuming that one of them does get drafted and ends up with a pro team. My question then becomes, why is it that so many professional athletes end up broke? Busted, disgusted, and can't be trusted! They look at me with deadpans faces. How can a person sign a multi-million dollar contract and within a few years have nothing? It's because their income took a leap beyond their mentality to deal with it. Because they didn't mature to the level necessary to keep pace with the money, it came back to meet their level of education. If they end up broke, what does that tell you about their level of personal development and education? It was obviously not up to par. Now's let's analyze something further. Next question, who ends up with all of their money? Answer, all of the people with education. The agents, lawyers, and businesspeople all have their education and are poised to pounce on people less versed in the nuances of business than they are. There is no getting around education. When athletes retire, most often, they are in their early thirties. How are they going to make a living with more than 40 years of life expectancy left?

Some people pray that they will hit the lottery. The fact of the matter is that most lottery winners end up broke because they are ignorant when it comes to understanding the fundamentals of managing money. So in a very short period of time for some, and a longer one for others, an erosionary process begins so that many end up in worse circumstances than before they won the money. Ignorance is not bliss! If you don't know something, then you'd better know someone who does. I call it the power of OPs. There's other people's money, other people's time, other people's energy, other people's knowledge, and the list goes on. The key is to use, not misuse, these resources to increase your odds of winning. In Napoleon Hill's classic book, *Think and Grow Rich*, he discusses the power of a master mind alliance. This involves building yourself a team of people who are well skilled in the areas where you may be lacking. They, in turn, can use the skills that you bring, creating a win, win proposition for all.

THE MINUTE YOU THINK YOU'VE ARRIVED, LOOK OUT!

There's an old adage that says, "The minute you think you've arrived, you're ready for the return trip back home!" In fact, 47 percent of the Fortune 500 companies ten years ago are no longer in business today. There's always someone looking to take your place, and if you're egotistical enough to believe that you have all of the skill you need, you are sure to be replaced in a short period of time. Your own ignorance will be the reason. I once heard someone say that you should constantly seek to replace yourself in the marketplace before your competition does. Long-term success comes to people who continually seek ways to get better. When you approach the future with this attitude, you have the formula for changing your life. Success is never a place where you can stay without continual learning. Technology is changing too fast! Just imagine the number of inventions that are on the drawing board that we haven't even heard of yet. It can be daunting!

AVOID INFORMATION OVERLOAD

Do you ever feel frustrated trying to zero in on what to learn? I do! I've had more than my share of headaches trying to determine where to start. The key for me has been to decide on a definite course of action. When I prioritize according to needs, I focus on the things that will give me the greatest return for the time invested. Take the time to craft a plan of action for yourself by deciding what things are most important for you to learn first. List why it's important for you to learn these things and what you expect to gain from them over the short and long term. This will keep you from feeling overwhelmed with all of the information that is coming to you at the speed of light. It's similar to a smorgasbord. On it, you find a tremendous amount of choices, but there's no way that you can eat them all. You choose some things and bypass others. This will give you a greater feeling of control as you face the information age.

DON'T CONFUSE COST AND WORTH

One of the things that I believe will change your life is when you decide to invest in yourself without hesitation. The first thing people ask when faced with the decision of investing in their future is what something will cost. I have a library in my house that has taken me years to build. I have books that line the shelves as well as audio and video training programs. People often come over and ask to borrow my books or tapes. I very kindly give them the name of the author and the price, as well as tell them where I purchased the material. Many are insulted when I say I don't lend out my material. They complain about the price. I tell them that instead of asking what something cost, they should be more concerned about what it's worth. They are asking the wrong question! I ask them if they are truly committed to learning, or simply interested. If they are merely interested, they probably wouldn't read or listen to the information if I gave it to them anyway. In fact, statistics show that fewer than ten percent of the people who buy books or tapes ever take the cellophane off. What will people do if they are truly committed to learning? They will make the investment necessary. Here's another thing I found out. Whenever I loaned my material to people,

I never got the stuff back! I had to replace many hundreds of dollars worth of material before I learned this most valuable lesson.

Many people are holding themselves back because they are too cheap with themselves. They aren't willing to invest the necessary time and financial resources that will enable them to get ahead. They spend their money on things that will only provide temporary satisfaction and offer nothing that will help them build a better future. You must be willing to bet on you. The old biblical saying is never more true. "If you take the coins from your purse and fill your mind, your mind will eventually fill your purse with coins!" I've seen the results of this philosophy in my life. If you are not willing to invest in yourself, why should anyone else? You must make the distinction between what something cost and what it's worth. When you are able to do this, you take a huge step towards understanding that your own personal growth and development is the key to your future. Many people complain that there is no job security. There is, however, employment security. You secure this by continuing to work on your core competencies. When you do this, the market will reward you. Please don't shortchange yourself! The information that can help you change your life is not in short supply. If you could afford to purchase this book, then you are already familiar with the process. Now just keep doing it over and over and over again, for the rest of your life!

CHALLENGE

*is a necessary prerequisite
for continued growth.
It's first cousin, CHANGE,
recycles probabilities,
potential and hope.*

—©*Saunni Dais*

DEALING WITH THE
CHALLENGE OF CHANGE

*"God give us grace to accept with serenity the
things that cannot be changed, the courage to
change the things which should be changed, and
the wisdom to know the difference."*

—*Reinold Niebuhr, 1943*

There was a man who was working on an oil rig overseas when it exploded! The platform caught on fire and was engulfed in flames. The man looked around everywhere for some means of escape, but could find none. Finally, he saw an opening and dove off of the platform into the ocean and the burning hot oil that was floating on the surface. He was able to swim over to one of the four posts on the base of the platform. He hung on for dear life! Fortunately, he was later rescued. Later that night the gentleman appeared on *Night Line* with Ted Koppel. Ted Koppel began to applaud and compliment the man for being so brave. After a few minutes of this, the gentleman stopped Koppel in his tracks when he said, "Hey listen, I don't consider myself courageous in the least! For me, it was a matter of common sense! I chose probable death over certain death! I knew that if I stayed on that platform, I was going to die for sure, so jumping into the ocean became my only option!" How many of us stick with old ways of doing things or old behaviors long after they've proven outdated and ineffective? Many times, people maintain behavior patterns that are detrimental to their lives, all in the name of familiarity. Sometimes it seems as though we must wait until our pant cuffs are on fire before we get off our duffs and do something. Don't wait until you're on a burning platform to change, because you could wait too long!

I once knew a young man who defied everything that his father told him to do. His father would take him to school and occasionally even walk him to the classroom. As soon as the car sped off, he would skip out of school and go right back to the pool hall. This went on for a period of years. One night the young man didn't come home. His father became worried. At 3 a.m. the phone rang. It was the police department, explaining to the father that his son had been shot in the neck. I know this young man intimately because he is my oldest brother. My brother lived in a wheelchair for seven long years as a paraplegic before his body deteriorated to nothing and he died at the age of 24. One day before his death as he was staring out of the window, I eased up to him to ask him what he was thinking about. He told me that he was looking back over the course of his life and thinking that he really wanted to change. He said that he had always told himself that he would, but unfortunately he didn't and was now paying the price. He told me, "Desi, it's not enough to just change! Man, you've got to change in time!" I get chills every time I think about that day. I keep hearing his voice saying, "You've got to change in time!"

There was another young man who had the same attitude as my oldest brother. He felt he could always beat the system. Even though he was a straight A student in school, he challenged authority at every turn. He loved to get into mischief, even as a young kid. As a teenager he went from one reform school to another. He was intellectually brilliant, but unfortunately, he always used his smarts for something devious. Finally, he took to robbing banks. He was successful at robbing several branch banks. By simply using a note that read, "Put the money in the bag or I'll blow your head off!" he was able to rob more than a dozen banks. He got away each time. His day of reckoning finally came when he went to a dealership to purchase a car. If you were to go into a dealership to buy a car and put down $20 thousand in cash without any evidence of income, the dealership would become slightly suspicious, to say the least. When this young man came out of his apartment one morning, he was stunned to find that he was surrounded by police officers, state troopers, and detectives with their guns loaded, cocked, and aiming at him. He would spend the next twelve years in prison. I know this young man intimately as well, for he is my youngest brother.

Years later, he called me from the penitentiary and told me that he had finally figured out why he was in there. After years of blaming everyone else, he said, "Desi, it took me a long time to come to grips with the fact that I'm the reason I'm in prision!" When he said that, I began to cry. He said that he had wished for many things over the years, but most of all, he wished that he would have changed in time. The tragedy of my brothers' lives taught me that it's not enough to change, you've got to change in time. In business, you've got to change in time before opportunity is lost. Many people are waiting for conditions to determine what they are going to do. You must realize that the only way things are going to change in your life is when you change.

I've seen many instances in my life where people lived in regret for the rest of their lives because they didn't have the ability to change their behavior. I once knew a man who chain smoked for years. I can remember the "smoker's cough" that accompanied his raspy voice. Many years later, when he was dying from cancer of the lungs, he told me, "If I had known I was going to live this long, I would have taken better care of myself!" Have you ever heard this before? My question is, why not change yourself in advance and experience the private victory that comes from knowing that you had the courage and discipline to make yourself do it? Don't wait until your situation is terminal before you try to change things. It may be too late!

Of the many abusive relationships that my mother encountered, she was involved in one that had deadly consequences. She was married to a rough and tumble biker guy named Jerry. He would beat her to a pulp and then go out on a drinking or drug binge. Then would come back and repeat the same cycle. When I would go to visit her, he would act like the sweetest guy in the world, only to return to beating my mother when I left. She kept this from me because she didn't want me to worry or get involved. I was a child and she felt she could handle the situation. This went on for years until one day he came home and beat her so badly that she had to go into the hospital. Before he was through, she took a .38 caliber revolver and emptied the gun into his body, killing him instantly. Later she told me that she had always thought about putting him out of her house, but somehow always found a reason to stay in the relationship. She told me that, even if you kill in self-defense, you can never imagine the feelings of guilt and regret that come from taking the life of another human being. Leaving this relationship in time could have prevented this terrible tragedy.

WHY IS CHANGE SO HARD?

Change is very difficult, but if you continue to do the things you've been doing, you'll continue to get the same results. Try crossing your arms in the traditional fashion, with your left arm folded over your right one. Now switch positions with your right arm now placed over your left. How does it feel? Does it feel a bit awkward? Of course it does! It always will! Every time you seek to make a change in your life it will feel uneasy at first. You must be willing to work through this uneasiness. This is one of the main reasons why so many people live lives filled with failure and regret. They are not willing to be uncomfortable long enough to grow. You must be willing be operate with a certain degree of uncertainty if you want to become more than you currently are. Change is a process that requires patience. Often, you will not see results immediately, but you must stay the course nevertheless. Even when things look bleak, you must keep on going. Resiliency plays a huge role in implementing any lasting changes in your life. You cannot let temporary setbacks deter you from the changes.

STUCK ON STUPID

There was a guy who used to walk around campus at the University of Minnesota. We all called him "Walking Phil." He was quite a contradiction. He looked like a bum, always wearing tattered clothing, with an old fishing hat perched on top of his head. He walked with a real strut and always carried a copy of the *Wall Street Journal*. He could always be found walking through an area of campus called "Dinky Town," with restaurants and bars where students hung out. He loved to stop students, and in particular, athletes. I always seemed to be unfortunate enough to catch his eye whenever I was on my way to practice or to and from class. He would grill me as to whether or not I was attending class on a regular basis and taking care of business. He smelled so bad that I would often have to take a step back. Walking Phil was extremely articulate and spoke with as much confidence as he exuded when he walked. He even gave me a stock tip one day that I later checked out with my stockbroker, to only find that it was with one of the fastest growing companies in the country. I could never quite figure him out. He was a walking paradox. How could such a smart man be in such dire circumstances? Walking Phil has been walking around campus for better than 20 years now. I still see him from time to time when I'm around the University. He has been through generations of players, from David Winfield to Tony Dungy.

After doing some investigating, I found out that Walking Phil had a master's degree as well as a Ph.d. from the University of Minnesota. After graduating from college, he fell madly in love with a woman who eventually left him for someone else. He subsequently snapped, and has never been the same. This one incident in life caused him to get stuck. He lacked resiliency. The ability to bounce back is what separates winners from losers. Walking Phil is stuck on stupid and it's ridiculous for him to give up on his entire life because of a soured relationship. I'm sure that woman has gotten on with her life and probably doesn't spend much time thinking about him. A change in philosophy is often needed in order to get out of a stupid state of mind. As smart as this man is, he remains ignorant in terms of the wisdom necessary to move on.

THE PHILOSOPHY OF NEXT

Let's say you go in to the doctor and a patient goes in before you. Let's say that the patient dies. Does the doctor come out and say, "Well that last patient died and we're closing!" I don't think so! The doctor will come out of his office into the waiting room. He will look to the left and then to the right and say one word, "NEXT!" Let's say that another patient comes in and dies. They send him down the chute into a big box that awaits him in the alley. Does the doctors office close? Answer, no! He comes out of his office into the waiting room. He looks to the right and then looks to the left and says, "NEXT!" It's always NEXT! In the past, when I gave a seminar, I would become disappointed if everyone didn't leave excited. I would often blame myself for the one or two people that would give me negative feedback on my questionnaires, I would ask myself, "What seminar were they attending?" After a while you come to the conclusion that some people get it and some don't. Some will use the material and some won't. I'm not responsible for that, they are. So my philosophy of life has changed over the years to NEXT! It doesn't matter if they say, "Desi, we love you and we're gonna get in there with you and burn it up in five seconds!" I say, "Great, NEXT!" If they say, " We think you stink and are the worst speaker we've ever heard!" I say, "Great, NEXT!" NEXT is all you have. You cannot spend years dwelling on a situation that has long since past. Walking Phil could probably have been a successful lawyer, doctor, or politician. When that woman left him, after getting the crying out his system, he should have stood up, dusted himself off, and yelled to the top of his voice, "NEEEEEEEEXXXXXTTT!" I would suggest that you do the same thing.

THE INCREASING IMPACT OF CHANGE

There are three major reasons for the increasing impact of change. They are volume, speed, and the complexity of the world in which we live. There's no guarantee that what is working for you now will work as even as long as tomorrow. New ways of doing things and new products, services, and philosophies all make it necessary for you to adapt. When you feel that change is coming at you at a faster rate than you can handle, the natural tendency is to become overwhelmed. We all come into this world with an imaginary bucket of water. Have you ever gotten to the point where your bucket was full? If someone tried to dump more in it, but it was over-flowing, you exploded by saying, "Get your own bucket, Jack, because mine is full!" We all come into this world with a certain number of assimilation credits. These credits represent the amount of tolerance that each of us has for change. We all deal with it in different ways, but each time you are faced with change, you use a certain number of assimilation credits to make the transition. These credits are the water pouring into your bucket.

I have identified three different kinds of change; macro, or-ganizational and micro. Macro change involves interest rates, tax rates, who's president, and the price of a paper clip. It in-volves things that are outside of your ability to control but that you can still influence, with your vote, for example. Organi-zational change occurs when your company asks you to change jobs in order to give the organization more bench strength, enabling you to become a more valued employee by learning a different skill set. If you own your own business, it involves making changes because of market demands. For example, when the tax laws changed in the mid-eighties, it forced wholesale changes in the real estate industry. The macro change of tax reform caused organizational change within every business affected by it. Micro change is when something affects you personally. Anyone who has ever had their house broken into, been divorced, had major medical problems that arose after once being healthy, or had a close relative of theirs die, has been faced with a micro change in their life. This is the level of change that requires the largest number of assimilation credits for change adaptation. Once your bucket is full of life's changes, it overflows just like water in a bucket when the faucet is left running. It is at this point that you feel stress. A remedy is needed.

At this point, I want to ask you a question. If you have a glass and it is filled to the rim with water, can you get the glass to hold any more water? The answer is yes, if you pour some of the contents of the glass out first. Life is the same way. You must be willing to give up something in order to get something. Holding on to past beliefs or old ways of doing things just because they are comfortable is an ironclad guarantee that your life will not change in any significant way. Change does not always have to come by means of things that are done to you. I call this the "Victims of Circumstance" syndrome. You can implement changes in your life any time you decide to by simply making some key decisions. I know of people who are involved in jobs, and relationships, that they know are not in their best interest, but they stay, stay, and stay, until circumstances push them out on a limb. Meanwhile, they have lost the most precious commodity, time. Make the changes before they make you!

UNDERSTANDING HOW CHANGE FEELS

When undergoing change, know that you will feel awkward at first. It's only natural. The first thing you will think about is what you are giving up, which in some cases, ain't much! You may often feel alone. You may feel that the whole world is coming down on you and that you can only handle so much change. Give yourself a break, because people are at different readiness levels for change. You may have to start slowly, but please, get started! You may be concerned that you don't have enough resources, which is often the concern when people start their own businesses. Get started with what you have, right now! Remember also to hold yourself to certain standards of behavior, because if you don't, you will revert back to your old behavior, and nothing will happen. You must work through the initial pain that you may have to endure. Believe me, it will pale in comparison next to the pain of regret that you will experience as you look back over the course of your life and know that you didn't do what you should have. Life is no dress rehearsal. You only go around once! When it comes to change, no pain, no gain! I wish there was some other way to put it. Let me also say that the pleasure is well worth it. You will become a different person because you will know in your heart that you've got what it takes to make things happen in your life.

CHANGE YOURSELF FIRST!

Change requires that you adjust your attitude. Don't think about the things you may be losing because those same things may be the ones that are holding you back. Don't think, "There's no way I can do this!" Think to yourself, "Sure, this is tough, but so am I! "I can and will handle this!" Make positive affirmations to yourself and say them both aloud and silently to yourself each day. Please make sure to perform the exercises in the study guide. They will help you tremendously! You must be willing to let go of your past. When your fist is balled up too tightly, nothing gets out, but nothing gets in! When people are trying to hold on to the past, they go through periods of denial by saying, "This doesn't mean anything. I'll just hang out and eventually things will get back to normal!" When they are asked to make changes on their jobs, they immediately say, "How can they do this to me!", "I hate doing things this way!" or "Poor little me!" When this doesn't work, they move on to bargaining with change. They say, "OK, I'll do this part the way that change dictates, but I'm keeping all other parts the same. Some people act as if to say, "I don't care what they say, I'm not changing no matter what!" Here's what you need to understand. Change doesn't care how you feel. It is not going to ask for your permission. Change just is. When it comes, it waits for no one. The question is, are you ready? When you get those subtle signs that you need to make a change in your life, do you ignore them or do you act?

Moving From Neutral To Overdrive

*"What a wonderful life I've had! I only wished
I'd realized it sooner."*

—Colette

Some people go through their lives in neutral. Don't let this happen to you! They act as if they postpone making a decision, the situation will go away. It never does! The power of decision is what it will take to move from neutral into drive and then overdrive. When you are in neutral, you know what you should do, but you still aren't doing it. Don't worry about having to do everything right at the begining. Make a commitment to keep trying. Each day as I wrote this book, I created my own brand of stress about sitting down at he computer and getting started. I would often sit there for 30 minutes or more with a blank screen. Sometimes I would get frustrated when nothing would happen, but I stayed the course and eventually I found my hands moving briskly across the keyboard. You never know what you are capable of unless you try, and that includes writing a book. When you take the first step towards change, you will move to a new beginning and start a new chapter in the story of your life.

A Plan For Life Change

1. Weigh the pros and cons of the change. If the pros outweigh the cons, it's time to try something new. So do it now! Don't wait another day to make the necessary changes.
2. Break the desired change into small parts. Write a specific statement of affirmation for each change and a definite deadline for its accomplishment.
3. Enter into a written contract with a close friend or coworker who can serve as a compassionate observer or coach. Make sure it is someone, though, who will hold you to your promise as stated.

4. Start with the easiest part of the change. Give yourself a fighting chance.
5. Write a statement of positive self talk. Think about all of the reasons why this will work and how you will benefit from making the changes. Make this your focus from now on.
6. Work on one change at a time. Complete one part of the change process before moving on to something else.
7. Be patient. To change a behavior, you must practice it for at least 30 days consecutively.
8. Recognize that change will be awkward at first, but once you get the hang of it, it will seem no different than before, except that you will be much better off.
9. Celebrate your success, no matter how small.

THE "DO IT NOW" CHANGE PROGRAM

Complete the exercise below on how to change your life.

The change I will make is as follows: _____

_____

_____

_____

Below list the pros and cons of making the change.

<u>**PROS**</u>   <u>**CONS**</u>

This change can be broken into the following steps:

STEP	COMPLETION DATE
1. _____	_____
2. _____	_____
3. _____	_____
4. _____	_____

Write a statement of positive self talk, including the benefits of making the change.

Example: I want, deserve, and will have (your object of change) _____

_____

_____

_____

Choose the form of celebration after the change. _____

_____

_____

_____

THE EVOLUTION OF CHANGE
IT'S THIS SIMPLE

"If I never try anything, I never learn anything.
If I never take a risk, I stay right where I am.
If I hold myself back, I trade appearances for the
opportunity to find out what I'm really like."

—*Unknown*

KEY QUESTIONS

1. What do you want to change about your life?
2. How do you want to go about making the changes?
3. When do you want to make the changes?
4. Are you absolutely committed to changing your life for the better?

CHANGE TIPS

Learn to change yourself first! Don't worry about trying to change someone else. Remember: change is good, change is necessary, change is imminent, and change takes time, but

DON'T TAKE TOO LONG!

GOAL TENDING

Belief will manifest your
Presence if you can fashion
the magic of focus. Will
exerted, can forge the
mystery, oft times, yielding
honorable notice.
Synergy stands ready to aid
your grand, and truly, heartfelt dreams. Watch out
my friend, for the
"Doubt Most Monster"
that cannibalizes Esteem!

—© Saunni Dais

UNLEASH YOUR GOAL POWER

"Nothing contributes so much to tranquilize the mind as a steady purpose, a point on which the soul may fix its intellectual eye."

—*Mary Wollstonecraft Shelley*

When I was growing up in St. Louis, on any summer night you could go downtown near the St. Louis County jail and hear the inmates yelling and screaming out of the windows in their cells. I would often wonder how they ended up that way. What was the difference between being outside and inside? Why couldn't many of these people see a brighter future and a larger vision of themselves? It always scared me to think that with a few wrong moves and bad decisions on my part, I could end up in the same place, yelling out of that jailhouse window and wondering how in the world I got there in the first place.

SUBTLE CLUES

I will never forget the time when I got caught stealing in a small neighborhood grocery store. We had moved into a rather tough neighborhood, and I started to hang out with some tough kids. In order to be accepted, you had to prove yourself everyday. If someone extended you a challenge, you had to deal with it or be labeled. Your nerve, courage, and will were tested. If you were found to be weak, you were finished. People would prey on you each day, taking your money, clothes, and anything you had of perceived value. Many of these kids came from large families, and if you happened to get into a fight with one of them, you could literally be fighting for weeks as they all took numbers to stand in line for a shot at you. Talk about peer pressure. Well, that was how I ended up in that store with a Lucky Cake in my coat pocket. Some other kids had been stealing from this store and had not gotten caught. I was told that if I wanted to be initiated into a gang, I would have to pass this test. If I didn't do it, I was risking alienation, and that meant constant beatings and harrassment from gang members. I felt like I was about to pull it off. The game went like this. We would all go into the store and some kids would pretend to be looking at items to purhase while I stole the Lucky Cakes from the bakery section. What I didn't realize is that the couple who owned the store were watching me through one of the mirrors strategically placed throughout the store. As I stepped to the counter to purchase the penny candy as my disguise, the woman said to me, "Hey, what do we have here?" Her husband was a huge man. He grabbed me and threw me into the meat locker with all of the cold cuts, which were still uncut and hanging from the ceiling. He told me that he was going the call the police and have me picked up. I was petrified! I began yelling and screaming, "Mr., please let me out! I'm sorry! I promise I will never come back into your store again! I didn't mean to steal from you!" What I feared most was not the police. It was the beating my mother would have given me had she found out about it. I knew that she would skin me alive! All that I could see was that ironing chord whipping across my backside. Fortunately, after listening to me scream for the better part of 20 minutes, the owner felt sorry for me and let me go. Before he did though, he gave me a mini lecture and told me that if I didn't change my ways, I would end up in prison one day. He also told me that he could tell that I wasn't a hard kid, and that I should stop hanging out with the gang. He said he knew that some of them had stolen things from his store, but he had not caught them yet. I thought, "Why me?" At the age of ten, it was a valuable lesson that helped to detour me from further stealing, but not quite yet.

HEROES CAN HELP

After moving to a better neighborhood in the suburbs, we seemed to have a new lease on life. I went to an intergrated school for the first time in my life. My brother I and were able to make friends quickly, and developed a relationship with two boys about our ages who lived across the street. Their names were Ronnie and Adrian. I really envied them because they were from a wholesome family with very strict parents who really made them toe the line, but also were kind. Their father was a huge man of few words. You could tell that he was no one to fool around with. His presence demanded respect. The last thing in the world that the two boys wanted was to experience the wrath of their father.

There was a vending company that operated just two blocks from our respective houses, and my brother and I talked Ronnie and Adrian into robbing one of the trucks while the place was closed. One night after the business was closed, the four of us took bricks, knocked out the windows of one of the trucks, and hit the jackpot. We had more candy, gum, and soda pop than most stores. We made off with the goods in a shopping cart and hid them in an abandoned building. We thought that we had gotten away with something, but we hadn't. Our consciences would not allow us to sleep at night. The next day, we saw the Marvel Comic Book cartoons on television for the first time. There was Thor, Captain America, Spiderman, and the Submariner. We decided that we would each adopt one of the characters and become them, doing what was right from that day forward. We took the stolen goods back to the owner the next day and told him what had happened and how sorry we were. We also pleaded with him not to tell our parents. He promised that he wouldn't and told us that we did the right thing by bringing the stuff back. He told us that the fact that we had learned such a valuable lesson about life and had the courage to come forth was more valuable than any subsequent discipline. He was a nice man. Thank goodness! Had my mother found out about this, she might still be whipping me to this day! Many young people end up in miserable circumstances because they have not learned how to set goals. Had most of the young men I grew up with set goals, many of them might still be productive members of society rather than dead before their time. Many people are dead but haven't left us yet. I call them the walking dead. These are people who live their lives with no clear sense of direction or purpose. They have no goals. Once I committed myself to the process of goal setting, my life changed immensely and has never been the same since. I promise you that if you will allow yourself to become engulfed in the process of planning your life, it will reward you accordingly. The key is to first decide what you want and then put a plan of action into place.

It's a sad fact that most people spend more time planning a vacation than they do setting goals. If you don't have goals, you will surely drift through life and, more often than not, you will not be happy with the outcome. You must decide for yourself what you want out of life and commit it to pencil and paper just as you would write a contract.

THE COACH WHO WOULD BE KING

I really admire Lou Holtz, the coach at the University of Notre Dame. I've been a fan of his since his days at the University of Arkansas. He is a man who had to overcome great odds. Growing up in East Liverpool, Ohio, he was a scrawny little kid with a lisp. One of his teachers told him he didn't have brain power enough to graduate from Kent State University. How did this outcast go on to coach the New York Jets and become one of the greatest coaches in the history of college football?

He was coaching at the University of William and Mary when the entire coaching staff was fired. His wife was pregnant with their third child. He said later that he had never been so depressed and despondent in his entire life. Coach Holtz also said that he made a commitment to do something that would change the course of his life forever. He sat down with a pen and paper and wrote down more than one hundred things that he wanted to do with his life. He set goals to appear on the *Tonight Show*, which he did on more than one occasion, land on an aircraft carrier, and play some of the world's famous golf courses, which he did. One of his goals was also to one day be head football coach at the University of Notre Dame. He did that as well, after coaching at the University of Minnesota and taking a team that had finished a dismal 1-10 two years before to a bowl game.

How did Lou Holtz become so successful? He set goals

and made the commitment to see them through. You can do the same thing if you are motivated. You must be disciplined and care about your life enough to think about it and write out a detailed game plan. This is your blueprint for the future. Just as an office tower must be built from a set of blueprints, so must your life. How it would be to sit back in your rocking chair as an old person and look back at missed opportunities and unfulfilled dreams because you simply never took the time to plan your life? Goals must be set, prioritized, and reset in order to keep you on track. You never get to the point where you can coast through life without paying the toll. Part of the price for success is goal setting. Corporations or any other businesses, for that matter, start out each year with a business or annual operating plan. No business is more serious than that of living your life. If you don't take the time to set goals, be prepared to take whatever comes your way! After reading this chapter and doing the subsequent exercises in the action planner at the end of the book, you will be ready to realize your dreams and reach for the stars.

FIND SOME MENTORS

We can all make excuses for not setting goals in life for fear that they will not come true. I've heard people ask, "Why even try to do this or that?" No other black, white, red, green or brown person has ever done that. I felt that way about professional speaking. I had a mental block because I didn't see any examples of black speakers who were successful in the industry. I'm not talking about athletes who do the lecture circuit, for few of them can be categorized as professional speakers. Many are simply athletes who speak. I wanted to see someone who had come from a similar or worse background than myself who was making it and I saw no one at this point. I was working for Pepsi Cola Co., which is an awesome company to work for. It offers challenge and growth, and demands that you stretch to realize your potential. I was doing well in my job, but I had always had a burning desire to become a professional speaker. I picked up the yellow pages one day and looked under training. There was an organization called Professional Sales Trainers, which taught the Tom Hopkins training curriculum. I called the owner and asked if they were hiring trainers. He told me that they were not because he had not found anyone that he trusted enough to leave one of his classes with, but he was interested in potential salespeople. I went on to talk with him, not about becoming a salesperson, about becoming a speaker. I asked him if he was willing to let me pay to take his class. Afterwards, I asked him to give me one opportunity to stand before the class and give a presentation, and if he didn't like what he heard, we would forget all about the prospects of me doing any training for him. He took me up on my offer, and I subsequently taught the night training class for him for three years. He and I made some big plans. We began to change the curriculum of the program and we moved from a video facilitation format to that of teaching every aspect of the program ourselves. I got better and better. We would spend time together every Saturday creating and designing new material. I thought that we were going to build a business together, and I was crushed when I was told that they no longer needed me. I was convinced that I needed him. I had become dependent. I felt like he could get into doors that I could not because he was white. I figured I could sneak in the back door behind him and get noticed. I was crushed because I felt that this was my one chance. I saw no other examples of black speakers who were doing what I wanted to do. This gave me a convenient and temporary excuse for giving up on my dream. At that time, I seemed to find solace in the fact that I thought no other black speakers were out there. I was relieved that I actually had legitimate reasons for not moving another step forward. I later learned something very valuable in life. There's always somebody out there! At that time, I needed a sign. I asked for one, and it was provided. Please, read on!

THE TURNING POINT

The turning point for me came on a restless Sunday afternoon in 1984. I was flipping through the channels on cable when I ran across a young black man on BET (Black Entertainment Television). His name was Les Brown. He was dynamic, exciting, and doing what I wanted to do. He talked about how you had to enlarge your vision of yourself. He said that you had to believe in yourself! He told the story of how he became a disk jockey at a local radio station. He was from a negative background just as I was, and had suffered with misery and disappointments. I immediately got up off of the couch and began to take notes. Les talked about how you've got to be HUNGRAY! When I saw him that day, it changed my life forever. I thought to myself, here's a black man who is doing what I have been thinking about. If he can do it, so can I! I will be forever grateful to him for keeping his dream alive. When I saw Les Brown, I no longer had an excuse. Whatever you want to do in life, someone else has done it before. I had a goal from that point on: to meet Les Brown. I didn't know when or how it would happen. He has often said setting the goal is the major thing. How is none of your business! He is now a national celebrity, is married to music legend Gladys Knight, and is one of the most sought after speakers on the planet. Les Brown is a goal setter. I believe that goal setters are pace setters.

It freaked me out one day when I got a call from Renée Strom of the Speakers Bureau in Minneapolis. She told me that Les Brown had been asking about me and wanted to talk to me. She gave me the phone number of a hotel in New York where he was staying. I immediately called him. He picked up the phone after two rings and we spoke. He mentioned that he had been hearing good things about the work I was doing and wanted to congratulate me. He went on to say that he was putting together a cadre of speakers to travel around the country and speak to different orgainizations. He asked me to send him my material. Fortunately, what I have today is much better than the material I sent him at that time, but that wasn't the most important part of the call. The important thing was that goal setting worked. When I wrote down just a few years earlier that one day I would meet this man, I didn't know when but I knew it would happen. Goal setting works. I have had many other mentors even though I've never met most of them personally. When I first decided that I wanted to start a real estate business, I sought out two books. They were *Nothing Down* and *Creating Wealth,* both beautifully written by a man named Robert Allen. He became my personal mentor even though I've never personally met him. I used his philosophy to get where I wanted to go at a much faster rate. Since reading his books I have amassed a real estate fortune worth far in excess of one and a half million dollars. You can find and use mentors the same way. The many that I've used over the years include Dr. Norman Vincent Peale, Mary Kay Ash, Mary Parker Follet, Napoleon Hill, Dr. Martin Luther King, Dr. Robert Schuller, Jim Rohn, Muhammed Ali, Tony Robbins, Les Brown, John Johnson, Donald Trump, Russell Conwell, George Clason, Og Mandino, and many others. These people have all helped me to increase the quality of my life and accelerate my progress. Mentors help you gain confidence if you are disciplined enough to read and listen to their works and then take appropriate action on the ideas that stimulate you most. Within their stories, you will find the courage to write your own script and build your life to order. You will find that some of them overcame tremendous obstacles to achieve their dreams. They all have one thing in common. They all had goals that drove them to take action and get the results that they wanted from their lives. When you set goals, your mind gains focus and your body performs the activities necessary to help you achieve. It is a process that you must learn to trust! I am a perfect example of the power of what can happen. It's strange to think back on all of my years of formal education and realize that no one ever taught me to set goals.

It wasn't until I was 24 years old that I learned how to, and my life has never been the same. As I travel around to speak to Fortune 500 companies, and consider the fact that I'm the author of four audiotape programs, and a videotape series as well as this book, plus earn as much money in one month as I previously earned in a year, I can only tell you that all of this comes from setting goals. Before writing this chapter on a bitterly cold morning on New's Years Eve, I sat down at 6:00 a.m. to craft my goals for the year. This is a process that I've been following now for the last sixteen years. I couldn't imagine my life without them. Without written goals, I would have never gotten to the point of writing this book, which was also once a written goal that has now been accomplished. Think of all the things you take for granted. For most of us, learning to drive a car was, at one time, a goal. Once we learned to do it, we moved on to something else because we took for granted the fact that this goal had been accomplished.The key thing here is to understand the process by which you achieve something. Once you have been successful doing something, you have proven to yourself that you can be successful. The main objective is to move from simple successes to higher and higher levels.

WHERE DO YOU START?

"Even if you're on the right track, you'll get run over
if you just sit there."

—Will Rogers

I would suggest that you start wherever you are right now. The time will never be more right! Don't let another day go by without taking the time to assess your situation and make definite plans to change your life into whatever you want it to be. No matter how dire your circumstances may seem you have the ability to plan your way out of them. It's all a matter of perspective. During the stock market crash of 1929, many people lost all of their money. People committed suicide in record numbers. Others resorted to begging in the streets. But also during this same time period there were people who became millionaires. How could that happen when the country was in an uproar and so many people were losing their grip? It all depends upon how you look at it! I would venture to say that many of the people who succeeded at that time probably had some goals. They had some idea of what they wanted to do and how they wanted to go about doing it. In today's society, we are faced each day with the national debt, corporate layoffs, and softness in the economy, all of which are causing people to live with a great deal of fear and apprehension. Believe me, you cannot afford to take chances by guessing what the future holds for you. You must know where you want to go, how you plan to get there, and when you expect to arrive.

STOP PROCRASTINATING, NOW!

"When you get right down to the root of the meaning of the word 'succeed,' you find it simply means to follow through."

—*J.W. Nichol*

Whatever it is that you want to do with your life, you've got to start taking action immediately. I remember when I was 18 years old and 40 seemed like it was far in the future. I used to say, "Man, that's old!" I was working out with some young guys at a health club not long ago, when one of them asked me how old I was. When I told him forty, he said, "Man, that's old!" I thought to myself, "What a minute! That's my line! I'm the one who use to say that to older guys! Now I'm one of them!" We have got to make sure that we don't get left behind because time waits for no one.

Don't let the fact that it's spring, summer, winter, or fall keep you from the task of setting goals. Goal setting requires that you use your mind. This can be more demanding than physical labor because thinking forces you to deal with the depths of your being. It requires you to answer tough questions about yourself, and sometimes you will find that you don't have answers to important issues in your life. That's OK! Goal setting can help lead you to answers in many cases. Many times a goal in one area of your life will lead you to answers in another, but you will never find them if you aren't willing to struggle. There are many different types of goals, such as family, career, health, financial, spiritual, social, and fun. You must develop the courage to design your life.

One of the things you must learn to master is the ability to focus. You cannot afford to let the telephone, dust in the corners of your office, the fact that's it's a sunny day, or anything else get you off track. Sometimes you have to learn to say, NO! Say it with me three times, NO!, NO!, NO! You will certainly have interuptions and they will always seem to happen during the time that you have set aside for goal setting. This used to happen to me constantly. I would sit down to begin my planning session and the phone would ring, or someone would stop by the house unannouced for a social visit and provide me with a convenient excuse to put it off again. Because I speak on motivation among other topics, people would often call me for pep talks when they were feeling down, and I would always respond by taking the time to rev up their engine. The only problem was that it often left me out of gas and the time to do the necessary things to keep my own house in order. If someone comes by unannounced or calls for social talk in the middle of something important such as planning, I simply tell them I'm busy. If they push, I tell them to let me call them back or stop by at a more convenient time for the both of us, but that at this time, I've got to keep moving. Sometimes we don't do this because we feel that we will alienate a friend or acquaintance. Nothing could be further from the truth! If a person is truly in your corner, they will understand and appreciate the fact that you're trying to increase the quality of your life. If they can't, maybe you need to reevaluate whether or not this person is truly a friend. This is important because many people spend years putting things off for what they perceive to be a little bit better time. The reality of the situation is twofold. Number one, they don't have the ability to distinguish between the urgent and the important. The urgent is often the easier of the two, but often provides the least reward in terms of real productivity. Number two, they haven't become disciplined enough to make a real commitment to setting goals, and therefore will continue to get the same or worse results because they have not made any significant changes. Many people suffer from the manana syndrome, saying I'll get around to that tomorrow, tomorrow, or tomorrow. Unfortunately, tomorrow never comes. This deadly disease is one of the main reasons for failure. As Nike says, JUST DO IT!

GOAL SETTING CAN SET YOU FREE FINANCIALLY

I'll never forget a goal-setting evening that changed my life forever. I was sitting in a hotel in Rapid City, South Dakota, one evening in 1985, bored out of my mind. I decided that to become more productive, I would spend the evening setting some goals of a purely financial nature. I was earning about $40,000 a year at the time. I played a game by setting a goal to pay myself a certain amount of money each time I was paid. At that time I was getting paid every two weeks, and I wrote the plan according to how I was paid. I wrote these goals down, month by month, year after year, through the year 2003. I didn't give myself any raise and I treated the situation as though I would never make more than $40,000 a year. An interesting thing happened. By the time I played this scenario out to the year 2003, I found that I would have more than two million dollars in cash. All with a simple savings plan! I thought to myself that if I only did half as well as my projection, I would still be in great shape, and certainly in better shape than if I had no plan at all. Most of us will run in one of two circles for the rest of our lives. One is a circle in which we run around frantically working for money. The other is where money runs around in a circle working for us. You will never get to the circle where money works for you if you have no plan. This is why less than five percent of the people in this country are able to retire with any degree of financial security. The majority of people simply have no plan, so their resources get away from them. Don't let this be you.

YOUR GOALS WILL TEACH YOU

Goal setting is important not so much for what you get at the end of the rainbow, but what it makes of you in the process. Can you imagine walking up to the chairman of General Electric Co. and asking, "How did you get here?" He probably wouldn't say, "Well, I just kept showing up for work each day and that kept promoting me!" Can you imagine going up to Sir Edmund Hillary after he scaled Mount Everest and asking him, "How did you get here?", and him saying, "Well, I don't really know, I just went out for a walk and here I am."? Of course not! Things don't just happen, they happen just. Your goals will help you to learn things that you didn't know before about yourself and other people. For this reason I always suggest that couples set goals together. Simply take out a blank sheet of paper and put together what I call your dream list. This requires that you relax and sit back in the comfort of you favorite chair and simply dream about the things that you want. You must dream as though failure does not exist. What would you dream about doing if you knew for sure that you could have it? You would probably dream much bigger! Allow yourself this essential part of the process. You may want to listen to some relaxing music as you go through this process.

After you've spent five to ten minutes dreaming, get your notepad down and start writing down your goals. Don't try to analyze and judge them. Just keep writing until you written down at least 50 or more items. The goals can be as simple as cleaning out your garage or as challenging as becoming a state senator. The key is to get your thoughts down on paper. After this, you can go through your list and prioritize your list according to a time frame. You can then organize your goals so that you accomplish the most immediate ones first. After this, you can plan for the achievement of your goals in one, three, five, ten, or twenty year segments. You will have short-range, intermediate, and long-range goals augmented by the daily tasks that you must perform daily to achieve them. I tend to be fanatical about goal setting because I know that it works. My wife and I set a goal to have a child. So I wrote down a goal in the fall of 1990 that reads as follows. We will have a healthly child in the fall of 1991. This goal will be completed by November 30, 1991. My daughter was born on November 8, 1991. My wife said, "I want to get pregnant before I get too old to have children!" I said, "Boom! No problem!" Now, I realize that this process had a lot more do with things other than simply setting goals, but please don't miss my point. Goals give your life direction and will help you to crystalize your thoughts, your actions, and your future!

YOUR GOALS CAN CHANGE

You don't have to feel as though your goals have to be cast in stone, holding you hostage for all time. Your goals may change depending upon your situation and your priorities. My goals changed when I decided that I no longer wanted to be an actor and opted instead for a career in business. This doesn't mean that you've failed. It simply means that you have changed. Sometimes these changes will result in you accomplishing even larger goals or finding greater happiness with smaller ones.

As I mentioned in an earlier chapter, Tony Dungy is a young man that I really admire. He helped to recruit me to the University of Minnesota. Tony was always a very goal- oriented, dedicated person. That is one of the reasons why he became one of the top young coaches in professional football. Since he became a professional football coach, there has been much speculation as to when he would become one of the few black head coaches in the NFL. It was long thought that he would be the first to be named as such, until Art Shell became head coach of the then Los Angeles Raiders. Tony's name invariably came up whenever a head coaching job was mentioned, but he had yet to be made an offer. I saw him not long ago at the health club and had the opportunity to talk to him about this. I told him that if people knew him as well as I do, they would know that the media and everyone else is a lot more worried about this than he is. He told me that he was completely happy performing his duties as a defensive coordinator and could happily continue to do this for the rest of his coaching career. He said, "When they're ready (meaning the NFL), I'm ready! I don't spend my time worrying about things that I can't control!" He went on to say that when he got the job, he wanted it to be for all of the right reasons. Here is an example of someone who continued to find happiness and joy in what he was doing even though he had not achieved what he ultimately wanted. His goals were not any smaller, they were just put into a different perspective, a more healthy one that happened to work for him.

On January 22nd, 1996, his dream finally came true. After fifteen years as an assistant coach, Tony Dungy became the head coach of the Tampa Bay Bucaneers and the third Afro American to coach in the National Football league. He paid his dues! Tony represents what persistence and perserverance are all about. There's no doubt that he will make history as one of the most successful coaches in the league. He's that kind of a person! The key is to maintain balance by not worrying about the uncontrollable, while definitely controlling the things that you can. Please complete the excercises in the back of this book on goal setting in order to understand the process.

Everything is Relative

Walk quietly and deliberately
into the storm. Think peace-
fully so your thoughts will
keep you warm. Stand at the
helm of your heart's true
desire. Discovery can lift your
spirits so much higher. Move
with purpose toward what
makes your soul heal and glad-
den. Then witness yourself
receiving the wonderful things
that can happen! Peace be
with you in every way.
Patience will keep anxiety at
bay! All honor comes from
standing and daring to begin.
Even when you fall and have
to stand and start again.

—© Saunni Dais

DISCOVERING YOUR
CORE VALUES

*"I found that values, for each person, were
numerous. Therefore, I proposed to write my value
names and to annex to each a short precept—
which fully expressed the extent I gave to each
meaning. I then arranged them in such a way as
to facilitate acquisition of these virtues."*

—*Benjamin Franklin*

On a late Sunday night back in 1988, I found myself lying in the middle of my living room floor with my head hurting so badly that it felt as if it were going to burst. I knew that this was much more than a typical headache. I had experienced the worst of migranes from my head-on collisions on the football field, but nothing even came close to this one. I couldn't hold my head up because that only seemed to intensify the pain. The pain went from my head down through my lower back and into my legs. I thought I was having a stroke. All I could do was call my wife with a faint cry that sounded like a wounded animal in distress. She bounded down the stairs to see what was wrong with me. As she helped me to my feet, all I could do was plead with her to get me to the hospital quickly. The pain was increasing with each step to the car. I begged her to hurry as she sped through the lights on the way to Fairview Southdale Hospital. Once there, I was promptly rushed in to see a doctor and was kept in the hospital overnight.

After a battery of tests, I was diagnosed with a severe sinus and ear infection that could have killed me had we not taken immediate action. What was more disturbing was the additional diagnosis by the doctor. I was also told that during the EKG, the doctor noticed some unusual patterns that were caused by an extreme amount of anxiety and stress. I thought, "How could this happen to me?" I was young, only 33 years old, and by most standards I seemed to have more outward success than most. I certainly had more than my background would have predicted. What was the problem? The doctor told me that he had seen this pattern in type A personalities before. After dealing with, sometimes, years of stress and anxiety, the body and mind take a vacation. He went on to tell me that whatever I was going after in life wasn't worth killing myself for. He told me that I'd better back off and try to enjoy life more than I seemed to be. As I sat on the chair in his office, with my head hung down, I knew in my heart that he was right. I was shocked that we were even having this conversation. I thought that this was the kind of thing that happened to other people. Not me, the big strong, macho, ex football player. But, here I was, stressed out and in an emotional struggle for survival. Why me?

I should have noticed the signs six months earlier. My 33rd birthday should been a time of great celebration. I was driving a Mercedes Benz, lived in a beautiful, new three-bedroom townhouse, owned more than one million dollars worth of real estate, and had enough money in the bank to satisfy any immediate or future needs. In spite of all these material things, it was the worst birthday I've ever had. I struggled that entire day from stress and anxiety. Why was I so unhappy? I found that it was because I didn't really know where I stood in my own mind. I knew in my heart that I never would be happy until I learned to respect my own progress and give myself credit for my own accomplishments, no matter how big or small. I must, as you must, never worry about what someone else is doing so much that you take your eyes off of your own crystal ball. We all come into this world at different times, have different challenges, and have varying degrees of advantages and disadvantages. The key is to focus on your own business. Read and learn what you can from and about others, but write and live according to your own script. Most of the unhappiness many people experience comes from an obsession with comparison.

NEVER COMPARE YOURSELF TO ANYONE

"The hook is your desire to be approved of by others. The bait is any kind of reward. The minute you go for the bait, the game is playing you. You are no longer playing the game. You become a victim."

—*Laurence G. Boldt*

I was miserable because I was comparing myself to other people. I found that when you make the mistake of doing this, you will always lose. You will never measure up when you place someone else on a pedestal ahead of yourself. I became a victim of the very same programming that helped to create my success. I would read about people like Donald Trump, Adnan Khashoggi, and Warren Buffett, and proclaim to myself that what I had was nothing compared to these people. I would read about the awesome success of people like Curt Carlson, Carl Pohlad, and Irwin Jacobs, and feel that I wasn't even scratching the surface. I felt totally inadequate. I believed that I could work as hard as humanly possible and still never be worth the kind of money that these people were worth. This scared me. The more I read about the Forbes 400, the more like a loser I felt. I found myself having panic attacks. The thought of how hard I would have to work to be worth $100 million dollars didn't bother me. I felt that I needed to find a vehicle to get me there, and it wasn't the great job that I had at the time. My life was spiraling out of control. I was not the kind of person to break the law in order to succeed. That was against my constitution. My problem was that my life was tremendously out of balance! Money was my number one priority in life and it was making me miserable. What caused me to feel that I needed so much? I had become a victim of the mad rush of the eighties mentality that said, "Get as much as you can, while you can!" For a period of about a year, I felt as though I was cracking up! There was so much coming at me so fast that it was hard to ascertain what to take from the table of success and what to leave. Every business magazine that I read offered 1,001 different ways to go after the brass ring. I was stressed out trying to keep up with it all. Every time I would read about another Horatio Alger story, I would mentally throw whatever I was focusing on at the time into the dumpster and start thinking about the latest new fad in franchising, direct mail, or telemarketing. I didn't realize that as long as I was making measurable progress in a reasonable amount of time, I was succeeding!

I have since found a much healthier perspective for myself. This experience taught me that to compare yourself with anyone is wrong. Never compare yourself to anyone! You came here at a different time than others and you will probably leave at a different time. Envy will blur your focus. People often value the success of others without understanding the circumstances or price that was paid in order to achieve it. Furthermore, why should you care in the first place? It has nothing to do with your life or success. There will always be people in life with more or less than you have. Life is not fair and never will be. The thing I learned is to do the best I can with what I've got. As the U.S. Army says, "Be all you can be!" That has to be good enough. The stories in the early nineties about the rise and fall of some of America's moneyed elite helped me to gain a much better perspective on life. One thing I learned about myself is that I was a very ungrateful person at that stage of my life, ungrateful because I wasn't thankful for my blessings. I couldn't enjoy anything because I was always looking for the next thing. A friend of mine told me something one day that really hurt my feelings, but I knew that it was true. He said, "How sad it is for a man to awaken to a wonderful morning, walk in a beautiful garden, or look at a gorgeous sunset, and not even notice!" That was me, always rushing through life in an effort to accumulate more, more, more! Everything I watched and read was about making money. I had no other interests. If my friends didn't serve a purpose towards that end, I distanced myself from them slowly but surely. I knew that I had to change before I destroyed my life and the friendships that I had spent years building. I've learned to read about and respect the accomplishments of others only to the extent that I can make distinctions, but not to the point where their success or failure becomes an object of personal comparison for me.

The eighties was a decade of greed and I was a product of it. Ingratitude is a sin and the offspring of it is unhappiness and despair. I look at some of the people that were my heroes at that time. Many of them will live the rest of their lives in shame. They have lost their integrity, which is something that can never be bought, and all for the love of money! Some of those people will spend the rest of their lives in prison for their greed. Charles Keating, Ivan Boesky, Dennis Levine, and a host of others were all idolized for their ability to make money. Now, they would only find themselves elected to the hall of shame. They left a trail of financial collapse behind for the rest of us to clean up. They were out of balance in their lives, and this lead them to become out of control. Being a one-dimensional person will cause you to lose perspective, because life is made up of so many different aspects. We need a system of values to help keep us on track. Ambition is good and greed is bad. Greed causes destruction and ruin. The love of anything to the point of obsession can cause problems in your life. Before you know it, you will find yourself spinning out of control and into the "Twilight Zone!" DO, DO, DO, DO, DO, DO, DO, DO!

FOOD FOR THOUGHT

"No man is an island, entire in itself; every man is a piece of the continent, a part of the main."

—*John Donne*

One of my heroes in American business is Reginald F. Lewis. He was the Chairman and CEO of Beatrice TLC. His $1.7 billion leveraged buyout of that company in 1987 was an unprecedented accomplishment for blacks in the history of corporate America. He went from a working class neighborhood to Harvard and finally into business circles reserved only for the elite. He was a brilliant businessman who knew what he wanted and how to get there. Over the years, I have collected just about every article ever written about him. He was, indeed, something special! His autobiography, *Why*

Should White Guys Have All The Fun, profiles his life. The book told of his incredible drive, awesome determination, and how he pushed himself beyond the realm of what most people would consider humanly possible. I was saddened by his premature death in January of 1993 from brain cancer. He was only 50 years old. I was stunned at the affect that his death had on me. I felt as if I knew him.

I wondered what part stress and anxiety may have played in his illness. I thought back to stories in the book about his fast-paced life and unbelievable travel schedule. I thought about how often this man might have gone without the proper sleep or diet. He travelled all around the world in order to keep track of his business dealings. How did he keep all of this in his head? The awesome demands that were placed upon him by his own ambition had to have an effect. I'm not a doctor, but common sense would tell me that a lifestyle that intense would have to lead to severe consequences. It is well known that stress and anxiety can cause a chemical breakdown in the body, leaving you open to sickness and disease. It only seemed reasonable to me that this played some part of the early departure of what I consider an American hero. I learned a tremendous amount about life and death from a man that I only met through the media. He helped me to get a better grasp of my own life by learning to take time to smell the roses. I'm learning to move through life not only with a sense of purpose and passion, but also an understanding that life is also made to enjoy. No matter how much you accumulate, it will only be a pittance compared to the vast riches of the world. The key for me was to find that delicate balance that would allow me to achieve my goals and yet not sacrifice an emotionally healthy life. Ambition has its place in life, but it must be harnessed if it is to serve rather than enslave us. A system of values will help you approach life with a sense of calm and serenity, knowing that everything in life must be balanced and must occupy its place in your life at the proper place and time. You've got to know where you stand! If you asked the average person to list their top five or ten values, many people would struggle to come up with more than one.

WHAT ARE YOUR VALUES?

"Values are the foundation of our character and of our confidence. A person who does not know what they stand for or what they should stand for, will never enjoy true happiness and success."

—*L. Lionel Kendrick*

One of the most difficult things that I've ever done in life was to sit down and come to terms with my values. Your values are the things you cherish most. They represent a set of principles, standards, or qualities that you consider worthwhile or desirable. A system of values will keep you whole. They will help keep you out of trouble as you travel through life's maze. A friend of mine, Rick, and I went through a month-long process where we helped each other create a list of our own personal core values.

The operative question in discovering your values is this: What's most important to you in life? What's most important to you about marriage, children, insurance, career, education, health, religion or anything else? Success is not determined so much by getting what you want as wanting what you get. This is manifested by a clear understanding that getting there does not require that you sacrifice the things that will make you happy along the way. How many stories have you heard about people who gain the world but lose their soul in the process? What good is success if you lose your family, friends, integrity, and maybe your health? Pyschologists' offices are filled with people who have broken dreams because they sacrificed too much to get the things that they thought would make them happy. They got to the top of the mountain only to jump off in desperation. There are successful businessmen who are miserable failures as husbands or fathers. There are successful women who have given their entire lives to their careers, only to wake up later in life and realize that the material trappings of success fall very short of the happiness they might have experienced through a loving relationship or family life, if that was their ideal. Sometimes you can go along for years pursuing a course of action that you think will make you happy only to feel emptiness at the end. Had you asked me a few years ago, what my number one value in life was, before I discovered my own core values, I would have told you it was money. I thought it was the most important thing until I had a chance to really step back and think about it. It doesn't even make the top five. I sat down and really began to analyze my life and my feelings towards it, creating what I call my own constitution. Here's how it looked. There are two things to note here. A value is what I deem most important and a rule is the behavior that I must demonstrate in order to live a value so that I remain congruent. The thing to keep in mind is that these are my values. In no way do I wish to impose them on you. You must take the time to sit down and calmly think about your own life and what's most important to you. Only then can you come to grips with your own system of values.

> *"Nothing gives so much direction to a person's life as a sound set of principles."*
>
> —*Ralph Waldo Emerson*

DESI'S VALUES (MY CONSTITUTION)

These are my values

1. GOD . . .To be one with GOD and all of his creations.

> RULE: To be GOD like in my thinking and deeds.

2. HEALTH...To maximize my physical health so as to operate my body and mind at peak efficiency.

> RULE: To cherish my body and mind with cleanliness and moderation. To do nothing that would VIOLATE my health either mentally or physically.

3. FAMILY...To maximize harmony and closeness in my family

> RULE: To approach my family life with as much enthusiasm as I do my business. To nuture and empower my family relationship to be the best that it can be. To make time for my family, achieving balance between work and family.

4. PERSONAL DEVELOPMENT . . .This is the foundation of my life. The major key to my better future is me. It's not what happens to me that determines the quality of my life, but what I do about it that makes the difference.

> RULE: To make learning a lifelong journey. To always STRETCH BEYOND THE NORM FOR EXCELLENCE TO LEVEL 20. Then Level 10 becomes a normal and natural way of operating. To read, study, and model excellence each day, realizing that it's not what I get, but what I become that will make me happy. I will always invest in myself without hesitation.

5. FREEDOM . . . To have the ultimate power of choice free from the decisions of others. To spend the rest of my life doing work that I love . . . . Speaking! To make everyday my day!

RULE: My thoughts, decisions, and actions must manifest this destiny of total freedom. The only power things have over me is the power that I give them.

6. INTEGRITY . . . To be honest and fair in my dealings with other people. To always seek a win-win solution to problems. To look for not who's right, but, what's best.

RULE: To treat people with dignity, respect, and truth. To call things as they are and not as I want or wish them to be. To make people feel as though they are the most important people in the world.

7. FINANCIAL INDEPENDENCE . . . To be wealthy enough to amplify all of the governing values in my life. To have money work for me instead of me for it. I deserve success and will have it in direct proportion to the value that I deliver to the marketplace.

RULE: Always make saving and tithing a priority in order to create the foundation for freedom.
   A. Only look at long-term approaches with solid returns. (NO PIE IN THE SKY)
   B. Only take advice from those who are competent through their own experience to give it.
   C. Do not lose money. Maximize the power of accumulation through compounding.
   D. Do not speculate, INVEST!
   E. Eliminate consumer debt, maximize investment debt.

8. PATIENCE...I will master this virtue as part of everything that I do in life, realizing that patience is its own reward. It is a major key to my lifelong success!

RULE: Direction is more important than speed! It takes time for things to develop. The bigger the goal, the more time required. I will exercise faith as the cornerstone of patience. LIFE IS NOT A DESTINATION, IT'S A JOURNEY!

9. PERSISTENCE....I will succeed in my goals no matter how long it takes! My life has no limits in terms of what I can do.

RULE: I will never give up! Rejection only makes me feel stronger and teaches me to find new and better ways of doing things. I will never entertain the thought of quitting in the quest of my goals.

VICTORY OR DEATH! "I'd rather die on my feet than live on my knees!"

—James Brown

10. MASTERY OF EMOTIONS...I will master my emotions by continually exercising the power of focus.

RULE: I will focus my attention on the things that I want. I will think positively and live my life with forgiveness, passion, and impact!

As I look back at my list of values, I realize how important this list was to me at a turning point in my life. It was not put together without a great deal of thought and soul searching. I was forced to go inside of myself like never before. I was forced to make some tough decisions. Which values would come first? Why? How would the hierarchy of my values affect my behavior and subsequently the results I get from life? All of these questions are part of the values discovery process. For example, when I placed GOD as my number one value, it caused me to think. I thought, is this to say that I'm perfect? The answer is absolutely not! But, at the same time, I felt as though no matter what, I will be a better person for trying to operate according to the standards set forth by the word.

I also struggled with my number two value of health. I thought to myself, "Am I being selfish by placing my own individual health ahead of my own family in the hierarchy?" I then came to the conclusion that if I don't take care of myself, I won't be around long enough to take care of them. From this discussion with myself, I decided health would be my second most important value.

> *"Many a businessman feels himself the prisoner of the commodities he sells; he has a feeling of fraudulency about his product and a secret contempt for it. Most important of all, he hates himself, because he sees his life passing him by without making any sense beyond the momentary intoxication of success."*
>
> —*Eric Fromm*

There was also a bit of conflict between my sixth and seventh values. My number six value used to be financial independence, with integrity holding the number seven slot. My friend, Rick, then asked me if I would steal or sell drugs in order to make money. I assured him that I would never do anything illegal or unethical for financial gain. He suggested that I consider moving my value of integrity ahead of financial independence. That way whenever I need to make a financial decision, I will never sacrifice my integrity. By exchanging these values in my hierarchy, I will always make the right decision. Do you see how going through this process could benefit you?

I promise you that this excercise will change your life. If you dont' know what you value most in life and in what order, you will find yourself making decisions that may not be in your own long-term best interest. In my opinion, in order to live a happy life, you need to know what your values are. If I know your values, I know what motivates you. If I know what is most important to you, I can predict your behavior. By the same token, if you know what's most important to you, you can predict your behavior in any situation. A great deal of misery comes into the lives of many because they don't have the ability to determine what's most important to them. They end up victims, and that's no way to be!

Financial independence is still a very important value for me, but in order to control my desire for it, I found it necessary to give it a lower priority in order to experience peace. You will have to do the same relative to your own list. You must do this on your own. I can promise you this, you will learn more about yourself than you ever knew before. When people attend one of my LifeTime Management seminars, they will often write and tell me that the discovery of their core values was the most valuable part.

A QUESTION OF VALUES

How Inland Container Corporation Was Born

There was a man who dreamed of becoming a high ranking corporate executive. He worked for years to reach his dream, but seemed to get no further than middle management. Then one day he finally got the call. He was brought in to the chairman's office and told that he was being promoted to the level of senior vice president because of his performance and years of dedication to the company. The chairman also informed the man that there was a meeting to be held the next morning. There was only one rule, when the time came for a vote on several key issues, he was to vote as the chairman voted, no questions asked, no matter what. This was not open for negotiation. The next morning before the meeting, the man went in to the chairman and resigned. When asked for an explanation, the man said that he was not about to be a puppet for anyone, no matter how badly he wanted the job because it was against his value system. When the man got home, his wife asked him what he was doing home so early. He explained to her that he had good news and bad news. The good news was that he had finally gotten the job of his dreams. The bad news was that he quit!

The next morning as he sat reading the newspaper, he got a knock at his front door. It was three of the senior managers that worked at the company. They informed him that they had also quit and wanted to work for him. He told them that he appreciated their loyalty, but that it would be hard to work for someone who didn't even have a job. That day, the four of them sat down around his dining room table and Inland Container Corporation was born. It has since become one of the most successful companies of its kind in the world.

ME AND MY DAD

It took my father many years before he was able to put his values in order. As I mentioned previously, he always worked like a demon in an effort to provide for his family. I suppose he worked so hard because he never had much growing up, and he overcompensated from the fear that came from the memories of being poor. When he was a younger man, his entire focus was on making money. For a period of time, he was possessed. There were many times when I needed him. Whether it was taking me to a movie or sitting in the stands on Parents Day during football season, I always found myself attending those events alone. It would make me feel bad to see the parents of all my teammates come into the locker room after the game and know that there would be no one waiting for me. By the time he looked up, I was grown and out on my own. Before he knew it, all that time had passed. Fortunately, over a period of years, he learned that money is not the most valuable thing on earth, but a tool to be used to increase the quality of our lives. In your pursuit of money and for the sake of what it can buy, be careful that you don't sacrifice all of the things that money can't buy. As I look at my own children, I will never forget the loneliness of those past experiences. I will be there for my children. My father and I now have a wonderful relationship and I am grateful for that. He taught me something valuable about the priorities of life. When you die, few people will ask you how much money you made, or how big your house was. The things that will matter most are family, a few close friends, and the people you touched along the way. Whether you are an existing parent or parent to be, make sure that you spend time with your family. The time passes so fast that you won't believe it!

HERE AND NOW

This event has cast upon my time a shadow that follows me. It tugs and certainly pushes the best that always lives in me. It pulls me toward the conception of my dream. Destiny will have it's way, it would seem.

It fulfills me, not with doubt, but with confidence that I'LL TRIUMPH, I'LL WIN! It assures me that all my glory will come from seizing the opportunity to begin. Today, all the fascination and challenge of fulfilling my Dreams are here at last! Better days are here to carry me to a place where my future and I shake hands, at last!

—©Saunni Dais

LEARNING FROM LIFE'S LESSONS

"It is the chiefest point of happiness that a person is willing to be what they are."

—*Desiderius Erasmus*

WHEN LIFE KNOCKS YOU DOWN, GET UP!

The summer of 1987 was, indeed, an exciting time in my life. I had just gotten married that spring and had bought my first business. I was working as a franchise manager for PepsiCo Inc., but my ambition was to have my own business. After months of looking at different things, I had finally found it. It was a business that included two stores specializing in window treatments. The name of the business was Rainbow Custom Window Fashions, and it specialized in selling window treatments of all kinds such as mini blinds, micro blinds, vertical blinds, balloon shades...You name it! I felt as though this was a no miss situation. When I thought about the number of windows in the Twin Cities, I began to salivate over all of the cash coming my way.

The gentleman who sold my wife and I the business was a 32-year-old entrepreneur named Mel Buchta. He was getting out of the retailing end of the business and was building a facility in his home to manufacture blinds. He wanted a very close relationship with the person who bought the business because his idea was to use the two stores as a conduit to get his product into the marketplace. He was going to give us pricing that would knock the competition out, as well as show us the ropes in running the business until we felt comfortable enough to fly solo. My wife, Sue, had been an interior decorator for more than ten years, so we all felt as though this business was a natural fit. We all looked forward to building a profitable business together.

I will never forget the feeling when I walked out of the closing. It was the most exhilarating feeling in the world. I had finally found a business! It was a profitable business with a seven-year track record and a seller that was going to be our supplier. How could we lose? I had visions of appearing on the cover of *Entrepreneur Magazine* with a pair of sunglasses on and the headline would read..."BLIND AMBITION...How Desi Williamson Created a Multi-Million Empire By Looking At Windows!" The sun was beaming down on my face and

I felt as though I could walk on water. I thought, "A business of my own! Everyone should have the opportunity to feel what I'm feeling, just once!" These feelings would be short-lived!

Mel Buchta was also excited about the opportunity. He and Sue got along great and he was relieved to find that we were a couple of people he could work with. This was an important part of his motivation for selling to us. He wanted to sell the business to people he liked. His reason for selling the business boiled down to the fact that his wife was nine months pregnant with their second child and he wanted to spend more time at home with them. He had a two-year-old daughter as well. He was a real family man who loved to spend time at home. He had found what he felt was the perfect combination.

Fourth of July weekend that year marks a time in my life that I will never forget. Mel went up north to Brainerd, Minnesota, for a weekend retreat. He told me that he was celebrating the sale of the business and wanted to get away. You could feel the excitement in his voice. He was really looking forward to this trip.

When the Fourth of July weekend was over, I was ready to get started. I couldn't wait to talk to Mel and discuss what course of action we would take in getting this venture started. Little did I know, that I would never talk to him again. I got a phone call on Monday morning at around 8 a. m. It was from Mel's wife. She was sobbing, and from the sound in her voice, you could tell that she was exhausted from crying. He had apparently jumped into a lake, off a dock headfirst into shallow water and broke his neck. He was floating in the lake when they found him. I broke down and started to cry when Sue came into the room. When I told her, she cried as well. After hanging up the phone, we both sat in the room together in total shock that something like this could happen. The aftermath of Mel's death made us numb. We couldn't even think about the affect that it would have on our lives from a business perspective because there were more important issues at hand. He had children that he would never raise, friends that would never see him again, and a wife that would have to raise two children alone without the husband that she dearly loved.

After the funeral was over, the reality of running the business without any direction set in. We were horrified! I had talked Sue into giving up a secure job that she had held for ten years with a well-known company in the interior design business. She had given up benefits as well as retirement plans. We were the blind leading the blind. The two stores were on opposite ends of town. One was in Golden Valley, Minnesota, a suburb about ten minutes from our home in Edina, and the other was in Apple Valley, which seemed like a world away. The Apple Valley store was in a small strip mall that was dying. I knew that if we were to have any chance of surviving, we needed more foot traffic. I decided to move to a larger mall but there was one major risk factor. The mall had more traffic, but the rent was three times as much as we were paying. We made the move anyway. This mall had strong anchor tenants and we had an ironclad, four-year lease with an exclusivity clause. Our space was well located in the mall, and we went on to invest some $20,000 in leasehold improvements. Things looked promising. Our first full year in the business, despite losing Mel, we made a small profit and were able to pay Sue a salary. We felt great!

In the spring of the following year, we learned that the mall was going to get an achor tenant much stronger than any of the existing ones. We knew the name Budget Power very well. It was owned by a one hundred million dollar company called Thompson Enterprises. They were strong and even though they sold ready-made blinds, we felt no threat because our products were all custom-made. Our customers paid 50 percent down upon placing an order, and the balance upon installation. We knew that Budget Power had the ability to draw and the fact that we were less than 50 yards from them could do us nothing but good! Our sales continued to climb over the summer as Budget Power moved in and got themselves accustomed to doing business in Apple

Valley. We relished the thought of having people come into our store to compare the difference between ready-made blinds and custom. There was no comparison! My exclusivity agreement protected me against competitive activity in custom window treatments and life was good.

In the fall, things would change. I noticed that our sales were starting to slump miserably. I couldn't figure out why. It's one thing to be off ten or twenty percent, but when you go down thirty and forty percent, you better apply a tourniquet fast, before you bleed to death. I decided to visit Budget Power and was shocked! They had almost an exact replica of my store inside of theirs and were selling at my cost. Because of their huge volume purchases, they could buy at better discounts and were ripping us to shreds. To make matters worse, the people we hired to manage our store would often not show up on time or at all. Some would steal from us and others just didn't care. I learned the hard way that people who work for you don't necessarily share your dream. I was petrified! All of a sudden, our volume hit the skids. We had to close the Golden Valley store and put our focus on the Apple Valley store, because we had a larger financial commitment there and it had the most potential. The Golden Valley store was only an office with no retail traffic. Each month the volume went further down the tubes. It got to the point where Sue would come home with this horrified look on her face. I knew immediately what it meant, that more money would be needed to take care of our monthly expenses. What would the figure be? That was the only question. For three months, I drained our personal savings in order to meet our monthly debt service. I've never felt so helpless and desperate in my life. We had more sleepless nights than I care to mention. I was finally forced to deal with the inevitable confrontation with the man who owned the mall where my store was dying.

I immediately contacted him to let him know how furious I was about the fact that he had breached our contract by allowing the big corporate conglomerate to come in and ruin my business. I told him that I would no longer pay him rent as long as Budget Power was allowed to sell the same products at my cost. I was put on notice by him that if I breached the lease he would sue me for the balance, which totalled four more years worth $30,000. I felt sick to my stomach. I felt all of the things that I had worked for up to that point were going down the drain. In addition to the monthly cost of running the business, we still had a household to support. There were mortgage payments, car payments, and all of the other things associated with living. I also had a real estate business to run, not to mention a full time job at PepsiCo. Pepsi is a very demanding company in a competitive industry. It demands an eight to ten hour a day commitment from executives, just to keep up. I felt as though I was losing my grip many times, but I was determined not to let this situation wreck the one thing that was giving us any level of security, the job. Each day, as I reported to work, I offered a giant smile and pleasant attitude that only served to mask the inner civil war that was going on inside of me. I knew that I had to take drastic action, and soon! I knew that it was only a matter of time before my bank account was going to dry up from paying huge monthly expenses. I listed our house and started the process necessary to sell it. At this juncture, I was more than $100,000 in debt and was bleeding badly, one pinprick at a time. I hired a lawyer. He told me that my situation didn't look good because the guy who owned the mall was worth millions and could drain me dry if I tried to sue him for breach of the lease. He went on to tell me that he would be willing to take my money if I chose to pursue litigation, but advised me that it might be necessary to cut off the arm in order to save the body. He advised me to close the business and negotiate with the owner on a settlement that would terminate our agreement. He said that he could buy me some time through written communications with their lawyer and through sending a demand letter with the threat of a lawsuit that would never be carried out. This bought me 90 days.

We went back and forth. Finally the owner felt sorry for me and let me out of the agreement for a total of $3,000. I was able to pay this over the course of the next 90 days. I found out later that the only reason he agreed to this was because he had already found a tenant who was to move in at the end of the 90 days and enjoy the fruits of the time and effort that my wife and I had put into this store. We felt as though we were losing a child. We cried the day we sold our countertops, chairs, and other equipment that we'd bought just months earlier. But at least we were done with this episode. This would only provide temporary relief because there was still the problem of the bank and the $100,000 that I owed them.

We began to think about what we could do to pay off what seemed to be Mount Everest at that time. The only place to look was to the real estate that we owned, and the piece of property with the most promise was our house. Fortunately for us, we had bought a small house on a quarter acre lot in a very desirable part of town that we had dramatically improved over the years. The house was now worth more than $300,000 and we owed only $108,000 against it. I had a strong relationship with a banker who was willing to loan me 80 percent of the value. That meant that we could get as much as $240,000, more than enough to pay off the bank and protect our credit rating. We, of course, had a much higher mortgage payment, but that seemed insignificant compared to having an albatross of $100k hanging around our necks. When interest rates hit a 20 year low, we were able to secure a seven percent interest rate, which put our house payment back to the level it was, at our lower mortgage amount.

We've all heard the saying, "One day I'm going to look back and laugh at this!" I certainly didn't think so at the time. It was anything but funny. I can now honestly say that I can look back and laugh. This is one of the best things that ever happened to me. Why? Because it taught me that when life knocks you down, get up! What if it keeps knocking you down? You keep getting up, again, again, and again! This life lesson taught me that there's nothing that can't be overcome with enough faith, tenacity, and belief. The only way to fail is to quit. I'm grateful for this failure because it has given me a depth of understanding about myself and other people that I never otherwise would possess. This experience made me a much wiser person and has set me up to earn far more in my future ventures because I will approach each situation with more savvy. Whatever you're faced with in life, a failed relationship or business, the loss of a loved one, or a huge financial setback, know that none of these situations are greater than your ability to overcome them. This faith will give you the power to move beyond or through obstacles to reach your ultimate destination.

SHE WANTED TO LIVE

My grandmother is the strongest person that I have ever known. She is a woman of extremely high character and moral fiber. At 90 years old, she lives alone and takes care of herself despite the massive pain that racks her body daily due to arthritis and respiratory problems. Each day she gets out of bed before seven a.m., puts on her makeup, and gets dressed as though going to work. She suffered a stroke one night and while reaching for the phone, she noticed that it wasn't sitting in its usual place on the nightstand on the right side of her bed. She was frantically gasping for breath when she stood up to look for it. She immediately fell to the floor in pain as she remembered that the phone was on the opposite side of her bed where she had placed it while talking on it earlier. She told me that she crawled around to the other side of the bed and dialed 911, and then called my father to come and get her. The ambulance beat my father to the house, and my grandmother crawled to the door and was waiting for them when they knocked. I knew something was wrong when I called her on a Monday night and there was no answer. She's always home in the evening unless she's out of town, and I always know when that is. It upsets me when I call there and she is ill and noboby has told me. She does this because she doesn't want me to worry. Do you have any relatives in your family like this? My grandmother later told me that all she could think about was getting up off that floor. She told me that she never entertained the idea of dying as she was crawling towards that phone to call 911 and to the door to wait until they got there. She told me that it took everything inside of her to drag her 220 lb body around that house in the dark, and for that time, all she could think about was getting up! She said that she thought about me, her children, and her grandchildren. "Those are the things that kept me alive!" is what she told me later. When life knocks you down, get up! If my eighty-seven year old grandmother can do it, what's my excuse? My question to you is, what's yours? There is none! If you can look up, you can get up!

DON'T JOKE AROUND!

"Some jokes aren't funny. Afterwards you might find that the joke has been played on you!"

—*Desi Williamson*

A few years ago, I played a very mean practical joke on a friend of mine who lives in Tampa, Florida. I called him one day and pretended as though I was from the IRS. I told him that he needed to call the regional office and set up a time to see an auditor about his tax situation. I had a hard time pulling this off without laughing out loud. I held my hand over the receiver in order to keep from blowing my cover as I laughed quietly to myself. His voice cracked as he responded in a whimpering tone, "Where is it that you want me call?" I was in stitches on the other end of the phone. I was laughing so hard the tears began to flow down my checks. Finally, I could no longer help myself. I laughed out loud and he automatically knew it was me. He didn't think it was very funny, but he eventually admitted that he was horrified, which let me know that I hadn't lost my touch as a supreme master of the practical joke.

I couldn't believe it when three weeks later I went to the mailbox and got my mail. It was a letter from the Internal Revenue Service. If you've ever had that sick feeling that comes from getting something in the mail from Uncle Sam, you know exactly what I'm talking about. I opened the letter, covering one of my eyes in terror, only to have my worse nightmare realized. I was being audited on two separate issues. I was sick inside from that day up to the day of the audit. Fortunately, I came out of it in good shape, but I learned a valuable lesson. Never play practical jokes on people because you may find that the joke just might be on you.

You've Got To Be Bold

I have cousin named V.S. who gives a whole new meaning to the word cheap. He is so tight that he squeaks when he walks. His idea of fine dining is a bucket of fish and chips from Long John Silver's. He's a wealthy man with incredible savings habits. A few years ago, we happened to be travelling in separate cars on a trip from Los Angeles to St. Louis, when we found ourselves stranded in the mountains a few miles past Williams, Arizona. The state troopers would not let us go any further and were turning people around on the freeway. We were forced to go back to Williams to find a place to bed down for the night. This would be a long night. One family seemed to own everything in this town, including the gas station, the convenience store and the only motel in town. It was snowing so hard that you could barely see two feet in front of you. We asked if there were any rooms and were told that there was only one room left. The owner told us that she and her husband would give us a special price because the room had some shortcomings. We asked her how much of a discount and she said, "Ten Bucks!" The regular rack rate was $40. It sounded like a great deal until we got to the room. The room had no beds, no television, no phone, and no heat! The woman threw us a couple of blankets, two pillows, asked us for her $30 and said good night. We huddled together on that cold floor and attempted to fall asleep in the hopes that morning would come as soon as possible. My cousin jumped up out of what appeared to be a dead sleep, got his coat, and headed for the door. When I asked him where he was going, he shouted, "I'm going to get some of my damn money back!" It was three o'clock in the morning.

The couple lived right on the premises in a small house a few doors down from us. You could hear my cousin, for probably a mile, banging on the door of that couple in a blinding snow storm. A few minutes later, he emerged from the elements with cash in hand. He had two ten dollar bills. He gave me one of them, stuffed the other in his hip pocket, climbed back underneath the blankets on that cold floor and fell fast asleep as if to say, "I feel much better, now I can get a good nights sleep!" Ten bucks seemed to be an adequate price to pay for such a room. I've been laughing from that day to this one. I couldn't believe that anyone could be that bold. To go and get that couple out of bed, at that time of morning, took some guts. I'm sure that they are still in shock. I would imagine that they weren't often awoken by a black man in the middle of the mountains, in a blinding snow storm, at three in the morning.

I couldn't have done it. His boldness taught me a valuable lesson. Boldness has its place in life. Any time something happens that cuts against the grain of your values, you have got to be bold enough to question it. You can't just let it slide, because that will only teach you to compromise in other areas of your life. I tease my cousin about this cross-country mishap every time I see him and we get a big laugh out of it. It has been said that there's genius in boldness. I believe this to be true. You will find out things about yourself that you never knew were possible when you do something bold. Sometimes it is not enough to merely knock on a door. Sometimes you've got to knock it down!

PAY ATTENTION TO WAKE-UP CALLS

"Never for a moment do we lay aside our mistrust of the ideas established by society, and of the convictions which are kept by it in circulation. We always know that society is full of folly and will deceive us in the matter of humanity. It is an unreliable horse, and blind into the bargain. Woe to the driver if he falls asleep."

—*Albert Schweitzer*

It was 2:30 a.m. on a warm summer morning and I was sitting alone, in my car, half asleep while a friend of mine went in to a restaurant to order something to eat after we attended a party. I sat in the car with the window rolled down. I was caught completely off guard when I felt the cold barrel of a .357 magnum crash against my temple . The assailant then hit me in the head twice with the gun, walked around to the passenger's side, climbed into the car and told me to drive. I was scared out of my wits! As I drove him all around town, with the barrel of that gun pointed at my gut, I knew that this man had the potential to kill me at any time because I knew who he was. His name was Lucky and he was known all over St. Louis as a ruthless person who had killed people and gotten away with it. I had briefly attended elementary school with him and even then he was known as a crazy person who would do anything on a dare. I was terrified because I knew that he had the ability to kill me and would, if I provoked him. This death journey went on for 90 minutes before he jumped out of the car and very casually said, "Later!" He assured me that if I reported this occurence to anyone, I would surely end up dead! I knew that he meant every word of it. I went home, jumped under the covers, and shook in terror the rest of the night. This was a wake-up call. Had I been more aware that night, this would possibly not have happened. I lost track of the kind of neighborhood that I was in. It was certainly no place to fall asleep in my car in the wee hours of the morning. I learned a valuable lesson that day. Pay attention! Pay attention to everything around you at all times. Unfortunately, a few years later Lucky would be shot in the head, falling prey to the the same misery that he heaped upon others. I had my wake-up call, and he never paid any attention to his. It cost him his life! Have you ever had one?

If you've ever been in a situation where you've been daydreaming while you were driving and suddenly found yourself slamming on your brakes, only to land a few feet short of the car in front of you, that's a wake-up call! A negative performance review in your job is a wake-up call to get in line. Bad feelings in a relationship that erupt into harsh arguments are wake-up calls that can have devastating consequences if gone unchecked. Lagging sales, or the resignation of key people in your business, are wake-up calls that tell you to take stock and change your management style before it's too late. Each day of our lives we get them, yet few people are smart enough to stop, take a deep breath, and really learn from these incidents. The person who slams on their brakes inches from an auto collision and then continues to drive like a person possessed until finally they end up dead or killing someone else did not heed their wake-up call.

JEWEL'S LAMENT

There was a kid who grew up across the street from me in St. Louis named Jewel Meeks. He was a loud kid who was always talking back to adults and anyone else who crossed his path. He was very disrespectful to just about everyone he met. He would pick fights with people just for fun, because he knew that most of the people he challenged would back down. He had five brothers who were all eager to fight any place, any time. There were often fights between his brothers and other families because of something he did. He thought that he was really doing something. I always found the best course of action was to avoid him completely! Everyone in the neighborhood felt that way. One day, Jewel's mouth would catch up with him. He had many wake-up calls in his time, but never paid any attention.

One day he was visiting another neighborhood and walked across the lawn of an elderly man, who was known as a nice man, but no one to fool around with. He didn't play! Jewel was walking all over the man's property, talking loud and using all kinds of profane language. There's an old belief where I grew up, that you should give older people their respect, especially old men. Old men who end up with anything in life have gone through hell and back to get it. They will take you out of the game if you try to take advantage of them. Respect is their basic criteria, and they are not about to tolerate abuse from some smart mouthed kid.

When the old man told Jewel that he would appreciate it if he would get off of his property and curtail the use of profanity in his presence, Jewel told him what he and his brothers were going to do to him. The old man asked Jewel once again to remove himself from his property. Jewel stood steadfast, all the while continuing to hurl obscenities at the old man. The old man went inside, emerged with a .38 caliber revolver, and shot Jewel dead! No one was surprised. Certainly, the old man was wrong for the course of action he took. Murdering someone is anything but the correct way to resolve conflict. That didn't make any difference to Jewel. He was dead! Had he paid attention to many of the wake-up calls he had along the way, he might still be alive today.

I will never forget dating a very pretty girl one summer who lived across the street from me and a few houses down the street from Jewel. Her name was Emily. We had a weird relationship throughout elementary school. When I liked her, she didn't like me. When she decided to like me, I didn't like her. We started to go out in high school. She was always more attracted to the thuggish, gangster kind of guys. That summer, I learned that she was available to date me because her boyfriend was in jail. He sent a message to the streets that anyone who was messing around with her was dead meat when he got out of the joint. Wake-up call! Needless to say, I immediately ended the relationship by exiting stage left!

I was on vacation in St. Louis one fall day and happened to be driving home from my father's restaurant to get some much needed rest. It was one of those dark, rainy, overcast days where the only thing on my mind was to get home, lie down, and forget about things for a while. So I wasn't in any hurry, taking my time to drive a route that I'd taken a thousand times before in my life. I was having some rather pleasant thoughts as I drove past Fairgrounds Park, a landmark in inner-city St. Louis. I played Little League baseball and football in that park. It was there that the whole dream that led to a football scholarship at the University of Minnesota got started. Even though I was daydreaming, I was very conscious of my driving because of the cold, wet, Seattle, type of mist that was falling that day. I had my speed locked in at 25 mph in a 35 mph zone. What could possibly go wrong? They trained us in drivers ed to watch out for the other guy, and I was clearly doing that. As I crossed the oncoming intersection, I noticed a car coming towards me in the opposite lane. No reason to get excited. The next thing I know, this car was attempting to turn left without stopping at the stop sign in front of him. As he turned towards me, I braced myself for an inevitable head-on collision. I turned my wheel hard to the right in an effort to avoid him, but could not. As I readied for the crash, I saw my life flash in front of me. I saw my wife, my seven-month-old son, my three-year-old daughter, my father, my mother, and my beloved grandmother. I thought that I might never see them again. My heart raced! This scared me to death because I saw possible death staring me in the face and could not get out of the way. As the cars collided, the impact turned my car around 180 degrees. My head hit the dashboard, and my body twisted like a pretzel. There was smoke and steam everywhere!

As the 77-year-old man ascended from the remains of his

new Lincoln Continental, he appeared to be in much better shape than I. The next thing I know, I'm lying in the emergency room at the hospital. Wake-up call! It dawned on me at that point that no matter how quick, well prepared or defensive you are, there are some things that you can't anticipate. Life can still catch you on the blind side. Sometimes life will force you to deal with it right at the point of impact. This will allow you to understand the true meaning of a wake-up call. That's why it's so important to approach life with a grateful mind. All too quickly, it can be taken away by something as simple as the turning of a steering wheel by a good person, who happens to be heading in the wrong direction at the wrong time. Sometimes it takes drastic action for us to realize how precious life is. The key is to recognize ahead of time how valuable the gift of life is. In my emergency, the thing that I feared most was the idea of never holding my children again, of not seeing them grow up, of not telling my wife how much I love her, of not letting my father and mother know, one more time, how much I love them, and of not being able to tell my grandmother again how much I appreciate her for believing in me. I was given another chance, to live, to love, to make a difference!

Many of us die each day because we don't pay attention to the subtle clues that something is out of whack. The next time something happens in your life that represents a wake-up call, stop, take a deep breath, slow down, and ask yourself, " What is the hidden message in this?" If you really take the time to think about it, you will find the answers. Don't ignore knocks on your door.

Have you ever met someone who continues to beat their head against the wall, making the same dumb mistakes over and over again, even when they know that the results will be ones that will cause them to suffer? This is a form of insanity that, if continued, can take you only one place, DOWN! From this day forward, keep your antennae up, and heed your wake-up calls.

SAVE YOUR MONEY

"Too many people spend money they haven't earned, to buy things they don't want, to impress people they don't like."

—*Will Rogers*

It's amazing to me that so many people suffer from financial ruin in a society that offers the richest way of life in the civilized world. Why is this? It's because the average person spends a lot more than they make. We live in a world where immediate gratification is the rule and delayed gratification is the exception. In order to really take control of your life, you must take control of your finances. This means that you must learn to pay yourself first! This sounds simple, doesn't it? Well, it is, if you are willing to make a real commitment. Many people have turned over their financial situation to the government as if life owes them a living. This is flirting with disaster! I don't care how much money you earn, if you don't have a plan for it, you will find it slipping through your fingers and you'll end up flat broke! People act as if gaining financial security in their lives involves some kind of magical formula. It doesn't! Getting control of your finances involves the following basic principles:

Pay Yourself First!—I've been fortunate enough over the course of the last 20 years to save more than 25 percent of what I earned each year. My good fortune came about only because I had the discipline to sacrifice immediate gratification in favor of much greater freedom later on. I don't care how much or little you earn. It's what you do with it that counts! If someone else has to wait, make them wait, but always, I repeat, always, make the first payment you make, to You, Inc. If you continue to do this, you will in time develop a healthy nest egg that will start you on the pathway to freedom.

Learn To Live On Less Than You Earn—Learn to allocate your money to best serve your personal interests.

> Learn to live on 60 percent of your income.
> Learn to use 10 percent for tithing to whatever cause you believe in.
> Learn to use 10 percent for capital creation.
> Learn to use 10 percent to invest in your future.
> Learn to invest 10 percent in your own personal growth and development.

If you choose to really accelerate your progress then learn to live off of less and less of your income. Imagine what would happen if you could live off of 40 percent of your income. You would then have another 20 percent available for investments. What if you could learn to really tighten your belt and live off of 30 percent of your income? You would have an additional 30 percent to invest in buying your freedom. You might be feeling a bit of discomfort about the thought of living off of such a small amount. Remember our lessons from the previous chapters. If you really want to achieve anything of significance, you've got to be willing to be uncomfortable. If you're not, you will keep getting the same old results.

If you aren't making as much money as you'd like, there are so many ways to invest that it boggles my mind. There are so many ways to start your own business for a small amount of money, it's amazing. There are opportunities everywhere if you just take the time to investigate them. Network marketing is one of the most powerful vehicles in the country and it is making more millionaires of people more quickly than any other business. There's Nutrition for Life, Excel, AmWay, Mary Kay, Herbalife, and Shaklee, to name just a few. The key is to find one that works for you. But again, this will require an investment of time and energy on your part. I'm not going to elaborate because this is not a financial management book. If you develop enough savvy to save a sizable nest egg, you will find the right places to put it if you surround yourself with the right people. You can't invest what you don't have! I felt compelled to write about this subject because I see so many people who are in financial straits and it affects every other area of their lives. *The Richest Man in Babylon* is a wonderful book that should be required reading for every one. It profiles the story of a wealthy man named Algamish, who had taken a particular interest in a young scribe by the name of Arkad. The young scribe was interested in how Algamish had become so wealthy. The old man explained that the way he became wealthy was by religiously practicing a simple principle: "A part of all you earn is yours to keep!" After suffering a series of setbacks over a period of years, Arkad would eventually take the place of Algamish as The Richest Man in Babylon and express the same principles. You, too, can achieve financial independence if you are willing to invest in yourself. I paid $1.95 for this book fifteen years ago. It has been responsible for my making many thousands of dollars and achieving a level of financial independence I never thought possible.

BUILD YOURSELF A MASTERMIND GROUP

In Napolean Hill's classic book, *Think and Grow Rich*, he talks about the power of having a mastermind group. These are groups of like-minded people who can help you reach your dreams. You must find a group of people with different skills who you can meet with frequently to help you in your quest for success. You must also bring a contribution to the group. The group size should be limited to somewhere between seven and a dozen people. The more diverse their backgrounds, the better. You need people who think differently than you, who can give you honest feedback about your goals and progress, and who will also encourage you to stretch beyond your limits. I can't stress the power of a group like this enough. My mastermind group consists of people who are smarter than I am in different areas such as real estate, financial planning, marketing, and investing. My relationship with these individuals has allowed me to make quantum leaps in terms of my progess both personally and professionally. I'm light years ahead of where I would be had we not put together this group. I also bring expertise to the group in terms of sales, marketing, consulting, and speaking. We all help each other get where we want to go at a much faster rate. When putting together a mastermind group, make sure that you involve yourself with people who will challenge you. So often, we are afraid that we will alienate friends by wanting to associate with people who will stretch us. Olds friends will say that we've changed now that we've made it. The reality of the situation is that they have not changed. That's their problem, not yours. If you want to be successful, be around people who are, or who have at least made a commitment to be something more than they are. This will have a dramatic and immediate impact on your life. When several like minds are brought together, a larger, more intelligent force is born. This is vitally important, particularly in the area of finance and investing. You need to develop a team of experts in the areas of insurance, tax planning, financial planning, estate planning, real estate, and investing. The old saying is true: "Once the mind is stretched by a new idea, it can never return its original dimensions!"

YOU'VE GOT TO SELL YOURSELF!

You are the first thing sold in any proposition that involves the exchange of value between two or more people. I've seen many situations where people didn't get the job or the sale they were after because they didn't understand the concept of self-promotion. You're always selling, no matter what. I often have people tell me that they are not involved in selling because they are a nurse, doctor, lawyer, or schooteacher. You are selling health care services as a nurse or doctor, your ability to get results for your clients as a lawyer, and ideas and education if you're a schoolteacher. If you're going to be exceptional in any walk of life, you're going to have to be good at letting people know what you bring to the table. Why should you have the job, get the promotion, or get the business vs someone else? Unless you can convince them that your USP (unique selling proposition) provides them with greater benefits than the others, you will not get the results. Your unique selling proposition involves what you can do for someone else that they cannot do for themselves. What service do you provide that can add value to what they're doing? Your USP must involve what specific expertise you possess that someone else would be willing to pay for. This core expertise involves continued education. You must find the classes, seminars, and books that can help you develop this core expertise that will distinguish you from every other wannabe who is going after the same thing that you are. You must be able to communicate this in less than 30 seconds.

WHAT'S YOUR USP?

In the space below, write your unique selling propostiton. After you've crafted your USP, hone it to the point where you can recite it in 30 seconds or less. I suggest you use pencil in case you want to make changes later.

_____

_____

_____

_____

_____

WHAT ARE YOU SELLING?

Many people don't succeed because they don't understand the difference between features and benefits. This is true no matter what they're selling, especially themselves! A feature is what something is, a benefit is what it does. This is the reason why most resumes end up in the scrap heap. They are filled with useless information about the prospective candidate instead of the results that can be derived for the company by hiring them. They then blame the company or fate when they continue to get rejected, instead of taking a look at themselves. You must market yourself on a continual basis no matter how successful you currently are. People have short memories, and you have to ensure that you continue to occupy and command your SOM (share of mind).

Back in 1979, I was hired as a sales representative for Johnson and Johnson. I was working for McNeil Consumer Products Company, which was the division that sold Tylenol. While driving through my territory one day, I noticed the marketing/sales manual that they had so beautifully constructed. I thought about what an advantage it would be for me to have a similar document that featured me as the major product. From that day, I began to collect and file documentation on everything that I did. This included letters of recommendation, sales reports, results from sales contests, awards, and any other information that would highlight the benefits that could derive from a professional association with me. I took this information and placed it in a portfolio in chronological order, taking it with me on every job interview from that point forward. When a perspective employer asked for a documented track record, I had one! This would sometimes blow my interviewers away! Some would be so insecure that this would scare them, particularly if they were my prospective boss. They figured that sooner or later, a person with this kind of foresight would be after their job. I didn't want to work for anyone like that, anyway. My portfolio helped to eliminate the companies that I didn't want to work for as much as it helped me to get hired by some great ones. I've had some great jobs during my career, but none of them were dropped in my lap. You've got to learn how to market and sell yourself if you really want to succeed in this world.

Just like any other product, you've got to continue to remake yourself every few years with new packaging and updated skills. You must continue to become new and improved!

Harvey Mackay is a man that I greatly admire. He is author of two best selling books, *Swim With The Sharks Without Being Eaten Alive* and *Beware Of The Naked Man Who Offers You His Shirt*. He is one of the most savvy marketers that I know. A master salesman from the word go. Through his mastery of the art of persuasion, he was responsible for keeping the Minnesota Twins baseball team in the Twin Cities at a time when we could have just as easily lost them. He was instrumental in going after a big name college football coach, Lou Holtz, and bringing him to the University of Minnesota at a time when most people thought it impossible. He was also largely responsible for bringing the Super Bowl to Minnesota when popular opinion said that the Twin Cities couldn't compete with other warm weather cities for such a coveted event. Harvey has continued to defy the odds because he knows how to sell himself first. If people buy you first, there are better odds that they will also purchase whatever else goes along with the package. Harvey knows that you are always selling something, however, the first thing sold in any sale is always you!

Do What You Fear Most, First!

"Our doubts are traitors and make us lose the good we oft might win by fearing to attempt."

—Shakespeare

I've found that the best way to overcome fear in life is to do what you fear most, first! Whether it's public speaking, a fear of water, heights, or anything else, the best way to confront these fears is head on. I've always had a terrible fear of water. When a good friend of mine asked me to go water skiing a few years ago, I told him that he was nuts! He kept working on me for about three weeks. Finally, I agreed to go, as long as I could wear at least two life jackets. Once I was able to get up on those skis, I had the time of my life. I couldn't believe that I was on a lake going 30 miles per hour on a couple of two by fours. I never thought for a minute that I would enjoy this experience, but afterwards, I couldn't wait to get out there again! You will often find the same thing to be true. Whatever it is that you are afraid of, just do it without worrying about the outcome. You will find that your fear will diminish after you discover that those gremlins were only figments of your imagination.

I was watching a program not long ago that profiled beautiful women who were alone and without a serious relationship. When asked why they were alone, many of them responded that men don't approach them because they are afraid of being rejected. This lack of confidence caused many of these gorgeous women to spend their lives without dates on special holidays such as New Year's Eve and Valentine's Day because guys didn't have the ability to simply go up and introduce themselves. When asked what advice they would give to these would-be suitors, these women said that they should come up and do it. What's the worst that could happen? The best case scenario is that you meet a great person that could possibly be your soul mate. The worst case scenario is that they tell you to take a hike. Guess what? No risk, no reward. It's just that kind of world!

Victor, the Wrestling Bear

For many years, there was a wrestling bear named Victor who stormed through the National Football League challenging any player who was brave enough to get into the ring. I had the opportunity to wrestle him as part of a promotion for a health club I was working at during my summers off in St. Louis. I was in great shape because I had the opportunity to work out while I was at work. Turner's Gym has been a fixture in St. Louis for more than 40 years for athletes of all kinds, including body builders, power lifters, and jocks. I was excited about the opportunity to wrestle this bear until the day of the event. It was 98 degrees outside with nintey eight percent humidity and Victor was not in a good mood. I went to the truck where he resided to get a look at him before the match and there were two huge fans blowing on him to keep him cool. I thought to myself, "I must be out of my mind!" There were hundreds of people outside waiting to see three football players, two from the pros and myself, a college football player, tussle with this bear. I would be the first to be so honored. When I climbed into the ring, Victor was on all fours, rocking back and forth. My heart was beating a thousand miles a minute! When his trainer clapped his hands, Victor stood up on his hind legs, right on command. He was eight feet, three inches, and weighed more than 600 lbs. His trainer clapped his hands again and Victor moved into action. He threw me around that ring like a rag doll, and what turned out to be two minutes seemed like two hours. Finally, Victor got tired of toying with me and upon a final command from his trainer, pinned me to the mat and began to lick me all over through his muzzle. It took me three days to get his smell off of me. When the next guy tried to get into the ring, Victor went after him with a vengeance. He was not playing this time. He was angry. I suppose the heat and humidity was causing him some discomfort. I was glad that I wasn't the next guy to get into the ring. We had all signed waivers releasing the club and the bear from any liability. Had that next guy gotten into the ring, Victor would have ripped him to shreds. His trainer, who, by the way didn't smell much better than the bear, jumped into the ring and popped Victor in the nose with a right cross. The bear fell to his knees. The trainer then grabbed the microphone and explained to the crowd that he and Victor had had a little misunderstanding and that everything was okay now. Meanwhile, Victor was holding his nose with both paws as if to say, "OUCH!" The trainer made up with his buddy by tossing him a two liter bottle of Pepsi which he devoured in around ten seconds, let out a huge belch, and proceeded to toss the plastic bottle over the ropes into the crowd. Everyone was hysterical with laughter.

I learned a great deal about fear that day. Courage is not the absence of fear, but the mastery of it! It's okay to be fearful. It's a normal emotional reaction. Just don't let it stop you from taking action. Do what you're going to do in spite of the fear. Take action anyway! As I think back, had I not taken advantage of the opportunity to wrestle this bear, I would have regretted it for the rest of my life. I would have always wondered what it was like. Whenever I think about some of the challenges in my life, and find myself racked with fear, I'll remember the time when I wrestled a bear. Many times the challenge at hand will pale in comparison, for few of the challenges that I've faced stood eight feet, three inches, and weighed a quarter of a ton. Don't let fear cheat you out of the opportunity to learn something new or something more about yourself than you knew before. That's where the juice of life flows!

IT PAYS TO BE NICE!

I once had an unused airline ticket that I wanted to redeem for a future trip. The airline had a rule that, without a written notice from a doctor, you were out of luck. I missed my flight the night before because my daughter was sick with the flu, but according their rules, I had to be the one sick. After spending 45 minutes in a heated debate with the reservations staff, I became frustrated. I asked to speak to a supervisor. It was apparent who the supervisor was when this huge guy with a thick mustache came lumbering over to the counter. I asked him if he had the authority to make a decision in this regard. He responded by quipping, "I can do anything I want to!" I explained to him that I was a frequent flyer with more than three quarters of a million miles to my credit. Then I hit him with the bomb. I asked him the following question. I said, "Sir if you could help me in this situation, why wouldn't you?" He stopped dead in his tracks for what seemed like 30 seconds, and then proceeded to verify my frequent flyer status and give me a new ticket to the city of my choice. This situation once again reinforced my belief that it pays to be nice. I could have exploded by losing my temper and exacerbated the entire situation, but this would not have brought me the result that I was looking for. You will find that this discipline will pay dividends more often than not in every aspect of your life.

Even if you have to deliver bad news, there is a correct way to do it. I was once getting into my car after running a short errand. I left the car running with the radio on. The radio was louder than normal because I had ejected a cassette tape that I was listening to and the radio was at a much higher volume level. This was in the middle of the winter, so both windows were rolled up. As I opened the door to get in, an old man came up to me and read me the riot act. He was screaming at me and telling me that he could hear my music as he was getting in his car and that I was causing noise pollution. A fews years ago, I would have told him in no short order where to get off. Because I've changed my ways and learned to be nicer, I simply paused and listened to the old man. I then very nicely explained to him that he should mind his own business. I did this for two reasons. One, because it was true. The second reason was because I didn't want him to get hurt in the future. I went on to explain to this man that he didn't know me from Adam and that some people may not take kindly to his getting so personal with them. I explained to him that people have gotten killed for less. He was fortunate because I was not the kind of person to lose it over such a trivial matter. These days people are hurting and sometimes it takes very little to send them over the edge. After explaining this to the gentleman in a fifteen second seminar, he actually thought about it for a minute and thanked me. I was in shock! I couldn't believe that those words were coming out of his mouth. I smiled as I got into my car. What could have been an inflammatory situation turned out fine. It always pays to be nice. You never know who might be watching!

REAFFIRMED

My Soul doth resonate
and the world can feel the
vibration of my thunder.

My spirit is resilient,
like a cockroach, it's a
natural wonder.

My mind sings a song
as sweet as an angel's.

My principles are rigid
lest they are bent to
positive angles.

—© *Saunni Dais*

TWELVE LIFE CHANGING PRINCIPLES

"Every individual has a place to fill in the world and is important in some respect, whether he chooses to be so or not."

—*Nathaniel Hawthorne*

Life is certainly a strange experience. I sometimes wonder whether it is a game designed to test us. I think so! That's what makes it so interesting. I've discovered that life really does come full circle if you meet it halfway. There are many principles that you must master in order to get off your assets and make your life work the way that you want it to. I want to give you what I believe to be some of the most powerful ones. These principles, combined with my own list of core values, have helped to center and balance my life. This list is by no means all inclusive, but it will give you the framework to truly jump start your life.

THE PRINCIPLE OF SELF BELIEF

"One comes to be of just such stuff as that on which the mind is set."

—Upanishads

This is a feeling of certainty about the outcome of something. You must learn to believe in yourself because if you don't, nobody else will. Will doubt ever creep in and try to wreck your plans? Almost always! You must learn that this emotion must be given a shot in the arm each day by you. The guy says, "I wish somebody would come along and turn me on!" What if they don't show up? You cannot afford to leave it up to someone else to get you started. Sometimes life seems to move at a much slower pace than we want it to. Sometimes you want something so much that you can taste it yet it can seem so far from you. I say hold fast to your goal and continue to believe in yourself as long as you have breath in you. You never know when your time will come. Tony Dungy said that he knew that one day he would get his chance to coach in the National Football League. He was prepared to continue to dream about and work towards that end, no matter how long it took. You must do the same thing. You can make it! Just don't ever give up, especially on you!

THE PRINCIPLE OF FAITH

"Be patient toward all that is unresolved in your heart,
And try to love the questions themselves."

—*Rainer Maria Rilke*

The concept of faith requires not only belief, but also perseverance. Faith is believing in yourself long enough. It's believing in yourself until you succeed! Anyone can exercise faith when things are going well. It's when you hit those bumps in the road that your faith will be tested. You will no doubt become sad, mad, happy, glad, depressed, worried, and frustrated during your journey to self-actualization. You need to be aware of these emotions, both consciously and subconsciously. There's an old Chinese proverb that says, "Even a hurricane only lasts a day". The Chinese bamboo tree can grow as tall as 90 feet in a matter of weeks. This only occurs after consistent watering from five to ten years. This is called "The Process." Does the tree really grow that tall in a matter of weeks? Of course not! It was all of the care and nurturing it had received up to that point that allowed it to reach its maximum potential. How tall will a tree grow? The answer is, as tall as it can. No one ever heard of a tree growing only half as tall as it could. Your life is the same way. You must continue to nurture your dreams for as long as it takes you to reach them. Your faith in a higher power as well as yourself will help you weather the hurricanes of life. Just don't give up!

"Our demons are our own limitations, which shut us off
from the realization of the ubiquity of the spirit . . . each
of these demons is conquered in a vision quest"

—*Joseph Campbell*

I once knew a very attractive girl who lived down the street from me, named Denise. She was the kind of person whom everyone liked. She had a very sweet demeanor. I was shocked to come home from school one day and find that she had committed suicide. In a fit of depression, she locked herself inside the garage at her house with the car running. It shocked everyone that a young girl with so much promise would take her own life. I thought to myself, "What kind of situation or feelings would create such an atmosphere of hopelessness that would cause one to take such drastic action?" If you ever feel that depressed, know that, "This too, shall pass!" Everything in life is temporary as is life itself. When you leave this earth, you'll be dead for a lot longer than you were ever alive. Do you agree that this is a fact of life? If so, why not give yourself every chance to succeed? As long as you have breath in your body, you're still in the game. Just keep believing in yourself long enough. You will eventually get where you want to go. I am to the point in my life where I don't worry about what other people think. Do I care what they think? Yes, I do care about how I'm perceived as a person, but I don't spend any time dwelling on others' opinions of me. I'm sure that I will have many critics who may not like this book. That's fine! That's their opinion. Some people wish that I had written yet another book about the helpless, pitiful plight of life in today's complex world. The world has enough propaganda about that. This is my book and I wrote it for you. If the critics want to, let them write their own book!

THE PRINCIPLE OF SELF LOVE

"Thoroughly to know oneself, is above all art, for it is the highest art."

—*Theologia Germanica*

"To thy own self be true." Never were truer words spoken. George Benson sings on his million dollar hit record, "Learning to love yourself is the greatest love of all!" I've found this to be true in every aspect of my life. You can't love anyone else until you first love you. Many people are looking for love in all the wrong places instead of first looking inside of themselves for the emotional support that they need. I know a guy named Glenn. He's 62 years old and has a body like Adonis. He walks with a swagger and an air of confidence that speaks not of arrogance, but of self love. I asked him what caused him to have such an incredible outlook on life. He told me to imagine being involved in an incredible love affair, the kind where you can't wait to see the other person. When you think of them, you get goose bumps. You can get through almost any difficulties that you may encounter during the day, as long as you know you will get to see this person at the end of it. The very thought of this person makes you excited about your life. He then marched me over to a mirror and told me to look into it. He then told me to imagine that the person that I was having this mad love affair with was myself. He told me that this was his secret. Glenn told me that it took him years to come to grips with this self-love concept. He had been through two marriages and raised three kids before he learned about it. He said when you learn to love yourself, life takes on a whole new glow. You wake up each day excited! People want to be around you because they want some of that to rub off on them. It's not about arrogance. Arrogance involves an outward display of emotion that usually centers around trying to impress or belittle someone else in order to make yourself look good. Self love in an internal thing. It comes from the inside out rather than the outside in. The key is to recognize the fact that you are enough to make you happy. If you base your happiness on anyone or anything other than you, you will more than likely be crushed when they don't meet your expectations. Keep the focus on you and what you can do on a continual basis to make yourself happy.

The Principle of Persistence

"Anyone who proposes to do good must not expect people to roll stones out of his way, but must accept his lot calmly, even if they roll a few more upon it."

—*Albert Schweitzer*

Persistence is the one thing that will definitely make the difference in whether you will reach your goals and live your dreams. Remember, the only way that you can ever fail in life is to quit. As long as you keep trying, you are a winner. No matter how well prepared or talented you are, be ready to have doors slammed in your face. It's just the nature of people. No matter how well received you are, there will always be someone who doesn't like you. One thing is for sure, if you give up without giving yourself every chance to win for as long as you can, you will fail.

Michael Jordan was cut from the basketball team during his sophomore year in high school. Who would have ever thought at that time that he would go on to be, without question, the greatest basketball player in the history of the game? I recently saw a program that profiled Michael Jordan's life and it was interesting to listen to his high school basketball coach try to justify his reason for cutting the greatest basketball player in the world. Michael didn't give up, thank goodness! Think of what we would all be missing. I've had to go through the same things in my life and so will you. Expect it, accept it, and deal with it! If you quit, you will be cheating the world as well as yourself out of receiving and giving the gift that only you can give.

The Principle of Proactivity

"All labor that uplifts humanity has dignity and importance and should be undertaken with painstaking excellence."

—*Dr. Martin Luther King, Jr.*

In Stephen Covey's best seller, *The Seven Habits of Highly Successful People,* he lists the the ability to be proactive as number one. This is the fourth skill necessary to achieve success once the others are firmly established. Whatever you're going to do in life, you've got to do it massively! Take massive action on a consistent basis and your results will change. Everything in life is a numbers game. The more often you try, the greater your chances of succeeding at anything that you try. Keep going, even when you don't feel like it! Even when faced with death, you will develop a belief system that could save your life.

My college football coach is a person of incredible belief. He is one of the few patients in the country living with another person's heart in his body. His name is Cal Stoll. He was one of the greatest recruiters in college football history. While coaching at Michigan State under the great Duffy Daugherty, he recruited players such as Bubba Smith, Clinton Jones, and George Webster. He's one of the greatest salesmen that I've ever seen. I called him not long ago and teased him about the fact that he coached four years in the Atlantic Coast Conference and 12 years in the Big Ten and didn't know anything about football. He told me that it didn't matter because he believed he would coach big time college football one day and belief was all that mattered. His belief allowed him to convince others that he could do it and he did. He then surrounded himself with people who knew what he didn't. Ironically enough, many of the coaches in the pros today came through his program at the University of Minnesota. Tom Moore, Moe Forte, Tony Dungy, Marc Trestman, and Roger French are all coaches who moved on to great things after being associated with Coach Stoll's program. When Coach Stoll was about to be wheeled into the operating room for his heart transplant, he told the head surgeon, "Look, it's fourth down, we've got the ball on the one-inch line, and there's only one second on the clock. Now, don't screw it up!" He told me that he never doubted for one second that he would come out of that operation alive. He did! Remember, you will not be judged in life by the number of times you fail, but rather by the number of times you succeed. The number of times you succeed is in direct proportion to the number of times you keep trying.

The Principle of Desire

"I have learned this at least by my experiment: that if one advances confidently in the direction of his dreams, and endeavors to live the life which he has imagined, he will meet with success unexpected in common hours."

—*Henry David Thoreau*

As a kid, I once knew a man named Freddy Blunt who used to talk about burning desire. You must possess an extraordinary amount of this success ingredient if you are going to be above average. Desire comes from the inside and can be fueled by your dreams and goals. There is no match for someone who has a burning desire. This comes from having a passion to do something great in life. That's not to say that it has to be something that will make you famous or will gain you notoriety. You do it because you love to do it. It will give you a feeling of contribution. When you get what is called "the eye of the tiger" you won't have to worry much about whether or not you will be successful. You will! A burning fire in your gut will keep you going. You will endure all the temporary setbacks and negative people that you will encounter along the way.

A Story of Burning Desire

It was mid-season, and Coach Knute Rockne of the University of Notre Dame was hospitalized with phlebitis, and a dangerous blood clot in his leg. Notre Dame was slated to play rival Carnegie Tech. Rockne left his bed to coach the game. He risked his life because he wanted victory more than life. Tom Leed came bursting into the locker room carrying Rockne in his arms as if he were a baby. As he sat Rock out on a table in the room, Rockne's eyes were glossy and staring ahead. The room was silent! The boys on the team said nothing. They looked like grade school kids sitting on the benches in front of him. They glanced at the ceiling, bit their lips, and did anything they could to keep the silence from driving them crazy. The boys went on to make college football history by winning 19 straight tough games in a row and two successive national championships. It would have been ludicrous if it had not been so serious. The great, strong, fierce, dynamic, indomitable Rockne being carried into the locker room like a baby. There were some wet eyes. You might think that this is a very silly business to become so emotional about, but it was 1929, a few years before the stock market crashed. A new era was about to dawn. This was Rockne and Notre Dame, it was Stephen and Carnegie Tech. This was the big game!

Behind the lockers, Dr. Maurice Keaney was whispering. He said that if Coach Rockne gets too excited and lets go and that bloods releases and hits his heart or brain, the chances are even that he'll never leave this locker room alive. These are close to the exact words that he said that day. Rockne said, "A lot of water has gone under the bridge, men, since I first came to Notre Dame, but I can't ever remember wanting a game as much as I want this one. Why do you think I'm taking this chance with my life? To see you lose? The other team will be primed, they'll be pumped, they think they've got your number. Are you gonna let it happen again, and again?"

Things got quiet for a moment. You couldn't see the boys' faces because their heads were down. But as you peeped through a space in the lockers, you could see that Rockne's face was racked with pain. He facial features were distorted with a look of determination. You see, this was the supreme effort of a great fighter. Now he shot the works! He said, "Go out there and crack 'em, fight 'em, fight to win! You've gotta

Win, Win, Win!" As the boys roared out of the locker room to take the field, they were yelling and screaming. They were excited! After the last player left the locker room, Rockne collapsed. The doctor continued to feel his pulse and mop the sweat from his face throughout. You see, Rockne wanted to win more than he wanted to live. The final score was Notre Dame-7, Carnegie Tech-0. That's what you call desire!

How will you know when you have a burning desire? You will know when you find something that gets you so excited that you have trouble sleeping at night. When you can't wait until morning so that you can hop out of bed and get on with it. These are the symptoms. The key is to drive that desire deep by surrounding yourself with all of the positive stimuli that you can find — people, books, tapes, and seminars. If you don't have something in your life that compels you at this point, don't despair. Just keep looking! If you look long and hard enough, I promise, you'll find it!

THE PRINCIPLE OF BENEVOLENCE

"Consciously and unconsciously, every one of us does render some service or other. If we cultivate the habit of doing this service deliberately, our desire for service will steadily grow stronger, and will make, not only for our own happiness, but that of the world at large."

—*Mahatma Ghandi*

I can't tell you how much I've seen this principle manifest itself in my life. I truly believe that the more you give, the more you get out of life. Many people are takers in this world rather than givers. When you learn to give, it opens up one of nature's laws. It's called the law of reciprocity. This law will provide all of the help you need in your quest for achievement. I could never find a better example than one from a story in *Ebony* magazine, about a woman named Osceola McCarty. She is an 87-year-old-washer woman who lives in

Hattiesburg, Mississippi. For years, she squirreled away a portion of the small income that she earned washing clothes in her back yard, until she accumulated a fortune of $250,000. She then made a personal scholarship endowment to the University of Mississippi of $150,000. Isn't that incredible? She could have taken that money and spent it on herself. She could have done anything with it, but she decided to give underprivileged students an opportunity to attend college. She was honored by the state of Mississippi as well as invited to the Congressional Black Caucus Dinner as President Clinton's special guest. There she was awarded the Presidential Citizens Medal. There's no doubt that she will continue to be blessed because of her giving heart. The same will happen for you, too. The more you give the more you get. The floodgates will open for you in direct proportion to the amount of your giving. Don't ask how much you get in a situation. Instead, ask how much you can give!

The Principle of Risk Taking

"Change and growth take place when a person has risked himself and dares to become involved with experimenting with his own life."

—*Herbert Otto*

No pain, no gain. No risk, no reward. You've got to be willing to take a chance on you. I've spent a good portion of the money that I've earned in life on me. I was once asked by a man at one of my seminars who was bankrolling me. I explained to him that I was bankrolling myself. I told him that I will bet on me every time. You should feel the same way about yourself. You cannot afford to keep waiting for a little bit better time. It will never be better than it is right now! Take a portion of your time and money and invest it in yourself as often as possible. Too much caution will kill your chances for success. I realize that you can be overzealous and make bad decisions, but ultimately you will have to get off your assets and make a decision if things are going to change. Life is so risky that we aren't going to get out of it alive, so why not just go for it? What if you're scared? I say, do it anyway. What's the worst that can happen? You learn something and move on! Moving in uncharted or unknown waters is always a little hairy, but worse yet is to do nothing but wait for things to happen. You can certainly do your homework before taking a leap of faith, but nothing you can do will ever take every element of risk out of a situation. Sometimes, life reserves hard knocks for us so that we don't forget. Don't run from these lessons. They're coming whether you want them or not! Take them, learn from them, and move forward. Even if you don't succeed at first, the worst that can happen is that you will learn something. A wise man was once asked to what he attributed his massive success in life. He said, "I attribute my success to my ability to make good decisions!" He was then asked how he learned the art of making good decisions. He said, "I learned the art of making good decisions from my vast array of experience. He was asked how he got all of his experience. He then responded, "From bad decisions!"

THE PRINCIPLE OF HONESTY

"All truth is an achievement. If you would have truth as its value, go win it!"

—*T.T. Munger*

Whatever you do, make sure that you are honest in your dealings with other people. You will only be cheating yourself if you're aren't. It always catches up with you in the end. Even when you think you've gotten away with something, there's an irrevocable law of nature that always evens the score. Look around you at all of the so-called high tech criminals who are now in prison. Don't try to beat the system. It was here long before you got here, and it will be here long after you're gone. I was watching *America's Most Wanted* a few weeks ago and saw a man who murdered his family. He was caught after 13 years on the run. He never dreamed that he would get caught. There are many reasons to be honest. I'm a big believer in the power of Karma. When you do good deeds with good intentions, things will swing back to you 360 degrees the same way. I can remember on many occasions in my life having the opportunity to capitalize on the misfortune of someone else, be it a lost wallet that I returned to the owner, an opportunity that I found out about that could benefit someone else rather than myself, or information that I found out about that could help someone else who wanted the same thing I did, and was better positioned to get it before me. The good fortune will return your way if you do what you know in your heart is right. You never know when you'll need Karma to come to your rescue. It will often come when you least expect it.

I once lost my wallet while watching a movie at a theatre in Seattle, Washington. I went back to the theatre later that night to try to retrieve it, but it was too late. I was frantic! I spent the rest of the night cursing mankind and all that it implied. Who would be so cruel as to find someone else's wallet and not return it? I left Seattle and flew back home to Minneapolis, wondering the entire time how much the culprit had attempted to charge on my credit cards. We sometimes think the worst at first, don't we? A few days after I returned home, I received package from Austin, Texas. It read as follows: I found your wallet in a theatre in Seattle. I hope it comes in handy. I found your wallet and decided that it would be best if I mailed it to you. I would have left it at the theatre, but I attended the late show and there was no one around to leave it with. Good Luck!

When that happened, I felt so ashamed. I thought about all of the wallets that I had returned to others over the years, and was thankful to the universe that, on this day, its Karma smiled upon me. It's not abnormal to think dishonest thoughts, just don't act on them. How many times have you gone into a bank and saw someone counting huge sums of money and wondered what it would be like to reach over the counter and grab a handful? You may think about it, but you don't do it, right? Honesty is usually the best policy is what I've learned throughout my life. If and when you must be the bearer of bad news, people will usually be glad that you told them in the end, particularly if you told them early in the game.

THE PRINCIPLE OF INTEGRITY

"Freedom consists not in refusing to recognize anything above us, but in respecting something which is above; for by respecting it, we raise ourselves to it, and, by our very acknowledgement, prove that we bear within ourselves what is higher, and are worthy to be on a level with it."

—Geothe

It is hard these days to find people who will do what they say they will. How often do you find yourself hiring people to do things for you and then find yourself doing a part or all of the work that you hired them to do? I once hired a woman to create some promotional material for me and found myself running all over town to make sure that things were done properly. The final straw that broke the camel's back was when I called to ask her about some pictures of me that were to be used on some audio albums. She told me that she thought I had them. I soon found myself going over to her house to pick up the pictures because she didn't have time to deliver them as promised. I then found myself talking directly to her vendors in order to ensure that the project was properly completed. Needless to say, I no longer deal with her. In fact I've done myself a huge favor by eliminating the thousands of dollars I was paying her. The money I spent with her was actually an investment, because by meeting her vendors, I was able to establish relationships with people that I would have never otherwise met. This will pay dividends for many years to come. People like this only get a chance to burn me one time. What they don't realize is that somehow I will profit from the experience and use it to gain a greater benefit at a later time. If you're looking to be successful over the long haul, always operate out of integrity. If you say you're going to do something, do it! Even something as trivial as returning a phone call can cost you major integrity points as far as I'm concerned. People will soon lose faith in you and your goose will be permanently cooked.

The Principle of Resiliency

"Our greatest goal must be in never falling, but arising each time we fall, for, in essence, this is the truest test of all great champions."

—*Unknown*

Resiliency is the ability to bounce back after a failure or disappointment. Expect failure to come. Open the door and welcome it into your domain and then beat the stuffing out of it with the principles mentioned previously. The key is not to worry about getting knocked down in life. You will! Just make sure that you don't stay down. You don't get the chance to fight another day if you pack up your bags and go home.

Many times, people will never know the pain you experienced to get where your are. You can be a star and nobody will know about your potential if you stop going for the goal. If you continue to try, the most important thing is that you will know that you are a winner. That's all that counts.

The Greatest Team That You'll Never See

In 1977, the University of Minnesota put one of the best teams on the floor in the history of college basketball. The team featured players like Mychal Thompson (Portland Trailblazers/Los Angeles Lakers), Kevin McHale (Boston Celtics/Minnesota Timberwolves), Ray Williams (New York Knicks, Boston Celtics), Osborne Lockhart (Harlem Globetrotters), and Phil "Flip" Saunders (Minnesota Timberwolves). This team was awesome. They went 24-3 that year and were one of the most dominating teams in the country. In fact, that same year Marquette University won the NCAA tournament and lost to the University if Minnesota by more than 30 points on their home court in Milwaukee. During the tournament, Al McGuire, the famed coach of the Marquette Warriors, commented that the best team in the country is not in the tournament. The university was not allowed to go the tournament because they were on probation for alleged recruiting violations. What was so impressive was to see these guys go out every night and lay it all on the line when there was supposedly nothing to play for since they were eliminated from tournament play. They made each team they played feel the wrath of their frustration. Even though the Gophers were barred from the "Big Show," there was no doubt that they left an indelible mark on the history of a sport with a tradition as rich as that of college basketball. They demonstrated an incredible amount of resiliency. They fought all year as though they would play in the tournament. That was a testament to their character. You can get the same results from your own life. Whatever level you strive to achieve, there will be challenges at that level to greet you. Just remember, the greater the challenge, the more glorious the victory!

THE PRINCIPLE OF FORGIVENESS

"I like the dreams of the future better than the history of the past."

—*Thomas Jefferson*

This is a powerful life principle that will free your spirit. Spite and resentfulness will destroy you. Trust me on this one, I know! I spent most of my life hating my mother. I hated her for the kind of life that she lead and for the kind of life I had to experience as a result. I suppose she felt the same way. We went for 30 years without seeing much of each other. I saw her a dozen times in a 30 year period. I knew that I loved her, but bitterness wouldn't allow me to make contact. It makes me sad now to think that 30 years went by without my mother in my life. As I got more involved in my speaking and training business, I kept having a feeling of hollowness and incongruity. Here I was, talking to other people through- out the country about their own personal development, and yet I had not gotten my own house in order. I knew that was hypocritical. That feeling kept gnawing at me. I knew that I had to do something about it! One Friday night, I happened to be in Orange County, California, conducting a seminar for Bax- ter/Kraft Food Service. It will always remain a pivotal moment because the night before was the ill-fated 30 mph chase scene between O.J. Simpson and the Los Angeles Police Depart- ment. In fact, he drove right past the Hyatt Regency Hotel, which was where the meeting was being held.

The next morning, after much deliberation, I called my mother. She'd moved to Los Angeles from St. Louis when I was in high school. I was sweating bullets. I hadn't talked to or seen her in more than 12 years. We talked on the phone for two hours, catching up. Finally, she told me that she had to go because her ride to church had arrived. I thought, "Church? We hardly ever went to church when I lived at home!" There was something different about her. I hadn't seen her since 1982 because it ripped me up so badly to see her on drugs. Sometimes I would walk into the house and it would be packed with lowlifes. Sometimes my mother would be so high off of wack, weed, sherm, or prescription drugs that she wouldn't even know me. It would take her awhile to recognize me. She would then spring to her feet and call my name, "Desi, Desi, Desi! This is my son, you all!" I would cry all the way back to the airport and for days afterward. This time, I realized that times had changed. I had changed. I was ready to bury the hatchet from the ugliness of the past and move on to a brighter future for the both of us.

After telling me that she had to go to church, my mother asked me to give her the phone number where I was. I told her to let me know what time she was coming back home. I didn't want to let her know that I was coming down into L.A. to see her. I wanted to surprise her. My next challenge was to hold myself together enough to make the two-hour drive down to the south central section of Los Angeles. I noticed people looking at me from their cars as I drove down Interstate 5, heading towards the city of Angels. I've often thought of it as the city of hell because of the things that happened to my family there. My brother was in the pen, and my mother and sister had fallen prey to the fast L.A. life there. People were looking at me as I drove because I was sobbing uncontrollably. I just let it rip! I had been holding in some of these feelings for years, and it was time to let it all out. This was going to be a day of healing old wounds.

I had attempted to go by her house many times in the past, but they were all weak attempts. I really didn't want find the house for fear of what I might find when I got there. This day was different, and my mother and I had both become different people. I could feel it over the phone. I knew that the time was right. It was time that I practiced some of the things that I was teaching to people throughout the country, things like persistence, forgiveness, and benevolence. I was committed to finding her house this time. I got out of the car and asked people, "Excuse, me can you tell me where 5563 Bangor St. is?" Several times I got lost and asked for directions, but eventually, I found myself edging closer to areas I recognized. My heart began to pound. I made a couple of turns and read the sign, Bangor St. I knew that her house was the last one on the right.

As I pulled my car in front of her house, I could feel sweat run down my arms. I hopped out of the car, ran to the front door, and rang the door bell. It was almost as if my mother had x-ray vision. I could hear her screaming, "Oh my, God!

It's my baby!" When she opened the door we immediately embraced one another. I could only say four words, and I said them over and over again. I said , "I love you, mama! I love you, mama! I love you, mama!" My mother kept repeating, "I love you, son! I love you, son! I love you, son!" We went inside and sat for five hours without moving, talking and talking. We spread pictures all over the floor as we caught up on 30 years. I surprised her when I told her that she had a granddaughter and grandson. She cried when I showed her pictures of them. She then told me something that changed my life forever. She told me, "Son, I'm sorry for all of the things that happened. I couldn't give you love because I never had anybody love me. I couldn't give you what I didn't have. I never knew my father, and my stepfather raped, beat, and took advantage of me constantly when I was a young girl. I wanted to let you know why things turned out the way that they did. I've spent the last 30 years in a mad search to find myself, and, through Jesus Christ, I've been able to do it. I love you, Desi. I've always loved you! I'll always be your Mama. No matter what happens, nothing will ever change that!" I called my father while I was there and put the two of them on the phone. They hadn't talked to each other in more than 30 years. It was a beautiful sight!

I felt so guilty for judging her all of those years. I didn't know what brand of hell she had been through in her life. I was too young to understand when I ran away from home. What right did I have to condemn her for the rest of her life because she didn't live up to my expectations. I had never walked a mile in her shoes. Think about how often you judge someone harshly without knowing what that person has had to deal with. There's a reason for everything. I always think about the biblical phrase, "Let he who is without sin cast the first stone!"

When I got into the car for the drive back to Orange County, I cried harder than I've ever cried in my life. But this time it was for a different reason. I was crying out of joy. The weight of the world had been taken from my shoulders. The wind ran through the open windows of my rental car as I sped down the freeway while the music of Yanni played in the background. We were both finally free to love each other unconditionally. I felt like a complete man for the first time in my life. My mother came to Minneapolis to visit her grandchildren that fall, and my wife finally became acquainted with a part of my life that had always been a mystery. Life really can come full circle.

I would encourage you to become a catalyst in your own life. If there's someone out there that you are harboring negative feelings about, you pick up the phone, call them, and heal the problem. Is there risk involved? Absolutely! But the bigger risk is living with the regret and pain that will come if you don't. What prompted me to really get off the dime and repair my past with my mother was the fact that many of my friends had lost their parents after years of bad relationships. The one thing that they all said with tears in their eyes was that they never had a chance to tell their parents that they loved them. They had the opportunity, they just didn't take it, and now they are living with regret. They will never have the chance to rectify the situation because they waited too long. I'm sharing this with you because I don't want you to blow it. Whether you realize it or not, this kind of burden will affect every area of your life. If you're not as successful in life as you'd like to be, healing old wounds like this will help to free your spirit and clear your head so that you can focus on your goals. If you feel that you're already successful, it will help you to become more successful as you create more balance in your life. I want you to pick up the phone and call the people in question. Tell them that you want to let them know that you are sorry for whatever it was that happened between you, even if it wasn't your fault. Tell them that you love them, how important they are to you, and how much you miss them. Tell them that you want to forget about the past and have the best relationship that you can have with them from this day forward.

Whether this person responds positively or negatively is

not the most critical thing. The most important thing is what it will do for you! You will have opened the door for the other person to walk through. Don't despair, for they may not have reached the level of emotional maturity that you have at this point. When they're ready, they will come around. You will find, more often than not, that the person in question will be feeling the same way you do. They just didn't have the confidence or courage to put their finger in the dial and call. If things are going to change, someone has to be man or woman enough to take charge. I promise you that it will change your life forever. All I can tell you is that it worked for me. Why not give it a try?

Bringing It Home

"Such gardens are not made By Singing: . . . "Oh how beautiful," and Sitting in the shade."

—*Rudyard Kipling*

There's no question about it. You play the most vital role in how things turn out in your life. It is my hope and dream that you have found some inspiration, motivation, and answers in the pages of this book. You have been so kind to invest your money and time in it. My goal has been to give you an unparalleled amount of value for each. If you feel that this has happened, then we both have richly benefitted.

The Lord said, "If you will plant the seed, I will provide the blessing of the sun, the seed, the soil, and the rain." This means that you must now go out and do something about what you've learned, what you know, and how you feel.

There's a story about a farmer who took an awful looking piece of land. There was glass, trash, rocks, and debris everywhere. This place was truly a mess! He took it and, WHOOSH! He transformed it into a beautiful farm and garden. There were rows and rows of corn, wheat, and soybeans. There were rows and rows of flowers, of all shapes and sizes. He had horses that could run like the wind. The farm house was beautiful, with perfectly manicured grounds. This place was really something special.

One day, a jealous neighbor stopped by to compliment the farmer on how beautiful this place looked, but he didn't want to give the farmer too much credit for this incredible transformation. He said, "My, my, what a beautiful farm and garden the Lord has blessed you with!" The farmer became a little perturbed by the cynical manner in which the neighbor delivered his praise. The farmer said, "You know something? You're right! If it wasn't for the Lord and the blessing of the soil, the seed, the sun, and the rain, there would certainly be no farm and no garden either. But let me tell you something, Jack, you should have seen this place when the Lord had it all by himself!" That means you must get off of your assets and do something. Everything that you need is already within your reach. The rest is up to you. You've got everything inside of you, right now, that it takes to be a winner. Most of all, you've got the winning spirit. What I want you do to from this day forward is unleash that spirit and let it explode!

Apollinaire said:

> "Come to the edge!"
> They said, "It's too high!"
> He said, "Come to the edge!"
> They said, "We might fall!"
> He said, "Come to they edge!"
> And they came.
> And he pushed them.
> And they flew!

—Christopher Hogue

Unleash the Power in You!

Desi Williamson

Workbook Action Guide
for Personal Achievement

Mission

To aid you in personal growth and development by offering solutions and ideas to assist you as you strive to achieve results in all areas of your life.

This ACTION GUIDE will provide you with the self empowerment and personal development skills necessary to discover and maximize your potential while achieving happiness, success, and more control over the conditions in your life.

In this ACTION GUIDE, you will learn how to:

- Program your mind for success.
- Change your life for the better.
- Use the power of personal development.
- Set goals that will change your life.
- Create a winning attitude.
- Discover core values that will change your life.

Unleash the Power in You!

Action Guide

Section One

Onward

*Every ending is a new
beginning! Life is an endless
unfoldment.*

*New opportunities give you
chances to win . . . again!
Some way you'll find
atonement.*

*Meet your new challenges and
goals with optimism and
determination.*

*Stand ready to lively up yourself if
it's rough going and you need
motivation.*

**SET SAIL!
DO WELL!
IT'S TIME TO EXCEL!**

—©*Saunni Dais*

Current Reality Questions

1. Are you happy with your current situation in life? Please explain why or why not.

2. What's good about your life at the present moment?

3. If nothing was your answer to number 2, please think about it again. The fact that you're alive is something to be excited about. Try again!

4. Is there more that you could be doing with your life than you currently are?   Please explain.

5. What is it about your current situation that you would like to change?

6. How would you go about changing it?

7. Do you feel successful at the present time? If yes, explain how. If no, explain why not.

8. What would it take to make you feel successful?

9. Do you have a positive or negative attitude about yourself? Your abilities? Your potential? Why? Please explain.

10. Are you easily influenced by others? Please explain.

11. Do you make good use of your time? Please explain how you do or don't.

12. Do you complete projects on time or find yourself procrastinating? If so, why?

13. Are you easily swayed by others or do you have firm beliefs and stick to them? Please explain.

14. Are you easily intimidated by others? Please explain.

15. Do you take good care of your health? Please explain.

16. Do you control your temper well? Please explain.

17. When you fail at something, do you learn from it and move on or dwell on it and beat yourself up? Please explain.

18. Do you communicate and express yourself well? Please explain.

19. Do you worry about minor issues to the level of excess?

20. Are there negative tendencies that you would like to overcome? What are they?

The Power of Adjustment

One of the reasons many people don't do well in life is because they don't have the ability to change their course of action when things aren't working for them. This one skill can have a dramatic impact on your life from this day forward. Many people simply give up when they meet a roadblock to their goals rather than finding new approaches to solving their problems.

Once you begin to adapt this philosophy to your approach, you will truly come to know that there's no such thing as failure. You always get results even though they may not be the ones you want. When winners make mistakes, they don't see it as failure, but rather as vital information they can use to make better decisions for future success. They take this information and figure out a new course of action!

Have you ever experienced rejection? How did it make you feel? Most people give up at the first sign of opposition! Rejection should never be taken personally, just keep going until you succeed!

Remember a time when you quit because you didn't achieve something. Write it down.

What did you learn from it?

How would you handle it the next time?

What adjustments would you make?

How would you use what you've learned in the future?

THE POWER OF PERSONAL IDENTITY

Your personal identity is the foundation of your life. It determines your self-image. Self-image is what you believe to be true about yourself. It determines your level of self-confidence and comfort with the outside world. Once I was able to really find the answers to some profound questions about myself, my entire life changed, and so will yours!

Exercise: In completing the answers to the following questions, there's a rule that must be employed. You cannot use labels to describe yourself. In other words, you cannot describe yourself by what you do for a living, but rather by who you are as a person. If we were attending your funeral, what would you want said about you? What effect did you have on the world? What was your gift to the world?

QUESTIONS TO PONDER

1. Who are you? How would you describe yourself? What are you about?

2. When writing this identity statement, list some of the emotions that you experienced.

3. Introduce yourself in one word, describing the emotion that you feel to be the most powerful of all. For example, you would say, "Hello, I'm...........<u>list emotion</u>.

NOTE: The key thing to remember here is that it's okay to feel whatever you felt. There are no right or wrong answers. The main thing is to come to grips with who you are as a person.

THE POWER OF PURPOSE

A purpose is often created by a personal challenge in life, something that compels us to take action. Many times we will do things for others that we will not do for ourselves. A personal challenge will give you reason to get up early and stay up late. It's like having rocket fuel for life. An unmotivated person is one who lacks a purpose backed by a burning desire. It's so easy to get caught up in the necessities of day to day survival that most people never take the time to really analyze why they do what they're doing. Don't let this happen to you! Life is too short not to get the most out of it, but you must take the time to think!

Exercise: In answering the following questions, be as honest with yourself as possible. If you don't know the answer right now, take the time to think about it.

What is your purpose? What do you want to do with your life? What would you have as a purpose if you knew you couldn't fail?

The thing that stops most people from succeeding is fear. We learned from this section that fear stands for. (Answer is listed on page 335.)

F-

E-

A-

R-

REASONS FOR SUCCEEDING

Reasons are a powerful force that will compel you to take action in life. You must learn to act on life or it will act on you. Let's pretend that we are 50 stories high, on the rooftops of two different buildings about 20 feet apart from each other.

You are on the rooftop of one building and I'm on the other. We are looking directly at one another. There's a 50 story drop and 20 feet separating us.

Let's say that I place an "I" beam from one building to the next so that you can walk from your building to mine. (An "I" beam is a steel girder that construction workers use to build large office buildings like the one we're standing on.) This "I" beam is about two feet in width. There's also a 30 mile per hour wind blowing.

If I held up an envelope and told you that there was $50,000 in it, and I would give it to you if you crossed that "I" beam from your building to mine, would you do it?

Answer:

Why or why not?

If I held up an envelope and told you that there was one million dollars in it, and I would give it to you if you crossed that "I" beam to get it, would you? The wind is now blowing at 50 miles per hour and remember, if you fall, it's curtains!

Answer:

Why or why not?

If I held up your mother, father, sister, brother, or child, and told you that unless you crossed that "I" beam, I would drop them, would you cross that "I" beam to get them? They are crying and pleading for you to save them!

Answer:

Why or why not?

Moral: We all have something that we would cross the "I" beam for, something or someone that we feel so strongly about that we would be willing to lay our lives on the line for it. When you find a purpose in life that you feel that strongly about, you will find a way to accomplish it!

There are many reasons for doing something. There's an old adage that says once a person finds out "WHY" they are doing something, they can deal with almost any "HOW" that they encounter along the way. Here are some of my reasons for wanting to succeed in life.

1. FAMILY—I want to be able to provide a nice home for my family and give my children a good start in life. My grandmother is elderly and I want her to be as comfortable as possible in her older years. She's 87 years old. She will want for nothing as long as I'm alive. I want to be able to help my mother and father, should they need my help, without sacrificing the needs of my wife and children. That means that I've got to work hard and really develop my skills.

2. MONETARY—I want to earn enough money to be financially independent. I want to be able to travel with my family and let them learn from seeing environments that are different from their own. I want to be able to help other people by establishing foundations so that they have a chance at success. I want to be able to live my older years in comfort without having to worry about money. I will never retire because I love to work, but this will give me the choice.

3. PERSONAL—I enjoy feeling like I've accomplished something. When I learn something new, I get excited because I've found a new and possibly better way to do things. I like the feeling of looking back over the years and seeing how much I've grown. I like the feelings that come from winning. This gives me confidence.

4. HEALTH—I enjoy the feeling the comes from being in shape. It gives me more energy and sets a good example for others when they see that I've got pride in the way that I look. For this reason, I eat well, exercise, and get the proper sleep, but mental health is also important, so I make sure to feed my mind with knowledge as well.

The key to discovering your reasons is to ask the question why? This causes all kinds of mental machinery to start working for you. It's like pressing the "on" button to a huge conveyor belt that will bring to you vital answers to the questions you need to make life changing decisions.

Think about it. From the moment little children are old enough to speak, they ask why? You tell them to do something, they ask why? They can drive you crazy with that one word! It's because they have a childlike curiosity that drives them to learn. They have to know! It's when we become adults that we become too skeptical and lose that edge. This exercise will help you bring back that curiosity that we all enjoyed as children. Remember, the list above is my list and is only an example to help you with the process. You must find your own reasons.

Exercise

In the spaces below, compose a list of reasons for succeeding that are so compelling that they cause you to get excited about your future. First list the reason, then why you want to achieve it.

1.

2.

3.

4.

5.

The key is to be perfectly honest with yourself.

THE POWER OF THOUGHT

Many people live in the past, constantly beating themselves up about past failures, or live in regret for not achieving their goals and living up to their full potential. Other people use lessons from the past to create an even better future for themselves. You can, too! You must learn from the past and use it as a launching pad to the future.

Exercise

I have identified three levels of thought. I would like for you to answer the following questions as honestly as you can.

Level One—(Negative Acceptance) I can't, It won't work, I don't know how.

> 1. In the space below, think back to a time when you talked yourself out of doing something because you thought you couldn't do it. Write it down. How did it make you feel?

Level Two—(Regret) I shoulda, I oughta, I coulda, Why didn't I think of that?

> 2. In the space below, think back to a time when you didn't do something that you now regret. How often do you think about it? How does it make you feel?

Level Three—(Integration) I can, I will, I shall, I must.

3. In the space below, list something major in your life that you are absolutely committed to changing right now. Write down how you plan to do it.

It's not what happens to you that will determine how your life turns out, it's what you do about it that makes the difference!

In the spaces below, under the appropriate subheading, take a few minutes to fill in your thoughts. Insight is what you've learned from the first section. Action is what you're going to do about it.

<table>
<tr><td style="text-align:center">**INSIGHT**
What you've learned</td><td style="text-align:center">**ACTION**
What you're going to do</td></tr>
</table>

*"What you think about affects every aspect of your life,
both consciously and subconsciously. Your thoughts
determine your actions and your actions will ultimately
determine your destiny!"*

—*Desi Williamson*

Unleash the Power in You!

Action Guide

Section Two

THE POWER OF INFLUENCE

Exercise

In life it's just as important to learn what not to do as what to do. Some people's lives are used as warnings while others are cited as examples. The people you associate with have an effect on you. Their influence either adds something to the quality of your life or takes something away. Some people, with their negative conversations and outlooks, can poison your thoughts and hold you back from reaching your potential. You must make critical decisions about the value of such relationships and be willing to remove yourself from their influence. Complete the following questions as they relate to the subject of examples and warnings.

1. Make a list of people you have known or have read about who represent a positive example of how to live successfully.

2. Make a list of people that you have known or read about who represent what not to do in life.

3. What lessons did you learn from both examples listed above? How can you use both to change your life for the better?

Never underestimate the power of influence. The people that you associate with affect you either negatively or positively. This greatly determines your attitude and ultimately the results that you get from your life.

Exercise

In the spaces below, answer the questions as honestly as you can about the people who have an influence in your life.

1. Who has a positive influence on your life? How will this association benefit you?

2. Who has a negative influence on your life? What is this association costing you?

3. What are some of the things that you are going to do about the people who negatively influence you?

The Power of Vision

The human brain is the most powerful computer on earth. Unfortunately, no one ever gave us an owner's manual to go with it. We must make a conscious effort to control our thoughts, continue to develop a larger vision of ourselves, and see ourselves doing the things that will help us to realize our dreams. It all starts here!

The power of vision comes in two forms. Sight is what you see with your eyes and insight is what you see with your mind. You must be able to project into the future a vision of yourself much larger than the one you currently have.

You Are a Human Computer

There are three components to a computer.

Screen—(Your Behavior) Pretend as though you are watching a computer screen and looking at your behavior. List some of the ways that you have been part of the problem in accomplishing your goals and ways that you can be the solution.

How have you been part of the problem? Please explain.

How can you be part of the solution? Please explain.

Keyboard—(Your senses and emotions) Close your eyes for three minutes and dream about what you would like to become. See yourself accomplishing the task. See yourself massively successful. What do you see? How does it feel? Write down your answers.

Disk—(Your Subconscious Mind) We are constantly influenced by the things we hear and see whether it's through television, radio, the printed word, or other people. List some of the things that you have seen or heard in the last week that have affected you. List whether the effects were positive or negative. List how you can better accentuate the positives and minimize the negatives in your life.

INSIGHT	**ACTION**
What you've learned	What you're going to do

"In order for you to get off of the treadmill of desperation and reach your goals, you must be willing to invest time in being uncomfortable. The comfort zone is a dangerous place to be, for never will you realize your true potential until you test the limits of your being."

—Desi Williamson

Unleash the Power in You!

Action Guide

Section Three

Exercise

Many people don't do well because they constantly focus on the negative things in life rather than the positive. Much of this comes from our negative programming as children. In the exercise below, called "Positive vs Negative," list something negative and then next to it list at least three positive things. They can be anything. There are no rules.

NEGATIVE	POSITIVE
1.	1.
	2.
	3.
2.	4.
	5.
	6.
3.	7.
	8.
	9.
4.	10.
	11.
	12.

Moral: If you had trouble listing more positive things than negative, it doesn't mean that you're a bad person. You simply need to change your focus so that you look for the good things in life even when something bad happens. Ask yourself a question: What's good about this? Remember, you get what you focus on in life.

FIVE STEPS TO MENTAL PROGRAMMING

Exercise

Write in the definitions to these five steps to the mental programming process. (Answers are listed on page 335.)

Impact—

Repetition—

Utilization—

Internalization—

Reinforcement—

FOUR LEVELS OF MENTAL MASTERY

Unconscious Competent—You are a master! You don't have to think about something before doing it. It's second nature!

Conscious Competent—You know something, but it takes every bit of effort you have to remember how do to it. You have not made the commitment to master it.

Unconscious Competent—You are aware that you don't know something, but haven't yet made the commitment to do something about it.

Unconscious Incompetent—You don't know something and you don't care. This is failure mentality.

THE THREE COMPONENTS OF HUMAN INTERACTION

Communication skills are important. In order to be effective in any walk of life, you must be able to express yourself well. The quality of your communication will determine the quality of your life. In the spaces below estimate the correct answers. Estimate what these qualities of communication represent. (Answers are listed on page 336.)

	Your Estimate	Actual
WORDS— (What you say)	_____%	_____%
TONE & PACE— (How you say what you say)	_____%	_____%
PHYSIOLOGY— (How you use your body when you talk, gestures, facial expression, volume, speed, tempo, eye contact, body spacing)	_____%	_____%

SELF TALK

What you say to yourself has a definite impact on how you think and what you do. It affects your performance as well as the results you get from life.

1. How do you feel about yourself when you've accomplished something that you set out to do? What do you say to yourself?

2. How do you feel about yourself when you've failed at something that you've tried? What do you say to yourself?

Exercise

What did you learn about yourself?

1. From now on I will....

2. My life is better because....

3. When I succeed, I feel....

4. I love to win because....

5. I will increase my skill level because....

6. I will be successful because....

7. I am a smart, capable person who will....

8. From this point on I will never again....

9. I'm looking forward to....

10. My life is better because....

11. I am the one who determines my....

12. One day I'm am going to be...

13. I will positively impact the world by...

14. I will help others by...

15. I will continue to develop my skills by....

16. I will become a better person by...

17. I will develop better health habits by....

18. I will become a better leader by....

19. I will acquire better reading skills because....

20. I will dream bigger dreams because...

THE MOST DEADLIEST CRIMINAL

The most deadliest of criminals is not he with a gun,
It's he who says that it can't be done!
A thief won't attack your character traits,
Your skills and abilities to your face.
It will more than likely be a well meaning friend,
Who simply crushes your will to win.
No, they don't rob you at the point of a gun,
They simply tell you, "It can't be done!"
When pointed to thousands who already are,
They say, "They're superior to you, personality wise
   and ability, too!"
"They're way ahead of what others can do!"
It matters not that their words are untrue,
Because you think they know you better than you,
   that's silly!
So you're robbed of your faith and hopes to succeed,
Robbed of material blessings received.
Robbed of your faith that says, "I can!"
Robbed by an ignorant, gunless friend?
So, the most deadliest of criminals is not he with
   a gun,
It's he who says that it can't be done.
For things taken by burglars can be gotten again, but
Who can replace your will to win?

—Anonymous

Exercise

   After reading this poem, write down your thoughts, its general
meaning and what specific value it has for your own life.

INSIGHT
What you've learned

ACTION
What you're going to do

Unleash the Power in You!

Action Guide

Section Four

Personal Development Power

Personal development is the starting point for all achievement. Most of us look for outside excuses when things aren't working out for us rather than looking inside at our own shortcomings and taking the steps to correct our deficiencies. You can learn new skills and develop a positive mindset that will eliminate the behavior that has held you back in the past. It's all a matter of choice. You have the ability to decide exactly how your life will turn out. The word "LUCK" means to "Labor Under Correct Knowledge." Many people are failing in life because they refuse to take personal responsibility.

When you finally decide to take responsibility for your growth and development, your life will change and you will take quantum leaps compared to what you've done in the past. The key is that you must actively seek out knowledge in its various forms and never stop learning.

Exercise

Fill in the missing blanks to the following questions regarding the subject of personal development. (Answers are listed on page 336.)

1. We get paid for the_____ we create in the marketplace.
2. Things get better when_____ get better.
3. In order for things to change,_____ going to have to change.
4. The major key to my better future is_____.
5. I can have more than I have because I can _____more than I am.
6. If it's to be, it's up to_____.
7. I don't get paid for_____, I get paid for_____.

8. There are two kinds of education,
   _____ and _____.
9. How much money I earn is a direct reflection of
   my _____ _____.
10. If I continue to do what I've always done, I'll
    continue to have what I've_____.

The Power of Learning

The process of learning involves education on many levels. There's formal education and self education. Formal education comes from our school system. Most of us in this country are fortunate enough to go through our educational system, which is the best in the civilized world. Unfortunately, most of us stop at this level and don't pursue active learning beyond our formal education. Self education is when you actively pursue knowledge on your own. This is a real act of maturity that will mark the beginning of your better future.

It doesn't matter how successful you have been in the past, you must seek to continue your education so that you remain a valuable commodity in the marketplace. Everything in life continues to change. You must expand your knowledge base on a consistent basis in order to remain on the cutting edge of coming changes.

There is big difference between knowledge and wisdom.

Knowledge teaches you what to do.

Wisdom teaches you how to do it.

Quantum Learning Process

1. Learn how to communicate.

-Expand your vocabulary

-Learn how to say it well

-Learn how to speak in groups

2. Learn to observe.

-Become a student of lifelong learning

-Become a reader (Spend at least one hour a day)

-Learn from the past

-Make life a study

3. Associate with successful people.

-Learn from successful people

-Look at how they did it

-Adopt some of their positive traits

4. Become a student.

-Success leaves clues

-Get around successful people and listen

-Ask questions, listen more than you talk

5. Get excited about your life.

-Be curious like a child

-Look forward to learning new things

-Wake up each day with an attitude of gratitude

Exercise

Answer the following questions regarding ways that you can increase your learning through the "Quantum Learning Process."

1. List three ways in which you will increase your communication skills over the course of the next year.

a.

b.

c.

2. What is it that you're really interested in learning? How many books have you read in the last year? What actions will you take to ensure that you improve your vocabulary and reading skills? How much time do you spend each day reading?

3. List people that you admire and are going to ask to be your mentor so that you can learn from them. Who do you admire that has written books or made audio or videotapes that you could use as a mentor by reading or listening to their work and becoming a student of their philosophy?

4. Explain why you think it's important to listen to other people, particularly those with more knowledge in a given area than yourself.

5. What is it about your life that you feel grateful for? How will you take this feeling and use it to your advantage?

6. List three things that you need to do over the course
of the next few years to improve yourself, and what
steps you're going to take to make it happen.

a.

b.

c.

If you really want to do well in life, you must make sure
that you maintain very close control over your time. You
must not allow yourself to spend major time on minor
things. If you could shrink your size and jump into the
briefcase of a very successful person, you would find that
they have very close controls over their time, how they
spend it, and who they spend it with. The average television
is on in each household across the country more than seven
hours a day.

If you sleep seven to eight hours a day, work or go to
school seven to eight hours a day, and watch television seven
to eight hours a day, it's all over. There is no more time! We
all have 24 hours in a day. If you want to make quantum
leaps in your own individual progress, you must make the decision to do the most productive thing possible at every given
moment. You will find that most successful people don't

spend their time watching television eight hours a day. Their time is too valuable! You must learn that your time is your most valuable commodity. When you learn to repect it, you will be taking a very important step towards increasing the quality of your life.

Exercise

Below, list the ways in which you use your time performing various activities outside of work or school.

Example:

Activity	Number of Hours Spent
Watching Television	20
Reading	16
Playing sports	20
Visiting with friends	10
Weeks Total	66

Activity	Number of Hours Spent

Activities	Total Hours

Review the activities you have listed on the previous page. Beside each activity, circle the hours that you devote to your own personal development. Total the hours you have circled and write it in the space provided below.

> Total hours devoted to personal development
> _____ hours.

Calculate the hours per week that you do not spend on personal development (Subtract the total you have just given in the line above from the "Total Hours" that you listed. (These are unproductive hours.)

> Total unproductive hours _____ hours.

I don't suggest that you use every waking moment for personal development, because you need to make sure that your life is balanced with activities that address your needs. It's important to spend time relaxing and enjoying yourself. However, you must be careful that you do not overindulge yourself to the point that "FUN TIME" becomes a way of life. It's this habit that you must work to overcome. Personal Development is fun once you begin to see yourself grow and move from one level to the next.

If you find that you are not spending any time on personal development, imagine what would happen if you decided to start spending 5, 10, or 15 hours on increasing your skills. What if you set aside one hour a day for reading? What would happen if you really spent quality time on your work assignments rather than rushing to get finished so that you could indulge yourself in play time? The difference in the rewards you will get are tremendous!

The progress you make will be in direct proportion to the amount of time you're willing to spend towards developing a better life for yourself. The more time you invest in doing the things that will give you the greatest return, the faster you will reach your goals.

In life there are always trade-offs. We exhange our time for the things that we think will benefit us in some way. I've found that we must ask not what it costs, but what it's worth. We must be willing to give up something in order to get something. It's not a question of having time because there's plenty. We all have the same amount! The question is, how will you use yours from this day forward?

Exercise

What activities could you give up that would provide you with more time to spend working on your personal development program? List what actvities you could possibly sacrifice, how many hours you would free up by doing so, and how you could better use the time.

What Could You Give Up?	Number of Available Hours	How Would You Use the Time?

Total Hours

How many hours could you now spend on developing a personal development program?   _____Hours

In what ways do you feel that this would build a better life?

INSIGHT
What you've learned

ACTION
What you're going to do

"Your life can be whatever you choose to make of it, for just over the horizon is the better life that awaits you. It's all predicated upon you becoming more today than you were yesterday, and more tomorrow than you are today!"

—*Desi Williamson*

Unleash the Power in You!

Action Guide

Section Five

GOAL POWER

Goals are critical to success. Without them, you will drift through life. This is how people become what is known as "VICTIMS OF CIRCUMSTANCE." When you set goals, you take charge of your life and decide what you want, when you want it, and how you plan to accomplish it. If you don't set goals, you will be left with what remains after the people who have set goals have chosen. Goals will make you a better person, not so much for what you get at the end, but for what you become in order to accomplish them.

With goals, you can design your life the way that you want it. They can revolutionize the possibilities for your future. In order to achieve success, you must plan it, for rarely do things of significance happen by chance. Many people don't set goals, because the prospect of accomplishing a major task quite often may seem monumental. Through a process called "CHUNKING," or the breaking of larger goals into smaller ones, you can gain confidence and celebrate by rewarding yourself along the way. Your goals must involve honesty, integrity, and benefit others as well as yourself.

There are certain rules of the goal-setting process that must be followed.

RULE OF SIX IN GOAL SETTING

1. Goals must be WRITTEN—This shows that you are serious about your future. Most people spend more time planning a vacation than they do their lives. When you write your goals down, it crystallizes your thoughts and allows you to communicate the things that you want in life. You must not be casual about the things you want in life because a casual approach creates casualties!

2. Goals must be SPECIFIC—It's not enough to merely say, "I want to get my degree!" You must set a definite date and time in which you plan to accomplish a certain goal. A better way to put it would be to say, "I will earn a degree in business from the University of Your Choice by attending class regularly and applying myself to the best of my abilities. I will graduate in the spring of 1999." This is a specific goal. With some goals, you can even be more specific by listing the month, day, and year in which you will reach an objective.

3. Goals must be MOTIVATIONAL—You must find what motivates you! Your goals must be based upon something that you feel excited about. What do you enjoy doing? What do you dream about doing or becoming? What do you enjoy doing so much that you would do it for free (outside of sports)? Motivation combined with the proper information will give you the inspiration necessary to realize your dreams!

4. Goals must be ATTAINABLE—Don't set a goal so difficult that you would never get there in a million years. Set a large goal and then break it into smaller parts so that it is more easily achieved. For example, if your goal were to become a millionaire, you would set the goal by first, 1.) Getting your high school education 2.) Deciding what college or trade school to attend in order to develop your skills, 3.) Finding work in your chosen field or perhaps starting your own business, 4.) Picking a set amount of money to set aside each month for investment purposes until you've reached your goal. Each of these steps is possible. Give yourself a chance to win!

5. Goals must be RELEVANT—They must be something that you feel strongly about. They must be important enough to you to grab your full attention. They must be the things that you feel will have the biggest impact on your life or the lives of the people you really care about. Sometimes we will do things for others that we will not do for ourselves.

6. Goals must be TRACEABLE—You must set up a system for keeping score. If you don't know how you're doing, you'll never know when you get there! You must give yourself constant feedback. How are you doing over the short term? Long term? You must constantly measure your progress! Feedback is the breakfast of champions!

Four Categories of Goals

1. VALUES GOALS—Values guide every decision you make. Values represent the things that are really important in life. They are the principles that determine how you live your life. They are of the highest priority. The operative question in determining your values is, "What's most important to you in life?" The same question could be asked about your education, job, family, friends, health, or any other subject. You will be doing a values exercise later in this program.

2. SHORT-RANGE GOALS—These represent the things that you would like to accomplish in the next one, three, or five years in order to reach your destination. Short-range goals can also be broken down into weeks or months in helping you

to realize your dreams as they roll into years. The key is to understand the things that are most important in the short term so that you are doing the most productive things at the right time.

3. LONG-RANGE GOALS—These represent the things that you would like to accomplish in the next 10, 15, or 20 years. They can even go beyond. What do you see yourself doing at more mature stages of your life? What do you want to be doing in the next 10 to 20 years? Where would you like to be living? What kinds of things would you like to have? These are the dreams that, with proper planning and execution, can be yours.

4. DAILY TASK GOALS—These are the things that you do on a daily basis that ultimately determine your destiny. It is suggested that you plan each day of your life out as carefully as possible with a "TO DO" list. There's a big difference between doing the most URGENT things and the most IMPORTANT. Urgent things are often things that come up at the spur of the moment and take our focus away from the things that will really help us move forward.

Exercise

The following values exercise will help you determine some of the things that are most important to you in life. In the spaces below list the top twenty. Place an "M" next to the ones that require money, place a "P" next to the ones that require the participation of others, and place a date next to it to determine when you want it. Finally, prioritize the list by determining your "TOP TEN" values.

What's most important to you in life? List your top twenty values.

1.	11.
2.	12.
3.	13.
4.	14.
5.	15.
6.	16.
7.	17.
8.	18.
9.	19.
10.	20.

Now reduce this list to your top ten most important values.

1.	6.
2.	7.
3.	8.
4.	9.
5.	10.

It's important to note that there are no rights or wrongs. These are your values and yours alone.

What did you learn about yourself from this exercise?

Refer to these values when setting your long-range and short-range goals. They will help give more meaning to your goals and help to keep you focused on what's most important.

REMEMBER: A goal is nothing more than a dream with a deadline!

Dream Big Dreams!

Exercise

I would like for you to take two minutes and relax in the comfort of your chair. Close your eyes and simply dream about the things you would like to have happen in your life. What would you like to become? What would you like to have? Where would you like to travel? Think about your top ten values as you dream. How do they influence what you dream about for your future?

Rule: There's no such thing as failure or limitations. Ready...Go!...(Two minutes only)

Next: In the space below, take five minutes to list as many goals as you can. Don't try to spend too much time thinking about them, just write as many of them down as you can get within the next five minutes. No matter what, please keep your pen moving.

Rule: Dream big dreams! What would you set as a goal if you knew you couldn't fail? If you can dream it, you can do it! Ready...Go!...(Five minutes only) Write them in the space below.

SHORT-RANGE GOALS

Exercise

Go back to your previous list of goals from your dream list and place a 1, 3, or 5 next the goals that you think you can accomplish in that time period. Write the goals below, that you placed either a 1, 3 or 5 next to and write the corresponding number next to it. After that, go to the next page marked Short-Range Goal Commitments and write a statement of positive affirmation about each goal. State how you are committed to accomplish each goal. Goal setting is work, and it's worth it!

Short-Range Goal Commitments

Exercise

List each of your short-range goals for one, three and five years. Make sure that you keep them in proper sequence. Write a short statement as to what date in the coming year(s) you will accomplish these objectives.

Goal: Read 24 books in coming year

Example: I will read at least 24 books in the coming year and this will be accomplished by: Month, Day, Year.

You could go even further by breaking this goal down by month and listing each book you plan to read and by what date. Chunking means that you would read perhaps two books per month in order to reach your goal of 24 for the year.

LONG-RANGE GOALS

Exercise

Go back to your original list of dream goals and place a 10, 15, or 20 next to the goals that you feel that you can accomplish in that time period. Write them in the space below, with the corresponding number next to the goal. Please do that at this time. Go to the next page marked Long Range Goal Commitments and write a statement of positive self talk about how you're absolutely committed to achieving each goal.

Long-Range Goal Commitments

Exercise

Long-range goals don't need to be as specific as shorter range ones because, as time passes, they will eventually become short-range goals. Take each of your long-range goals and write a commitment statement as to when you will achieve your 10, 15, or 20 year goals. Make sure to keep them in proper sequence. It is not necessary to write the month or day, but only the year in which you will have achieved a particular goal.

Goal—Nationally known author

Example: I will be known throughout the world as an author of books for self-development and empowerment. This will be accomplished by the year 2010, or whatever year is in question.

Daily Task Goals

You can use many of the day planners that are on the market to help you manage your time and ultimately your life. When planning your activities, you will find that you maintain more control over your time and operate more efficiently. Regardless of your age, you will gain enormous benefit from thinking about what you want to do and writing it down. By committing your task to paper, you are reinforcing in your own mind the importance of your actions.

Your tasks should ideally be broken into:

QUARTERS—By knowing what you want to do three months in advance, you can better anticipate what kind of year you will have. You will get better results and will be able to look forward to the future with anticipation rather than anxiety.

WEEKS—If you were to approach the beginning of each week knowing exactly what you had to do, it would change your life. By writing these things down in the form of a list, you will take pressure off of yourself to remember critical due dates. This will allow you to spend time on more productive things, and nothing of significance will fall through the cracks.

DAYS—Never start the day until you've already finished it! On paper, that is! As previously mentioned above, plan your next day the night before and you will awaken ready for action and gain much more control over the events of the day. (See three examples at the end of this section)

Note: Always keep your goals somewhere that allows you to look at them as often as possible. A binder or day planner is best. The more you review them, the better chance you have of keeping them "Top of Mind" and actually accomplishing them.

> "THE PERSON WHO FAILS TO PLAN
> IS PLANNING TO FAIL!"

INSIGHT
What you've learned

ACTION
What you're going to do

UNLEASH THE POWER IN YOU!

ACTION GUIDE

SECTION SIX

ENDURE

A wise woman had an inspiring story
she would sometimes tell, about a
young lass with eyes of light and
beauty fancied by every male.

She claimed that with every year that
came to pass, nothing blemished the
beauty of this bright eyed lass.

When asked by the town hags,
"What manner of woman is thee?"
The lass replied, "The beauty you envy
endures because of that inside me."

"The secret is to harbor no jealousy,
hatred or envious fear, then goodness
and laughter fill you with youth
each passing year."

"Beauty, more than skin deep, lasts
according to the attitude you keep!"

—Saunni Dais

Adjusting Your Attitude

The amount of happiness, success, and personal development you experience in life is a direct reflection of your attitude. As the saying goes, "Your attitude determines your altitude." Without a positive attitude, you cannot achieve anything worthwhile in life. The brighter your outlook, the greater your chances of achieving your goal. The world is filled with people who have talent but lack the proper attitude. Most of these people usually fall far short of their potential and end up victims of circumstances because they fail to realize that, "As you think, so shall you become!"

You can choose the way you think, which will ultimately determine how you feel. Your feelings will transform into actions, and your actions will determine your destiny. Can you see why negative thinking can destroy your chances for success, and positive thinking can help you build a better life? We are all aware of the disastrous effects of physical illness, but attitude illnesses are just as debilitating. You cannot operate at full capacity when you have the flu or even a common cold. By the same token, you cannot operate at full capacity either when your attitude is suffering from sickness.

In dealing with attitude illness, you must take inventory of everything that affects your life, including your goals, the people who influence you, what you watch, what you read, what you listen to, and how you think about your life.

Believe in Yourself, For I Believe in You!

Beliefs are powerful medicine for motivation. They are the compass and road map that will direct you to your outcome. A belief is a feeling of confidence or certainty about the outcome of something. You can condition yourself to believe in something. Our beliefs are a matter of choice. What you believe comes from a variety of sources, such as your environment, events, knowledge, wisdom, and past results. When you believe in yourself and the possibilities in your life, you create in your mind the experience you desire in the future, as if it were happening now. That's why it's so important to understand that the power of self belief is enormous. People who achieve greatness believe that they can. There is greatness in you! Why not give yourself every opportunity to succeed? The biggest mountains you will ever have to climb are in your own mind.

Exercise Note: Environment—In the spaces below, write some of the beliefs that come from your upbringing. Complete the following sentences.

    1. Because of the way I grew up, I am....

    2. Because of my background, I am not....

    3. Because of my environment, I can....

    4. Because of my upbringing, I will....

    5. Because of my past, I will no longer...

Exercise Note: Events—In the space below, list at least five major events in your life that have impacted you the most.

1.

2.

3.

4.

5.

Exercise Note: Knowledge—Below, list five positive things that you've learned from books you've read or people who have taught you something in your life.

1.

2.

3.

4.

5.

Exercise Note: Past Experience—In the space below, list five things that you have come to believe based upon personal experiences.

1.

2.

3.

4.

5.

Exercise Note: Resiliency—One of the most powerful skills is the ability to bounce back from disappointments. This is the difference between winning and losing. List a time that you were disappointed in an outcome in your life and how you bounced back from it.

1.

Exercise Note: The "Philosophy of Next" is important in helping you move from a position of being stuck into one of massive action. List something that's got you stuck. What are you going to do to move yourself forward?

1.

Exercise Note: Persistance—In the space below, list a time when you quit at something that you wanted to do. Also list at least two new ways to approach the accomplishment of this goal.

1.

New approach -1

New approach-2

Exercise Note: Disgust—In the space below, list something that you are really disgusted about in your life and what you will do to make a difference. What are you going to do about it?

1. What are you disgusted about?

2. What actions will you take to correct it?

3. What changes do you expect?

Exercise Note: Resolve—In the space below, list something that you are absolutely committed to doing to ensure that you become a better person tommorrow. Promise yourself you will do whatever it takes to make it happen.

1. I am absolutely committed to....

2. I promise myself that in order to make this happen, I will....

Exercise Note: Forgiveness—In the space listed below, list someone that you are not on good terms with or something that has happened that causes you to harbor bad feelings. Also list what steps you are going to take to change this situation and make it right so that you can move forward.

    1. What situation or person are you harboring ill feelings about?

    2. What are you going to do about it?

Exercise Note: Passion—In the space below, list something that you are passionate about and what you will do about it in the future.

    1. I am passionate about...

    2. Starting tomorrow, I will take action regarding my passion by...

INSIGHT	ACTION
What you've learned	What you're going to do

ANSWER SHEET

(Answers to exercise on page 267)
False Evidence Appearing Real

(Answers to exercise on page 286)

1. **Impact**-When any stimulus that you encounter causes you to take action. It's the force or impression of one thing upon another. For this reason it's important for you to learn to think for yourself.

2. **Repetition**-The act or process of repeating something. Repetition is the mother of skill and the father of learning. It is for this reason that you use it.

3. **Utilization**-To put to use for a certain purpose. If you don't use something, then ultimately you will lose it. The ideas in this material will do you no good if you don't put them into practical use in your daily life.

4. **Internalization**-To take in and make part of one's own attitudes and beliefs. When you follow the three preceding concepts, these ideas will become a natural part of your daily habits. You will become unconsciously competent. You become your own master!

5. **Reinforcement**-The strengthening of an operant conditioned response leading to satisfaction. An event, circumstance, or that which increases the likelihood that a given response will recur in a situation like that in which the reinforcing condition originally occured. In short, this means that if you really want these ideas to stick, then follow steps one through four on a continual basis!

(Answers to exercise on page 287)

1. Words—7 percent (The actual words you speak only comprise seven percent of the impact of what you say.)
2. Tone & Pace (The tone and pace of your voice comprises 38 percent of the impact of what you say.)
3. Physiology (The positioning of your body while you speak comprises 55 percent of the impact of your words.)

(Answers to exercise on pages 297 and 298)

1. Value
2. I
3. I'm
4. Me
5. Become

6. Me
7. Time, Value
8. Formal, Self
9. Skill level
10. Got

I've dedicated my life to helping people unleash the power within themselves. You can do remarkable things in life because you are a remarkable person. The key is to get started, make it a point to watch over the course of your life as a mother hen does her chicks. When you take charge of your life and plan it according to your purpose, values, goals, dreams, and take massive action, you will seldom be surprised by the outcome! Go for it!

I wish you the "Best of Success!" Have a great life!

Best Regards,

Desi Williamson

Desi Williamson

Faith

Doubt sees the obstacles
Faith sees the way.
Doubt sees the darkest night,
Faith sees the day.
Doubt fails to take a step,
Faith just soars on high.
Doubt asks, "Who believes?"
Faith answers, "I!"

—Unknown

"Time is the most valuable commodity on earth. Unlike other resources, you can't save it, stop it, or change it. The only thing that you can do with time is use it!"

—Desi Williamson

Order Form

YES! I want ____ copies of *Get off Your Assets!* at $29.95 each, plus $3.50 shipping and handling per book. ISBN #0-7872-2742-0.

Call 1-800-228-0810 to order by telephone or Fax 1-800-772-9165. Prepayment is required.

__ Check enclosed

__ Charge my account:

❑ Master Card ❑ American Express ❑ Visa

MC Bank # ____ Exp. Date __/__/__

Account # ________________

Signature ________________

(required for all charges)

Name ________________

Phone ________________

Address ________________

____

City/State/Zip ________________

Please make check payable to:

Kendall/Hunt Publishing Company
4050 Westmark Drive
P.O. Box 1840
Dubuque, Iowa 52004-1840